GHOSTS OF HALABJA

For Jules

Let's keep the embers of
until I am burning bright!
Great seeing you in San Diego.

All the best,

Mike

GHOSTS OF HALABJA

Saddam Hussein and the Kurdish Genocide

MICHAEL J. KELLY

Foreword by Ra'id Juhi al Saedi

PRAEGER SECURITY INTERNATIONAL
Westport, Connecticut • London

Library of Congress Cataloging-in-Publication Data

Kelly, Michael J., 1968–
    Ghosts of Halabja : Saddam Hussein and the Kurdish genocide / Michael J. Kelly; foreword by Ra'id Juhi al Saedi.
        p.   cm.
    Includes bibliographical references and index.
    ISBN: 978–0–275–99210–1 (alk. paper)
    1. Hussein, Saddam, 1937–2006—Trials, litigation, etc.   2. Trials (Crimes against humanity)—Iraq—Baghdad.   3. Trials (Murder)—Iraq—Baghdad.   4. Iraq. Iraqi Higher Criminal Court.   5. Anfal Campaign, Iraq, 1986–1989.   6. Halabjah (Iraq)—History—Bombardment, 1988.
I. Title.
    KMJ41.H87K45   2008
    345.567′470235—dc22   2008028215

British Library Cataloguing in Publication Data is available.

Library of Congress Catalog Card Number: 2008028215
ISBN-13: 978–0–275–99210–1

First published in 2008

Praeger Security International, 88 Post Road West, Westport, CT 06881
An imprint of Greenwood Publishing Group, Inc.
www.praeger.com

Printed in the United States of America

The paper used in this book complies with the Permanent Paper Standard issued by the National Information Standards Organization (Z39.48–1984).

10 9 8 7 6 5 4 3 2 1

For my boys,
Durham & Anderson

Contents

Foreword

Ghosts of Halabja. This title refers to a very specific crime - the chemical gassing of a Kurdish village in northern Iraq in 1988 by the forces of Saddam Hussein. He was to be tried for this crime before the Iraqi High Tribunal, but that trial against him will never take place. Saddam was executed in 2006 for the massacre of 148 men and boys from the town of Dujail. The attack on Halabja occurred during the Anfal campaigns, which were a military operation carried out against the Kurds of Iraq from 1987 to 1988. Saddam's execution occurred half-way through his trial for the Anfals.

I was the chief investigative judge for the Iraqi High Tribunal. As such, it was my office that indicted Saddam Hussein and his cohorts for the Dujail massacre and the Anfal campaigns. I spent many hours questioning Saddam and learned to avoid his manipulative personality in order to learn what he knew and what he was responsible for in connection with the crimes for which he was charged. I also spent many hours and days in the field at mass graves and with survivors of his atrocities. These trials represented a great turning point for justice in Iraq.

For decades, the Iraqi people were terrorized by secretive courts linked directly to Saddam's regime. The chance to finally hold Saddam and his government accountable for what they had done was too great an opportunity to squander by killing him. Bringing him to justice in the best way possible would help re-establish the basic concept of justice for Iraqis and show them that everyone, even the most powerful person, would be held accountable eventually.

It is unfortunate that Saddam Hussein was executed in the manner that was carried out and it is unfortunate that the Anfal trial against him could not be completed. This history of the Kurds under Saddam's regime that Professor Kelly has written helps to tell the story that could not be adequately told in court. The

Kurdish people are strong and very resilient. Their culture as a part of Iraqi culture is very rich and their heritage is one of which they should be proud. Saddam's regime could hurt them, and he did so grievously. But he could not bury their indomitable spirit. The courage and faith of the Iraqis in a better future should give us all hope—for a better Iraq and a better world.

Ra'id Juhi al Saedi
Former Chief Investigative Judge—Iraqi High Tribunal

Preface

This book is an extension of my previous research for *Nowhere to Hide: Defeat of the Sovereign Immunity Defense for Crimes of Genocide & the Trails of Slobodan Milosevic and Saddam Hussein* (Peter Lang Publishers, 2005). There, I chronicled the evolution of genocide over time from an accepted stratagem of warfare in antiquity to an international crime today, the erosion of sovereign immunity as a defense for leaders who commit genocide, and the prosecutions of Milosevic and Saddam as heads of state on charges of genocide. Milosevic has since died and Saddam has now been executed. Death allowed both men to escape completion of the genocide trials against them.

The unspeakable atrocities visited by Saddam specifically upon the Kurds of Iraq are explored here together with the trials of Saddam by the Iraqi High Tribunal—both the completed prosecution for the Dujail massacre against the Shi'ites and the incomplete one for the Anfal Campaigns against the Kurds. However, this work is more than a litigation history. It is also an exploration of the motivations behind and the depths of organized evil in the context of a single brutal despot at the helm of an artificially created multiethno/religious state lying atop massive oil wealth but situated in the most dangerous part of the world. Saddam's background and the context of his rule explain much about his actions, but not all. He remained an unpredictable tyrant to the end of his reign.

As this is not a treatise, I have omitted much cross-referencing and sourcing beyond major quotations, relying instead upon a general bibliography, which appears at the end of the book. This effort does not offer in-depth analysis of ancillary legal issues surrounding Saddam's trial proper, such as the illegality of the American-led invasion of Iraq under international law, the questionable legitimacy of the tribunal as established by the Coalition Provisional Authority, or treatment of prisoners in conjunction with the Geneva Conventions. Many, including myself, have written on these matters elsewhere and I invite readers to access those other projects.

Special acknowledgment must be given to the brave journalists and human rights activists who have consistently put their lives at risk covering the Kurdish genocide and the trials of Saddam Hussein. Human Rights Watch expended considerable resources to chronicle the atrocities perpetrated upon the Kurds during and after the Anfal campaigns, and it is their credible and corroborated reporting that I rely upon most heavily for my description of that unfortunate chapter in Kurdish history.

Many thanks go to my family, whose support allowed me to write this book, and to my research assistants, Kevin Tuininga and Caroline LaForge, for their meaningful contributions to this project. Thanks also to Vice President Patrick Borchers, Interim Dean Marianne Culhane, and Creighton University School of Law for their financial and technical backing of my work.

The National Security Archive at George Washington University has become a wealth of information for researchers in my field and its staff and leadership are worthy of commendation for finally compiling declassified documents in area specialties. I have included a handful of such documents with respect to the Iraq-U.S. relationship during the Iran–Iraq War in the appendix. I additionally want to recognize the efforts of Professor Michael Scharf, Director of the War Crimes Research Office at Case Western Reserve University School of Law, in marshalling the resources necessary to make primary materials of the Iraqi High Tribunal, like the English translation of the 900-page Anfal trial judgment, available.

Finally, I appreciate the comments provided by three Iraqi nationals on this manuscript to help make it as accurate and encompassing as possible: Judge Raid Juhi Al Saedi, Selwa "Silvy" Nasser Ahmad, and Kamaran Sabir. Their contributions, drawn from their personal experiences with delivering justice in Iraq, were particularly helpful. Judge Raid is owed a particular debt of gratitude for contributing a foreword to this volume that provides such an excellent framework for the discussion that follows.

This book is dedicated to my sons, whom I hope never experience the kinds of horrors Saddam visited upon the Kurds, but whom I also hope will come to appreciate efforts to bring such monsters to justice—imperfect as that justice may sometimes be.

Michael J. Kelly
Omaha, Nebraska

Introduction: Saddam Hussein and the Prelude to Genocide

As dawn broke over the Baghdad horizon on December 30, 2006, the morning call to prayer went up from spiraling minarets dotted across this ancient city. The hauntingly familiar song echoed back and forth against stone towers and down through the streets. The low-lying clouds tinted pink against the rising disk of the desert sun. In a nondescript gray concrete room, in the middle of a circle of masked men, the song of the muezzins mixed with that of a solitary rope—swinging slowly to and fro, stretching under the weight of a body clad in black. The rope was snapped by the hangman, and the lifeless body tumbled to the hard floor. Saddam Hussein was dead.

Eid ul-Adha had begun. Under Iraqi law, no executions may occur on a holy day. Eid ul-Adha is celebrated by Muslims in remembrance of the Prophet Ibrahim's (Abraham's) willingness to sacrifice his son Ishmael for God. Saddam died minutes before the holy day commenced. His executioners carried out the sentence of death pronounced on him six weeks prior by the Iraqi High Tribunal for the massacre of 148 Shi'ites in the village of Dujail.

At the time of Saddam's execution, he was additionally being tried for his role in the Anfal campaigns, a series of military strikes targeting the Kurdish population in northern Iraq. The charges included genocide. The prosecution had only presented half of its case when Saddam was executed. Five more trials had been scheduled to follow, including a trial focusing on the hideous gassing of Kurdish civilians by the Iraqi military in the city of Halabja. But because under Iraqi law, those who receive the death sentence must be put to death within thirty days of their final appeal, Saddam never finished the second trial, and the case against him on behalf of the victims of Halabja will never be made. Thus, the Kurds were denied their day in court against him; cheated of justice.

Yet, they were not surprised. The story of the Kurds is the story of a people buffeted by forces greater than they. The twentieth century offers ample example. For centuries, Kurds and Arabs served under the yoke of their Turkish masters during the Ottoman Empire. Then, when the Western Allies defeated Turkey, the moment came to finally be free. As the old imperial lands were being carved up into new nations, the Kurds were promised a homeland, albeit geographically crimped, by the 1920 Treaty of Sèvres in what is now modern-day Turkey. However, with the rise of Ataturk and establishment of the modern Turkish state, the Allies reneged on their guarantee and the Treaty of Sévres was replaced with the 1923 Treaty of Lausanne, which contained no provision for the Kurds and which folded Kurdish minority enclaves into Turkey, Iran, Syria, and Iraq.

Decades of mistreatment, repression, and outright hostility by their host governments hardened the Kurds, making them largely self-reliant. During the Iran–Iraq War, the Ayatollah cultivated Iraqi Kurds to fight with the Iranians, only to sell them out by making a separate peace with Saddam Hussein. Then, after the 1991 Persian Gulf War, President Bush incited them to rise up against Saddam, only to withdraw American support and leave them to be slaughtered by Iraqi forces. Thus, when the time finally came to bring Saddam to justice for what he had done to the Kurds, only to have him executed halfway through the trial and the charges against him dropped, the Kurdish people a rightly viewed this as yet another betrayal—this time by an Arab-dominated court within Iraq. No surprise, just more disappointment—a feeling with which they had become intimately familiar over the course of their troubled history within Iraq.

Who was Saddam Hussein? How did he come to be tried for war crimes, genocide, and crimes against humanity and executed before those trials could be completed? To understand that, one must understand how he came to power and ruled the sprawling multiethnic/multireligious country known as Iraq.

Iraq, like so many other offspring of the world's colonial past, is not a natural country. It is an artificial creation borne of convenience and connivance. France and Britain carved up the non-Turkish provinces of the collapsed Ottoman Empire after World War I and decided between themselves which provinces would be united into countries that they would each influence. France took Syria and Lebanon, and Britain took Palestine, Jordan, and Mesopotamia. In organizing Mesopotamia, the British cobbled together the old Ottoman provinces of Mosul (mostly Sunni Kurds), Baghdad (mostly Sunni Arabs), and Basra (mostly Shi'a Arabs), appointed a figurehead monarch, and dubbed the new creation "Iraq."

It was into this artificial and internally antagonistic country that Saddam was born in April 1937 in a small village outside Tikrit. As a teenager, he immersed himself in the prevailingly bitter anti-British (and anti-Western) atmosphere of the day. This profound disillusionment with failed promises from London to make Iraq a viable state, followed by more failed promises from the weak King Faisal to make Iraq independent of Western influence, affected Saddam at an early age. Perhaps this drove his deep cynicism, which would allow him to later use the West for what he could, to achieve much darker ambitions. At college in Baghdad, he joined the opposition Ba'ath Party and eventually, in 1956, took part in an aborted coup attempt.

After the ousting of the monarchy two years later, the young Saddam imprudently seized an opportunity to fast-track the Ba'athist rise to power by participating in a plot to kill the prime minister, Abdel-Karim Qassem. However, the conspiracy was discovered, and Saddam fled the country. He bided his time in Cairo—then a hotbed of Arab nationalistic activity, where he attended law school.

Five years later, in 1963, with the Ba'ath Party finally in control, Saddam returned and began jostling for a position of influence. During this period, he married his cousin Sajida. They later had two sons and three daughters. Turmoil followed Saddam. Within months of his return, the Ba'ath Party had been overthrown and Saddam was jailed; he remained in jail until the party returned to power in a July 1968 coup. An assessment of Saddam (see Figure I.1) in 1969 by the British embassy in Baghdad clearly identifies him as a rising power.

In a telegram issued one month later, after Saddam had risen to Vice-Chairman of the Revolutionary Command Council, British ambassador H.G. Balfour Paul described Saddam after meeting him as "a much more 'serious' character than other Ba'athist leaders; . . . . I should judge him, young as he is, to be a formidable, single-minded and hard-headed member of the Ba'athist hierarchy, but one with whom . . . it would be possible to do business."[1]

An older and more patient Saddam, as predicted by the British, eventually became the power behind the ailing president, Ahmed Hassan Bakr. In 1979, Saddam achieved his ambition of becoming head of state, succeeding Bakr. To consolidate his power, Saddam immediately executed sixty-six men he believed were working against him.

Once in power, Saddam was confronted with the problem of successfully governing a multiethnic, multireligious state. As Iraq contained both Shi'a and Sunni religious sects as well as an ethnic Arab–Kurd divide, political strength was required to hold the country together. Saddam knew such strength. In his rise to power, Saddam displayed shades of Stalin—ambition and cruelty coupled with paranoia. Faced with governing such an artificial state, Saddam overlaid these Stalinistic impulses with a cynical penchant for managing ethnic politics similar to Yugoslavia's longtime dictator Josip Broz Tito.

Like Tito, Saddam justified his brutal, iron-fisted rule as the only means of governing a state with such profound and ancient ethnic and religious fissures. Like Yugoslavia without Tito, Iraq without its strongman might fly apart into its constituent pieces, melting down into civil war in the process. For years, the West turned a blind eye, encouraging the continued territorial integrity and stability of nation-states (most of which they helped create) over human rights concerns.

With acquiescence from the West, Saddam was able to inflict grievous harm on those who opposed his regime in Baghdad. The religious beliefs of his own ruling clan within the Ba'ath Party were based in Sunni Islam—practiced by a minority segment of the total Iraqi population. That population, before the recent Iraq War,

CONFIDENTIAL

SADDAM HUSSEIN AL-TAKRITI

Born about 1937.   First came into prominence when chosen by the Ba'ath Party leadership in 1959 to assassinate Kassem and wounded in the attempt.   Provisional Secretary General of the Regional Ba'ath Command after November 1963.   Established himself thereafter as leading Party theorist in the background, emerging progressively into the limelight in 1969.   Headed Iraqi delegation to Libya immediately after the Libyan revolution.   Appointed Vice Chairman of the R.C.C. and deputy to the President November 1969, when he was also confirmed as Deputy Secretary General of the Iraqi Ba'ath.

A presentable young man.   Initially regarded as a Party extremist, but responsibility may mellow him.   Nephew of Khairallah Talfah, the Muhafiz of Baghdad and thus related to President Bakr by marriage.   Connected, as a Tikriti, with many of those in the corridors of power.

British Embassy,

BAGHDAD.

15 November, 1969

Figure I.1. British Assessment of Saddam in 1969. *Source*: National Security Archive, George Washington University.

consisted of 20 percent Sunni Arabs, 17 percent Sunni Kurds, and 60 percent Shi'a Arabs (see Figure I.2). This minority status caused Saddam to follow the pattern of other ethnic minority governments (such as in South Africa, the defunct state of Rhodesia, Rwanda, and Burundi) in brutalizing his own people to remain in power.

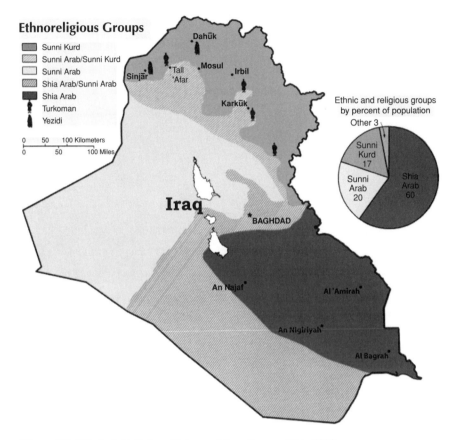

Figure I.2. Ethnic & Religious Makeup of Iraq. *Source*: CIA, 1992.

Underlying the political and power-based rationales for Saddam's approach to governance were economic concerns. As Figure I.3 indicates rather starkly, the distribution of oil wealth (Iraq's primary source of state revenue) is inconveniently concentrated in the Kurdish north and Shi'a south. The Sunni Arab lands in the middle have very little. The British recognized the value of the oil-rich Kurdish region (the old Mosul province) as the linchpin for Iraq's economy as early as 1917, when Sir Arnold Wilson, acting commissioner for Mesopotamia, noted:

> The idea of Iraq as an independent nation had scarcely taken shape, for the country lacked homogeneity, whether geographical, economic or racial. . . . It was scarcely to be hoped that the vilayets of Basra and Baghdad could maintain their existence as an autonomous state without the revenue it was hoped might eventually be derived from the economic resources of the Mosul vilayet. Yet three quarters of the inhabitants of the

Oilfields and Facilities

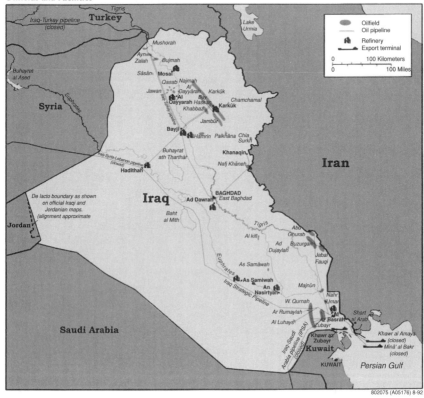

Figure I.3. Oil Wealth Distribution—Iraq. *Source*: CIA, 1992.

Mosul vilayet were non-Arabs, five-eighths being Kurdish, and one-eighth Christain or [non-Islamic Kurds].[2]

Consequently, to retain adequate control over the wealth of the nation, Saddam not only repressed the non-Sunni Arab populations in those areas, but also repopulated many districts with his Arab kinsmen—especially around the traditionally Kurdish area of Kirkuk. Mosul, mostly Kurdish under the Ottomans, became mostly Arab under Saddam. In the north, the "Arabization" of oil-producing areas meant eviction of Kurdish farmers, who were replaced with Arab tribesmen. Because the Iraqi Kurds were politically divided among themselves, Saddam could play the Kurdish factions off one another in return for favors from Baghdad. He was able to take advantage of this continual disunity to control them and eventually eliminate large Kurdish populations altogether.

Like many despots before him, Saddam was predisposed to criminality, brutality, and thuggish behavior long before assuming power. Saddam exhibited the same behaviors once in power. In that sense, Saddam shared a behavioral pattern with Stalin, and Hitler in particular who had to struggle within a political party apparatus to gain leadership as a prerequisite to controlling the state. And like Stalin and Hitler, Saddam proved calculating, retributive, and cunning in his intraparty maneuverings, as he lied, cheated, and murdered his way to the top.

Chaos of the times helps these situations unfold. For Stalin, it was the consolidation of Bolshevism in a young Soviet Union pulling itself together from near collapse after World War I and the continuing threat from within by other parties. For Hitler, it was the destabilization of Germany by worldwide economic depression combined with open warfare in the streets between the National Socialists and the Communists. For Saddam, it was an Arab world unsure of itself, embroiled in multiple wars with Israel, enmeshed in the deepening Cold War, and influenced by a Sunni minority struggling to maintain its grip on government within Iraq. Such engines produce strong leaders, to be sure, but also paranoid and cruel ones—paranoia from surviving the struggle to the top and cruelty as the proven means to get there.

Such characteristics, combined with impunity and lack of accountability, constitute a classic formula for atrocities on a mass scale that played out in Iraq just as in other contexts like Stalin's Russia, Hitler's Germany, Pol Pot's Cambodia, or Ceausescu's Romania. The list of Saddam's cruelties is long and the victims of his brutality many. This is the collective story of one people—the Iraqi Kurds, and the terrors they endured which culminated in the crime of crimes—genocide.

Part One _____

Genocide of the Kurds

Kurdistan (Introduction and Background on Region and People)

Known by the ancient Sumerians as the Karda and by the Babylonians as the Qardu, the land of the Kurds stretches across the northern part of what was known historically as Mesopotamia. Today, the 74,000 square miles of mountainous and heavily forested terrain that "Kurdistan" covers encompasses southeastern Turkey, northwestern Iran, northern Iraq, and northeastern Syria—an area the size of France (see Figure 1.1). The mighty Tigris and Euphrates rivers originate in the rugged mountains of Kurdistan; their life-giving waters cascading down to the lower plateaus of the Fertile Crescent.

From before the time of Xenophon (427–355 B.C.), this land was in the possession of the Kurds, who consider themselves indigenous to the region. Kurds are an Aryan people and an ethnic group distinct from the Turks, Persians, and Arabs, although the majority of Kurds share the Islamic faith of those populations. The Kurdish language, customs, traditions, and internal tribal structures are also distinct (see Figure 1.2). Numbering roughly 30 million, the Kurds are the largest ethnic group in the world without a state. Instead, they have been incorporated as minority populations within the larger surrounding states.

"Kurds have no friends but the mountains" is an old saying that continues to ring true. Indeed, virtual independence coupled with statelessness has been the fate of the Kurds through history. Wedged between the larger powers of Persians, Assyrians, and Babylonians, the Kurds were constantly pressed into service by the rulers of various empires up to and including that of the Greeks, which later gave way to their provincial incorporation into the Roman Empire.

From the demise of Byzantium to the rule by Arabs under the Caliph of Baghdad, the Kurds enjoyed a degree of autonomy which eventually gave way

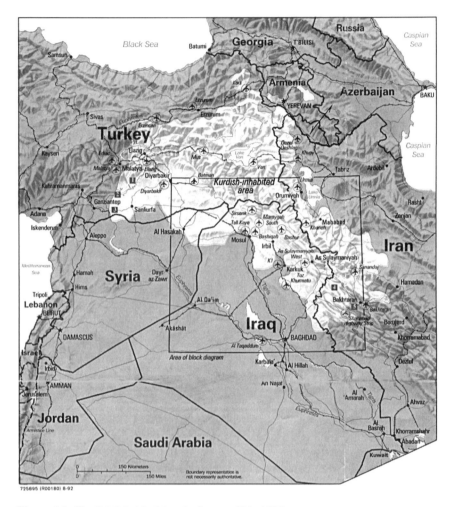

Figure 1.1. Kurdish Inhabited Lands. *Source*: CIA, 1992.

to virtual independence in the second half of the tenth century as Kurdistan was shared among the five largest Kurdish principalities: the Shaddadid, Rawadid, Hasanwayhids, Annazids, and the Marwanid. However, one by one, these principalities were annexed by the Seljuk Turks. Their greatest leader, Saladin, ruled during the Ayyubid period, but they later came under the influence of the Mongols during the thirteenth century, when Marco Polo made his famous trek across Asia to visit the court of Kubulai Khan, meeting and writing about Kurdish customs along his winding journey eastward.

Eventually, as their Mongol overlords receded back into Asia proper, the Kurds began forming independent principalities once again, only to be subsumed subsequently by foreign powers. The Ottoman Empire came to control much of

Figure 1.2. Traditional Kurdish Dress (from left—Mesopotamia, Mardin, and Diyarbekir). *Source*: Pascal Sebah, Les Costumes Populaires De Law Turquie, 1873.

Kurdistan early in the sixteenth century as Sultan Selim I defeated the Persian Shah Ismail in 1514. As a security measure, the Persians forcibly resettled hundreds of thousands of Kurds away from their new borders with the expanding Ottomans and into the interior of Persia. Removal of the Kurds from the Anatolia region was traumatic and devastating. Ismail's successor, Shah Tahmasp I, systematically destroyed Kurdish villages and the countryside as his forces slowly retreated eastward year by year from the advancing Ottomans.

In 1609, the Kurds rose up against their Persian masters, ruled by Shah Abbas I. They rallied around a fortress called Dimdim by Lake Urmia in what is now northwestern Iran. The Kurdish resistance, led by Amir Khan, capitulated after a yearlong siege led by the Persian grand vizier Hartem Beg who eventually captured the fortress and massacred the defenders. Shah Abbas then ordered the general massacre of Kurds in the surrounding cities and resettled Turkish tribes into formerly Kurdish areas.

The Kurds lived divided under Persian and Ottoman rules for centuries thereafter. Following the Russo-Turkish War of 1828, Kurdish uprisings over the next three decades were put down, Kurdish governors were replaced with Turkish ones, and garrisons were strengthened within Kurdish towns. Separatist activity continued at a low level up through World War I.

The collapse of the Ottoman Empire upon its defeat by the Allied powers in World War I offered the Kurds another chance at self-rule. Kurdish representatives lobbied the victorious Allies for an independent state to rise from the ashes of the rapidly disintegrating empire. Representatives of the crumbling Ottoman order signed the Treaty of Sèvres with the Allies in 1920 which formally dismembered the old empire into "mandatory" states under the supervision of Allied powers, as well as independent states. Kurdistan was assured of independence at last.

The method of triggering the creation of a Kurdish homeland was nuanced in the Treaty of Sèvres, as the section on Kurdistan reveals:

SECTION III.
KURDISTAN.
ARTICLE 62.

A Commission sitting at Constantinople and composed of three members appointed by the British, French and Italian Governments respectively shall draft within six months from the coming into force of the present Treaty a scheme of local autonomy for the predominantly Kurdish areas lying east of the Euphrates, south of the southern boundary of Armenia as it may be hereafter determined, and north of the frontier of Turkey with Syria and Mesopotamia, as defined in Article 27, II (2) and (3).

If unanimity cannot be secured on any question, it will be referred by the members of the Commission to their respective Governments. The scheme shall contain full safeguards for the protection of the Assyro-Chaldeans and other racial or religious minorities within these areas, and with this object a Commission composed of British, French, Italian, Persian and Kurdish representatives shall visit the spot to examine and decide what rectifications, if any, should be made in the Turkish frontier where, under the provisions of the present Treaty, that frontier coincides with that of Persia.

ARTICLE 63.

The Turkish Government hereby agrees to accept and execute the decisions of both the Commissions mentioned in Article 62 within three months from their communication to the said Government.

ARTICLE 64.

If within one year from the coming into force of the present Treaty the Kurdish peoples within the areas defined in Article 62 shall address themselves to the Council of the League of Nations in such a manner as to show that a majority of the population of these areas desires independence from Turkey, and if the Council then considers that these peoples are capable of such independence and recommends that it should be granted to them, Turkey hereby agrees to execute such a recommendation, and to renounce all rights and title over these areas.

The detailed provisions for such renunciation will form the subject of a separate agreement between the Principal Allied Powers and Turkey.

If and when such renunciation takes place, no objection will be raised by the Principal Allied Powers to the voluntary adhesion to such an independent Kurdish State of the Kurds inhabiting that part of Kurdistan which has hitherto been included in the Mosul vilayet.[1]

Although the United States was not a party to the peace settlement with Turkey, as the United States and the Ottoman Empire had not been at war, President Wilson was regarded by the other Allied powers as a player not to be ignored during discussions for a Middle East settlement. Specifically, Wilson was accorded the task of demarcating the boundaries of a new state for the Armenians, which was provided for in Articles 88–93 of the treaty. That Wilson took into account the Kurdish population neighboring a new Armenian state, and the potential for creation of a new Kurdish state, is revealed in his diplomatic note to the Allies explaining his rationale for the Armenian frontiers:

The White House
Washington
November 22, 1920

Mr. President: By action of the Supreme Council taken on April 26th of this year an invitation was tendered to me to arbitrate the question of the boundaries between Turkey and the new state of Armenia.... [T]he scope of the arbitral competence assigned to me is clearly limited to the determination of the frontiers of Turkey and Armenia in the Vilayets of Erzerum, Trebisond, Van and Bitlis. With full consciousness of the responsibility placed upon me by your request, I have approached this difficult task with eagerness to serve the best interests of the Armenian people as well as the remaining inhabitants, of whatever race or religious belief they may be, in this stricken country, attempting to exercise also the strictest possible justice toward the populations, whether Turkish, Kurdish, Greek or Armenian, living in the adjacent areas....

The conflicting territorial desires of Armenians, Turks, Kurds and Greeks along the boundaries assigned to my arbitral decision could not always be harmonized. In such cases it was my belief that consideration of a healthy economic life for the future state of Armenia should be decisive. Where, however, the requirements of a correct geographic boundary permitted, all mountain and valley districts along the border which were predominantly Kurdish or Turkish have been left to Turkey rather than assigned to Armenia, unless trade relations with definite market towns threw them necessarily into the Armenian state. Wherever information upon tribal relations and seasonal migrations was obtainable, the attempt was made to respect the integrity of tribal groupings and nomad pastoral movements.

From the Persian border southwest of the town of Kotur the boundary line of Armenia is determined by a rugged natural barrier of great height, extending south of Lake Van and lying southwest of the Armenian cities of Bitlis and Mush. This boundary line leaves as part of the Turkish state the entire Sanjak of Hakkiari, or about one-half of the Vilayet of Van, and almost the entire Sanjak of Sairt. The sound physiographic reason which seemed to justify this decision was further strengthened by the ethnographic consideration that Hakkiari and Sairt are predominantly Kurdish in population and economic relations. It did not seem in the best interest of the Armenian state to include in it the upper valley of the Great Zab River, largely Kurdish and Nestorian Christian in population and an essential element of the great Tigris river irrigation system of Turkish Kurdistan and Mesopotamia. The control of these headwaters should be kept, wherever possible, within the domain of the two interested states, Turkey and Mesopotamia. For these reasons the Armenian claim upon the upper valley of the Great Zab could not be satisfied.

The boundary upon the west from Bitlis and Mush northward to the vicinity of Erzingan lies well within Bitlis and Erzerum vilayets. It follows a natural geographic barrier, which furnishes Armenia with perfect security and leaves to the Turkish state an area which is strongly Kurdish. . . .

I have the honor to submit herewith the text of my decision.

Woodrow Wilson[2]

The Treaty of Sèvres, however, was rejected by the Turkish nationalist movement which was waging a military campaign against the occupying Allied forces under the direction of Mustafa Kemal Pasha, later to be known as Atatürk—the founder of a new secular Turkey. Atatürk was a battle-hardened veteran of the Galipoli campaign that repulsed repeated Allied attempts at landing on the narrow peninsula which had earned him grudging British respect. Before Kurdistan could be founded, Atatürk had parlayed vital support from the Soviet Union into a successful consolidation of the countryside and political assault on the weakening sultan that led to the military expulsion of Allied troops, abolition of the monarchy, and establishment of the Republic of Turkey. As historian Margaret MacMillan notes:

The great line of sultans that had produced Suleiman the Magnificent had dwindled to Mehmed VI. His main achievement was to have survived the rule of three brothers: one who was deposed when he went mad; his paranoid and cruel successor, so fearful of enemies that he employed a eunuch to take the first puff of every cigarette; and the timid old man who ruled until 1918. Mehmed VI was sane but it was difficult to gauge whether there were any ideas in his bony head. He took over as sultan with deep misgivings. "I am at a loss," he told a religious leader. "Pray for me."

The power of the throne, which had once made the world tremble, had slipped away. Orders from the government, reported the American representative, "often

receive but scant consideration in the provinces and public safety is very poor throughout Asia Minor." Although Constantinople was not officially occupied at first, Allied
soldiers and diplomats "were everywhere—advising and ordering and suggesting."
Allied warships packed the harbor so tightly that they looked like a solid mass. "I am
ill," murmured the sultan, "I can't look out the window. I hate to see them." Atatürk
had a very different thought: "As they have come, so they shall go."[3]

In 1923, the Turks of the fledgling republic under Atatürk signed a new treaty
with the Allied powers, who were not prepared to redeploy into Anatolia to fight
another war—especially since Atatürk was by then cutting deals with Lenin in
Soviet Russia. By that time, a smaller version of Armenia had been converted into
a Soviet Republic. The Treaty of Lausanne, recognizing the new political situation
in the region, revoked the promise of an independent Kurdistan and Armenia in
exchange for Turkey ceding claims to Cyprus, Iraq, and Syria and agreeing to
honor 40 percent of Ottoman debts.

Consequently, the Kurds were victims of global as opposed to regional poli-
tics. Abandonment of promises made by Western powers in the Treaty of Sèvres
was, from the perspective of the Kurds, a painful double-cross. It would not be
the last time they were abandoned by the West. The old Ottoman province of
Mosul, rich with oil fields, was attached to the new state of Iraq along with the
provinces of Basra and Baghdad. The Kurds who lived under Ottoman rule for
so long were thereby partitioned between Turkish and Arab rulers. Kurds in Iran
remained under the rule of the Persians.

The post–World War I settlement remains the geographic fate of greater Kurdistan. Each of the areas of Kurdistan has suffered different degrees of repression
from their foreign masters, perhaps mostly at the hands of the Turks and Arabs.
Iraqi Kurdistan has over time come to enjoy the greatest level of autonomy among
the larger Kurdish populations, but the journey to that level of autonomy has been
a long and difficult one. The struggle within Iraq began shortly after the war in
1918 and the struggle continues to the present day.

On December 1, 1918, during a meeting in Sulaimaniya with the British
commissioner for Mesopotamia, Kurdish leaders demanded support for a united
and independent Kurdistan under British protection. Frustrated, Shaikh Mahmoud
Barzani, a Kurdish leader based in Sulaimaniya, formed a Kurdish government
and led two revolts against British rule. It took authorities two years to put down
his uprisings. The first revolt began on May 22, 1919, with the arrest of British
officials in Sulaimaniya and it quickly spread to Mosul and Arbil. Afterward, the
British exiled Mahmoud to India.

In July 1920, tribal leaders called again for independence of Kurdistan within
the British mandate. British objection to Kurdish self-rule was driven by fear
that granting it would encourage the Arab areas of Baghdad and Basra to follow
suit, thereby threatening British control over all Mesopotamia. In 1922, Britain
restored Shaikh Mahmoud to power, hoping that he would organize the Kurds to
act as a buffer against the Turks, who had resurrected territorial claims over Mosul.

Mahmoud instead declared a Kurdish kingdom with himself as the king, though he later agreed to limited autonomy within the new state of Iraq. In 1930, following Iraq's admission into the League of Nations, Mahmoud instigated a third uprising which was suppressed with British air and ground forces.

By 1927, the Barzani clan had also become vocal supporters of Kurdish rights in Iraq. In 1929, the Barzanis demanded the formation of a Kurdish province in northern Iraq. Emboldened by these demands, in 1931 Kurdish representatives petitioned the League of Nations to set up an independent Kurdish government. Under pressure from the Iraqi government and the British, the most influential leader of the clan, Mustafa Barzani was forced into exile in Iran in 1945. He later relocated to the Soviet Union.

After the 1958 military coup in Iraq led by Abdul Karim Qasim, Barzani saw an opening for the Kurds and returned from exile to establish his own political party, the Kurdistan Democratic Party, which was granted legal status in 1960. Soon afterward, Qasim attempted to turn the *Baradost* and *Zebari* tribes against Barzani. In June 1961, Barzani led his first revolt against the Iraqi government with the aim of securing Kurdish autonomy. Qasim's government was not able to subdue the insurrection. The Ba'athist coup against Qasim in February 1963 resulted from his inability to deal with the Kurds forcefully. A ceasefire with the Kurds in 1964 caused a split among Kurdish radicals and traditional forces led by Barzani.

Barzani agreed to the ceasefire and expelled the radicals from the party. Seizing the opportunity of a crack in Kurdish unity, the central government in Baghdad moved against the Kurds militarily once again. This campaign failed in 1966, when Barzani's forces defeated the Iraqi Army near Rawanduz. Subsequently, the government in Baghdad issued a twelve-point peace program. The program was not implemented, however, because of a bloodless coup by the military in 1968 which installed the Ba'athist general Ahmad Hassan al-Bakr. The new regime began a fresh campaign to end the Kurdish insurrection, however the campaign was stalled in 1969 as an internal power struggle in Baghdad and tensions with Iran began to mount. Relenting to Soviet pressure to come to terms with Barzani, the al-Bakr government entered into a broadened peace plan providing for greater Kurdish autonomy within Iraq. The plan also granted Kurds representation in government bodies.

Simultaneously, the Iraqi government embarked on an Arabization program in the oil rich regions of Kirkuk and Khanaqin of Iraqi Kurdistan. Importing and resettling Sunni Arabs into the region became a priority for the Sunni-dominated minority government in Baghdad. In 1974, the government began a new offensive against the Kurds, pushing them closer to the border with Iran. Iraq negotiated with Iran to end Iranian support for the Iraqi Kurds in exchange for the settlement of border territory in Iran's favor. The 1975 Algiers Accords memorialized this agreement and Tehran cut supplies to the Kurdish movement. Support of the Kurds from the United States was also withdrawn.

Barzani, nevertheless, fled to Iran with many of his supporters. Others surrendered en masse and the resistance to Baghdad's control was quashed. The Iraqi government steadily extended its control over the northern region and advanced its Arabization program. In response to the government's repopulation policies, renewed clashes between Kurdish guerillas and Iraqi troops occurred in 1977. To punish the Kurds, Saddam's government leveled 600 Kurdish villages and forcibly removed 200,000 Kurds to other parts of the country in what was the beginning of a massive internal Kurdish diaspora.

Although the Iraqi Kurds had been severely mistreated under successive Arab regimes, it was nothing compared to what they would experience under the iron fist of Saddam Hussein who engineered his control over the government and the Ba'ath Party completely by 1977 and eased al-Bakr from the presidency by 1979.

2 _____

The Anfal Campaigns

To understand what happened to the Kurds in Iraq under Saddam Hussein, one must first understand the context of the Iran–Iraq War. Saddam never supported the 1975 Algiers Accords, which ceded 518 square kilometers of oil-rich territory adjacent to the Shatt al-Arab (a river on the border) to Iran in exchange for Iran's agreement to stop supporting Kurdish rebels in northern Iraq. And by 1979, the political landscape had changed dramatically. In Iraq, al-Bakr was dead and Saddam had emerged as the undisputed strongman. In Iran, the Shah had fled the country and the ayatollahs were completing their revolution amid continuing chaos. In the following year, having consolidated his power in Iraq and eliminated any immediate threat from his enemies, Saddam sought to take advantage of the turmoil in neighboring Iran and restore the Iraqi lands lost under the Algiers Accords.

Iraq's army crossed into Iran in September 1980, advancing to the outskirts of Abadan. Ayatollah Khomeni used the invasion to in turn consolidate his own power and rally Iranians to defend their homeland. Thus began the great clash between two large oil producers that would result in massive casualties on both sides during the ensuing eight years. As with most Cold War-era conflicts, the world took sides. Islamic countries were split between supporting the secular Islam, embodied by Saddam, and fanatical Islam, supported by the Ayatollah. The superpowers supported Iraq officially, but clandestinely assisted Iran—perhaps the most embarrassing demonstration was the Reagan Administration's secret sale of arms to Iran that secured funding for the U.S. intervention in Nicaragua.

By 1982, Iran had reversed the Iraqi invasion, restoring the border region. By 1984, Iran had driven into Iraq itself, secured the desert around Basra in the south, and cut Iraq off from the Persian Gulf. Desperate to restore the balance of the war and stem the gradual Iranian advance, Saddam employed chemical weapons against Iranian forces. These weapons proved an effective method of offsetting the advantage of Iran's much larger troop numbers, which Iranian generals had been sending across the border as "human waves." A recently declassified 1983 U.S. State Department memo assessing Saddam's use of chemical weapons quotes him as saying: "There is a weapon for every battle, and we have the weapon that will confront great numbers."[1]

Despite the use of chemical weapons against it, by the spring of 1987, Iran was making significant advances in the north, which Saddam correctly ascribed to assistance from Iraqi Kurdish sympathizers. Iran opened this second front in the rugged and easily defensible terrain of Iraqi Kurdistan. During the early years of the war, Saddam had ceded de facto control over much of the rural north to the Kurds and their *peshmerga* (guerilla fighters). But Iranian troops threatened to occupy more and more border territory with the mounting support of Iraqi Kurds. Thus, the vital Kirkuk oil fields, only a hundred miles from the border, were no longer safe from Iranian and/or Kurdish sabotage.

To handle what was referred to in captured Iraqi documents as "the Kurdish problem," Saddam tasked his cousin Ali Hassan al-Majid, leader of the Ba'ath Party's northern bureau, with the job of eradicating all resistance and granted him emergency powers to do so. Al-Majid then undertook a series of eight military campaigns against Kurdish "saboteurs" from 1987 to 1989. What began as a counterinsurgency during wartime ended in genocide, however. That the evidentiary trail of the ensuing military campaigns so clearly tells the story is a rarity in the annals of human rights, and is indeed a story in itself.

After Saddam's defeat in the first Gulf War in 1991, his beleaguered troops fell back under pressure from advancing forces led by Kurdish *peshmerga* militia fighters, who were reinforced by Kurdish refugees returning from their cousins' homelands in neighboring Turkey and Iran. This liberation of northern Iraq would prove fleeting as the United States withdrew its support, allowing Saddam's forces to later return en masse to put down the uprising. International nongovernmental organizations seized the short window of opportunity to get into northern Iraq and dispense aid to the returning populations as well as collect valuable evidence on the genocide many believed had occurred there three years earlier.

Middle East Watch, a regional division of Human Rights Watch, teamed up with Physicians for Human Rights to survey the mass graves that were being uncovered by the local Kurdish population. Over a ten-day period in 1991, several mass graves were exhumed near the Kurdish cities of Erbil and Suleimaniyeh. Large caches of Iraqi government and military records were also captured as hastily evacuated secret police buildings and government installations were stormed by advancing Kurds.

Peter Galbraith was dispatched by the U.S. Senate Foreign Relations Committee to broker a deal with the Kurds to secure the documents as Saddam was preparing to retake the north. Custody of the documents was secured with the assistance of Middle East Watch, and, in 1992, fourteen tons of documents were transferred to the Senate Committee where they remain to date. These, together with the forensic findings of Physicians for Human Rights and interviews conducted by Middle East Watch of 350 Kurdish survivors and eyewitnesses of the genocide, form the basis of a 1993 report: *The Anfal Campaign against the Kurds*.

This report recounts the initial systematic bureaucratic groundwork laid by al-Majid for his conduct of what would later become known as "the Anfal":

> In the first three months after assuming his post as secretary general of the Ba'ath Party's Northern Bureau, Ali Hassan al-Majid began the process of definition of the group that would be targeted by Anfal, and vastly expanded the range of repressive activities against all rural Kurds. He decreed that "saboteurs" would lose their property rights, suspended the legal rights of all the residents of prohibited villages, and began ordering the execution of first-degree relatives of "saboteurs" and of wounded civilians whose hostility to the regime had been determined by the intelligence services.
>
> In June 1987, al-Majid issued two successive sets of standing orders that were to govern the conduct of the security forces through the Anfal campaign and beyond. These orders were based on the simple axiom on which the regime now operated: in the "prohibited" rural areas, all resident Kurds were coterminous with the *peshmerga* insurgents, and they would be dealt with accordingly.
>
> The first of al-Majid's directives bans all human existence in the prohibited areas, to be applied through a shoot-to-kill policy. The second, numbered SF/4008, dated June 20, 1987, modifies and expands upon these orders. It constitutes a bald incitement to mass murder, spelled out in the most chilling detail. In clause 4, army commanders are ordered "to carry out random bombardments, using artillery, helicopters and aircraft, at all times of the day or night, in order to kill the largest number of persons present in these prohibited zones." In clause 5, al-Majid orders that, "All persons captured in those villages shall be detained and interrogated by the security services and those between the ages of 15 and 70 shall be executed after any useful information has been obtained from them, of which we should be duly notified."
>
> Even as this legal and bureaucratic structure was being set in place, the Iraqi regime became the first in history to attack its own civilian population with chemical weapons. On April 15, 1987, Iraqi aircraft dropped poison gas on the [Kurdistan Democratic Party] headquarters at Zewa Shkan, close to the Turkish border in Dohuk governorate, and the [Patriotic Union of Kurdistan] headquarters in the twin villages of Sergalou and Bergalou, in the governorate of Suleimaniyeh. The following afternoon, they dropped chemicals on the undefended civilian villages of Sheikh Wasan and Balisan, killing well over a hundred people, most of them women and children. Scores of other victims of the attack were abducted from their hospital beds in the city of Erbil, where they had been taken for treatment of their burns and blindness. They have never been seen again. These incidents were the first of at least forty documented chemical attacks on Kurdish targets over the succeeding eighteen months.[2]

Al-Majid employed a variety of chemical weapons during the Anfal campaign, including mustard gas, a blistering agent and Sarin, a nerve agent known as GB. His penchant for this method of extermination earned him the sobriquet "Chemical Ali," and a fearful reputation for brutality almost matching that of Saddam himself.

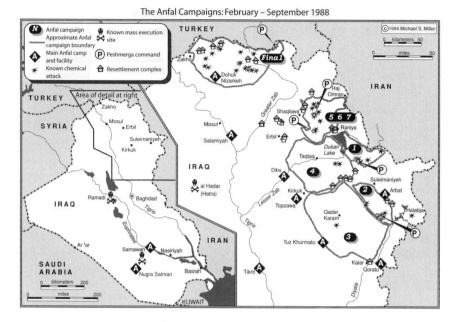

Figure 2.1. The Anfal Campaigns. *Source*: Michael Miller, Middle East Watch. © 1994 Michael S. Miller.

Galbraith, who secured the documentary evidence for the Senate and later went on to become ambassador to Croatia, characterized al-Majid as the "Josef Mengele of [the Anfal] operation," referring to the Nazi doctor who carried out experiments on Jews. "It was a deadly experiment to see which of these weapons were the most effective."[3]

One survivor of al-Majid's April 1987 chemical attacks on Kurdish villages in the Balisan valley described the effect of the pink, gray, and yellow gases drifting through the towns:

> It was all dark, covered with darkness, we could not see anything. . . . It was like a fog. And then everyone became blind. Some vomited. Faces turned black; people experienced painful swellings under the arm, and women under their breasts. Later, a yellow watery discharge would ooze from the eyes and nose. Many of those who survived suffered severe vision disturbances, or total blindness for up to a month. . . . Some villagers ran into the mountains and died there. Others, who had been closer to the place of impact of the bombs, died where they stood.[4]

The Anfal campaigns occurred over a large range of Kurdish-inhabited northern Iraq and, based upon the documents secured by Middle East Watch and witness testimony, can be subdivided into eight distinct military operations all sharing the same objective—elimination of the Kurds (see Figure 2.1). All shared the ultimate chain of command up through General al-Majid directly to Saddam Hussein.

FIRST ANFAL: THE SIEGE OF SERGALOU AND BERGALOU, FEBRUARY 23–MARCH 19, 1988

The Patriotic Union of Kurdistan (PUK) was a political and military force resisting the rule of Saddam. It was led by Jalal Talabani, who went on to assume the postwar presidency of Iraq in April 2005. The PUK and Mr. Talabani were high on Saddam's hit list, and the PUK's collusion with Iran during the war provided enough of a pretext for decimating the Kurdish civilian population that was supporting them. The PUK's main redoubt was nestled deep in the mountains of Suleimaniyeh in the Jafati valley. Its underground radio and communications operations were carried out in nearby Bergalou, which also housed a small field hospital. The *peshmergas*, PUK's military insurgents, operated out of Sergalou, a village of about 3,500 people.

Saddam's targets were clear, and on the night of February 23, 1988, between 1:30 A.M. and 2:00 A.M., his forces began shelling villages in the Jafati valley during a heavy rainstorm. At dawn, ground troops attacked. The *peshmergas* held out for three weeks and the villagers hid in local caves—about 250 people were killed during the siege. Then as Saddam's army began its breakthrough and village after village was razed, Kurds began fleeing en masse eastward toward the Iranian border.

It was still winter in the mountains and the bedraggled Kurds were harassed by bombers and warplanes as they fled. One survivor from Sergalou said, "We left behind all the properties accumulated over fifty years.... The people moved like a panicked herd of cattle through the mountains in the direction of Iran. It was raining. There were warplanes overhead.... Six people from Sergalou froze to death along the way, and another thirty from other villages in the same valley."[5] At least eighty people died from exposure during the long trek to the border. Stragglers were offered safety, only to be indefinitely detained and then ultimately disappear. Trick amnesties would become a ubiquitous tactic employed by the Iraqi military during the Anfals.

PUK's headquarters had fallen and the *peshmergas* had been dispersed. However, the Anfals had only just begun. The chemical gassing of the city of Halabja was next on General al-Majid's agenda. That atrocity, discussed in the next chapter in greater detail, unfolded on March 16, 1988.

SECOND ANFAL: QARA DAGH, MARCH 22–APRIL 1, 1988

By March 22, Saddam's forces had turned their attention to the lowlands of the Qara Dagh mountains and to three villages of PUK activity in particular—Takiyeh and Balagjar, which were easily overrun, and Sayw Senan, which suffered a devastating chemical attack on the first day of spring. A farmer named Omar who came to Sayw Senan after the attack recalled, "We saw the bodies of those who had died inside the village. I helped bury sixty-seven with my own hands in

Koshk village after we took them there on tractors. We laid them all in one big grave in the Jaji Raqa graveyard, with their clothes on. Another fourteen bodies were buried in Asteli Serru village. They had died instantly. They were bleeding from the nose; it was as if their brains had exploded."[6]

The ground assault began the next day, after the chemicals had subsided, leading to a mass exodus of the general Kurdish population. People fled into the hillsides to the north, hoping to eventually find sanctuary in Suleimaniyeh. They were harassed all the way by a confusing dragnet of Iraqi soldiers, Saddam's intelligence forces, and *jahsh* militia—Kurdish turncoats and informants working for Saddam. Women and children generally made it through, the men, however, did not.

The rest of the Kurds in the area fled south from Zerda Mountain toward Germian. Saddam's troops began systematically razing all the villages in the Qara Dagh region and continued their pursuit of the terrified refugees. The PUK's *peshmerga* fighters had been routed in the mountains and were fleeing behind the civilians. Artillery rained down upon the mass of moving people as they evacuated to Germian, a large rolling plain that would be the sight of the third Anfal once Saddam's troops had caught up with them.

THIRD ANFAL: GERMIAN, APRIL 7–20, 1988

By the second week in April, ragged *peshmerga* fighters and the weary Kurds from Qara Dagh had made their way into Germian villages along the Awa Su River, or the "white river" named after its milky waters. Unlike the strategic Jafati valley of the first Anfal or even the lowlands of Qara Dagh of the second Anfal, the great plain of Germian, bisected only by the small river, offered no geographic fortifications from which the remnants of Kurdish forces could hope to mount a viable defense and give the civilians a chance to flee.

Iraqi troop columns converged on the plain from eight directions. Massive pincer movements encircled *peshmerga* positions and funneled civilian refugee flows into designated "collection points." Military units reported back to their respective commands messages like this one from the Kalar column: "All the villages that the convoy passed through were destroyed and burned, since most of the villages were not marked on the map."[7] The names of obliterated villages correlated to sites of mass disappearances according to the Middle East Watch report.

The third Anfal was divided into three phases centering on Tuz Khurmata, Qader Karam and northern Germian, and Sengaw and southern Germian respectively. These campaigns differed markedly from the second Anfal—where military-aged men were the primary focus. Women and children disappeared in large numbers as entire villages were wiped out during this larger scale Anfal campaign.

Three task forces swept into the area during the Tuz Khurmata phase. British-supplied Hawker Hunter aircraft were used to drop chemical weapons sending up large clouds of white smoke. Aisha, one of the witnesses interviewed by Middle East Watch, was a twenty-year-old pregnant woman who watched the attacks from a hilltop. Upon descending in the evening, she discovered the bodies of twenty-five *peshmerga* and dead goats, cows, and birds—all victims of gas. She collected her children and headed for the hills. Eventually, she found refuge in a cave with other villagers. There, she gave birth to her baby. Too weak from hunger to nurse, she ventured out on the third day in search of food, but was picked up by a *jahsh* patrol and taken to a nearby school where people were being held.

There she found food and waited as more villagers surrendered themselves, filling the building. When the Iraqi army arrived and took over from the *jahsh*, soldiers began loading men into military buses and then women and children. Surprisingly, an officer took pity on her and allowed her to leave for Suleimaniyeh to the north. In one of the rare happy endings of the Anfal tragedy, Aisha was later reunited with the baby she had left behind in the cave with other villagers, although her husband, brothers, and twelve other family members did not return.[8]

The second phase of the campaign centered on Qader Karam and the northern sector of Germian. The thrust of this campaign resulted in villagers fleeing from scores of towns surrounding the recently emptied Qader Karam, including the many Jabari hamlets of the Zangana tribe, Mahmoud Parizad, Tazashar, Hanara, Golama, Bangol, Qeitoul, Garawi, and Qirtsa. Once evacuated, Iraqi troops torched the buildings and bulldozed the smoldering remains of the towns. Mass roundups of surviving and surrendering villagers commonly resulted in people being loaded onto buses that disappeared over the horizon. The refugee migration from this phase of the third Anfal flowed into four collection centers: Chamchamal, Qader Karam, Leilan, and Aliawa.

The third phase of the campaign likewise focused on collecting the panicked Kurdish population in some organized way while simultaneously crushing the remnants of *peshmerga* resistance. At the outset, nearly twenty villages were destroyed at the Awa Spi River's source, villagers were driven toward Chamchamal and the *peshmerga* were driven up against the southern edge of the Qara Dagh mountains. Similar tactics swept the southern sector of Germian clear as civilian casualties mounted; *pershmerga* were annihilated and villagers were relocated en masse on trucks or on foot. The collection centers for this phase of the campaign were Tuz Khurmatu and Qoratu.

Those interned at the collection centers were separated by sex and age. Many were beaten and malnourished. Most were ultimately removed to larger detention camps at Topzawa, Tikrit, and Nugra and Salman in the desert stretching to the Saudi border, and to the women's prison in Dibs. At Topzawa, which housed four to five thousand Kurds in a given week, the men were crammed into large holding halls so tightly that they could not lie down and had to squat all night—those who stood were beaten. Little provision was made for sanitation and all had diarrhea from the oily bone-laden soup that was served. The women and children were terrorized differently. Guards routinely removed children and infants from their mothers—taken away for the night only to be returned in some cases the next day without explanation. Some younger children died of starvation; soldiers threw their bodies into outside pits.

Brutality also reigned in the camp at Tikrit. Muhammad, a man in his sixties from Talau, witnessed abuses by the *Amn*—Saddam's intelligence agents:

> On the first morning, they separated the men into small groups and beat them. Four soldiers would beat one captive; the other prisoners could see this. About fifteen or twenty men were in each group that was taken a little way off to be kicked and beaten with sticks and [coaxial] cables. They were taken away in the early morning and returned in the afternoon. The soldiers did not gather the men by name, but just pointed, "you, and you" and so on. They were *Amn* from Tikrit and Kirkuk; butchers, we know them. When one group of beaten men returned, they took another and beat them. That night, I was in a group of ten or twelve men that was taken out and blindfolded, with our hands tied behind us. They took us in three or four cars to somewhere in Tikrit. We drove around all night, barely stopping. They asked me no questions. The captured men could not talk to each other. Everyone was thinking of his own destiny. Of the ten or twelve they took out that night, only five returned. The next night, when I was back in the hall, *Amn* came and asked for men to volunteer for the war against Iran. Eighty men volunteered. But it was a lie; they disappeared. A committee was set up by *Amn* to process the prisoners, who were ordered to squat while the *Amn* agents took all their money and put it in a big sack. They also took all our documents. The *Amn* agents were shouting at us to scare us. "Bring weapons to kill them," said one. "They are poor, don't shoot them," said another. And another: "I wish we had killed all of them." Later that night the *Amn* came back and took all the young men away. Only the elderly remained. The young men were taken away in Nissan buses, ten or more of them, each with a capacity of forty-five people. Their documents had already been taken; they left with nothing but the clothes on their backs. I never heard from them again. There were no messages, nothing. No one ever saw them again. Only Saddam Hussein knows.[9]

Dibs served as the women's prison—which was a step up from conditions at Topzawa. Women here could use the bathroom without restriction and rations were no longer near-starvation. The general treatment remained bad and many calamities befell the children. Buses would regularly appear and load up what appeared to be random prisoners for transport to a grimmer destination—Nugra Salman, in the middle of the southern desert.

Nugra Salman housed between six and eight thousand Kurds. It quickly became known as a last stop for the elderly and infirm. Inmates, infested by lice and beaten steadily, survived on bread and nonpotable water. Over 500 died here between April and September 1988. Bodies were left by guards to rot in the desert sun for up to three days before removal in bags that were taken out for garbage.

Those who had surrendered to the *jahsh* and government troops expecting amnesty ended up in these camps and had many months to languish and second-guess their decision if they survived.

FOURTH ANFAL: THE VALLEY OF THE LESSER ZAB, MAY 3–8, 1988

The remaining *peshmerga*, accompanying the fleeing civilians heading north along the Lesser Zab River, divided themselves into three forces to provide what protection they could for the large contingents of women and children. As Saddam's troops regrouped in the Germian to head north, his air force undertook a series of strikes against the towns of Goktapa and Askar, further north, where the PUK had tried to reestablish its command.

A formation of MIGs flew in low overhead, followed by eight "dull explosions" and spreading white smoke smelling of mint. The gas cloud drifted a couple of miles down to the river. Dead fish floated to the surface of water on the Lesser Zab where one of the bombs fell. Horrified villagers ran in all directions covering their faces with wet towels. Survivors claim to have buried 300 people from that attack. Yasin, a woman in her sixties who helped with the burials, said, "Some of their faces were black, covered with smoke. Others were ordinary but stiff. I saw one mother, nursing her infant, stiffened in that position."[10]

Twelve hours later, ground forces moved in—scattering the dazed population in all directions. The sluices of the nearby dam were opened and the waters of the Lesser Zab began to rise, preventing the refugees from crossing and pinning them along the valley. Most were funneled into Qamisha where the army was waiting for them. *Peshmerga* established rearguard actions en route, but to little avail. At Qamisha, Iraqi troops stripped Kurds of their money, valuables, and documents while homes were systematically looted and burned. The story was repeated at other small towns-turned refugee camps along the river. Those who managed to escape went beyond the valley, to where the Lesser Zab empties into the vast plain between Erbil and Kirkuk, and sought refuge where they could in Shwan area villages. However, with no meaningful defense, Iraqi forces swept the area quickly and routed them to collection points in Harmota and Taqtaq. From there, transport to the camps awaited them.

FIFTH, SIXTH AND, SEVENTH ANFALS: THE MOUNTAIN VALLEYS OF SHAQLAWA AND RAWANDUZ, MAY 15–AUGUST 26, 1988

This was the PUK's last stand. Jalal Talabani's loyal *peshmerga* resistance fighters had been dislodged from their stronghold in the Jafati valley after a fierce siege, pursued through the mountains of Qara Dagh, swept from the plains of Germian, and pushed out of the valley of the Lesser Zab. By the middle of May, they were preparing for their final battle—cornered in the steep mountains north of Dukan Lake, south of the town of Rawanduz and just west of the Iranian frontier.

The strength of *peshmerga* positions in the Balisan region explains why three separate campaigns occurred here. Unlike prior Anfals, the fifth and sixth failed to achieve their objectives. *Peshmerga* and civilians clung tightly to their cave hideouts and survived repeated gas attacks. Iraqi air force units, some of which were Russian-built Sukhoi fighter-bombers, dropped cluster bombs and chemical weapons relentlessly. But when the bluish smoke cleared, the casualties were not sufficient for Saddam's forces to consider the operation a success, although many corpses of horse and sheep littered the fields below. The fifth Anfal reached a stalemate on June 7, 1988. Captured military documents indicate that the Iraqi army was frustrated about its inability to effectively attack the Kurds in and around Korak Mountain, which rose 7,000 feet from the Alana valley.

During the break in the fighting, Jalal Talabani made his way to Washington, DC where he attempted to plead the case of the Kurds and make the Reagan administration aware of the genocide that was unfolding in the region. Only a mid-level State Department officer met with Talabani, and told him frankly that "because of his Iranian alliance, his group has enjoyed a certain degree of military success at the expense of the Kurdish population as a whole,"—echoing the official line from Saddam's regime, with whom the United States was still allied.[11]

On July 17, 1988, the Iranians sued for peace in the Iran–Iraq War, breaching the agreement they had struck with the PUK in 1986 that neither party would unilaterally strike a deal with Saddam. Realizing that the full force of Saddam's army now would be turned against them, the Kurds holding out in this sector decided that those who could no longer fight should take their families into the Kurdish lands across the border in Iran. Remaining *peshmerga* would stay behind and cover the retreat out of Iraq.

The sixth Anfal launched coordinated air strikes, making shambles of the escape plan. Multiple chemical bombardments in the main valleys (Balisan, Malakan, Warta, Hiran, and Smaquli) drove the people up into the mountain slopes to get above the gas clouds settling along their escape routes. Then, cluster bombs directed into the mountainsides drove them back down into the valleys— scattering people everywhere. Iraqi units quickly collected survivors and shipped them off to the dreadful Topzawa camp.

Despite the success of the sixth Anfal, Iraqi troops were not fast enough to close off two main escape routes into Iran. Assisted by sympathetic *jahsh* commanders, several families made it across. With the last of their people gone, the PUK dynamited its headquarters and fled the area. No longer was the Kurdish resistance a factor for Saddam. The seventh Anfal was a preparatory campaign to soften-up the Badinan area—home to Barzani's Kurdistan Democratic Party (KDP) faction.

FINAL ANFAL: BADINAN, AUGUST 25–SEPTEMBER 6, 1988

With the defeat of the PUK, Saddam's attention turned to the smaller KDP faction led by Mas'oud Barzani. With the close of the Iran–Iraq War, General al-Majid's Anfal operations were infused with new troops and equipment from the front and entire armies were redeployed from Fao and Basra in the south to Iraqi Kurdistan in the north. Unlike the PUK forces, which were spread throughout Kurdistan along the Iranian border, the KDP forces were concentrated in and around Badinan along the Turkish border between the Greater Zab River and the

Zargos Mountains. Although not as closely associated with the regime in Tehran as the PUK, the KDP had been traditionally allied with the Shah and continued to have enough ties with Iran for Saddam to easily use the same pretext for wiping them out as he had used against the PUK.

A small band of five to six thousand KDP *peshmerga* faced the now-inflated full force of 200,000 troops under al-Majid's command in addition to the *jahsh* fighters. The goal for this final Anfal was the elimination of the KDP and the destruction of 300–400 Kurdish villages along the mountainous border with Turkey. Fleeing into the Kurdish lands of Turkey would prove problematic, as Turkish forces were waging a low-level war against their own Kurdish insurgent group, the Kurdistan Workers' Party (PKK), led by Abdullah Öcalan. Consequently, Iraqi Kurds would be faced with the Hobson's choice of moving between conflicts or into Arab lands as there would be little sanctuary within the now cleared Anfal areas to the east.

The final Anfal was characterized by a heavier-than-usual reliance on chemical weapons. Saddam, apparently, had decided to use the remainder of his wartime supply on the Kurds rather than risk storing it. On the evening of August 24, 1988, KDP headquarters at Zewa Shkan was hit with gas. The following morning, Iraqi warplanes began bombing villages in earnest along a large strip of territory sixty miles wide by twenty miles deep.

A combination of mustard gas and Sarin nerve gas was used to deadly effect. A villager from Birjinni witnessed three planes making a pass overhead and dropping four bombs each, from which clouds of smoke rose "white, black and then yellow, rising about fifty or sixty yards into the air in a column. Then the column began to break up and drift. It drifted down into the valley and then passed through the village. Then we smelled the gas. It smelled of apples and something sweet. [Soon] it became bitter. It affected our eyes and our mouths and our skin. All of a sudden it was hard to breathe."[12] The final Anfal had begun.

The army later attacked on the ground, moving north in an attempt to seal the Turkish border. Those who lived along the frontier made it across (between 65,000 and 80,000 Kurds), and those who didn't were arrested and disappeared. Much of General al-Majid's firepower was concentrated on Gara Mountain, which forms a ridge stretching twenty miles. Between fifteen and thirty villages were targeted by the air force. The spread of the bombings was so wide that no village in the Anfal zone was more than twenty-five miles away from a chemical attack. Gas literally blanketed the area.

Realizing that a safe mass exodus across the border was not possible given the terrain, age of the refugees (majority of them were either old or young), vastly superior numbers of Iraqi troops, and that further resistance would trigger more chemical attacks, KDP headquarters issued an order to its *peshmerga* to advise fleeing Kurds to submit and hope for mercy. The occupation of Badinan and detention of the panicked Kurds was achieved on August 28, 1988.

Women and children were mostly spared in the final Anfal as KDP resistance faded early in the campaign. The men, however, were all suspected *peshmerga* and were specifically targeted for summary execution upon surrender. According to a former lieutenant colonel in the Iraqi Army, directives 3650 and 4008 from the military high command were clear: "We received orders to kill all *peshmerga*, even those who surrendered. Even civilian farmers were regarded as *peshmerga* if they were working within a prohibited area. All men in the prohibited areas, aged between 15 and 60, were to be considered saboteurs and killed. The prohibited areas were shown in red on the army maps, and they covered everything except the paved highways."[13] Mass firing squads were formed and group executions were undertaken under the authority of local army officers.

Well over 13,000 Kurds were collected and sent to a new camp established at Dohuk Fort, a Soviet-style concrete bunker. Dohuk Fort proved just as horrendous as the camp at Topzawa, if not more so, in that there was no attempt to feed the inmates. The survivors instead relied primarily on handouts from sympathetic villagers and guards. The detainees were crammed into cells "strewn with human waste"—which one prisoner recalled was like living in a toilet. Hunger and disease, interspersed with beatings and interrogations, became the order of the day.

Eventually, the younger men were massed and bundled onto outbound buses, never to be seen again. Women and children were also rounded up, but they were bused south to Mosul in large convoys. There they were detained for about two and half weeks outside the town of Salamiyeh on the east bank of the Tigris River.

AFTERMATH OF THE ANFALS

With the PUK and KDP no longer significant security issues, the depopulations of key Kurdish areas achieved, and the Iran–Iraq War over, Saddam issued a general amnesty for all Kurds on September 6, 1988. Decree number 736 came into effect immediately. The stories of the Anfals had been leaking out to the Western media from Kurdish refugees hiding in Turkey. General al-Majid was given special command powers to resettle the Kurds as they returned. However, they would not be settled in their now destroyed villages. Returning Kurds would be settled where General al-Majid wanted them settled and they would be permitted to build their own houses in designated areas.

"Repatriated" Kurds were forced to sign a statement which read: "I, the undersigned (. . . .) testify that I live in the governorate of (. . . .), in the section of (. . . .), residence number (. . . .), and I recognize that I will face the death penalty should the information indicated be false, or should I alter my address without notifying the appropriate administration and authorities. To this I affirm my support."[14]

The detention camps were emptied at regular intervals and buses driven north to over a dozen complexes set up to receive the former inmates. The trip north was as chaotic and traumatic as the trip south had been. Upon arrival, those who attempted to return to their ruined homesteads were executed. The city of Erbil became a makeshift staging area from which returnees left for their new designated areas—which were not supplied with food, water, building materials, or shelter. Influenza, hepatitis, and typhoid further depleted the ranks of returning Kurds, who survived only on the charity of the citizens of Erbil.

Vast "prohibited areas" were demarcated around where the Kurds resettled—devoid of human habitation or agricultural cultivation. Without the ability to sustain themselves, the Kurds became completely reliant on food aid from the international community.

All told, the Anfal campaign against the Kurds claimed between 100,000 and 200,000 lives by a conservative estimate. However, no single action accounts for all the casualties. There were multiple mass murders, multiple mass disappearances, forced displacement of hundreds of thousands of noncombatants, destruction of 2,000 villages that were classified in Iraqi government documents as "burned," "destroyed," "demolished," or "purified," and the razing of a dozen larger Kurdish towns and administrative centers. Altogether, 4049 villages were leveled.

The deadly combination of methods employed against the Kurds during the eight Anfals intertwines to form the most complete picture of genocide. Although the successive gassings are perhaps the starkest examples, conventional killing by shooting accounted for equal numbers of deaths. For instance, the majority of Kurdish detainees sent to Topzawa were registered and segregated. Adult and teenage males were then loaded onto closed trucks and taken to the execution grounds at places like Ramadi and Hatra, where they were lined up next to large pits and shot. The trenches were covered once full.

The elderly were mostly bused to the camp at Nugra Salman in the Iraqi desert, where death rates averaged four to five per day from exposure and infection. The women and children went elsewhere. They were usually taken to Dibs, a camp close to the Kirkuk-Mosul highway, where many of the children succumbed to dysentery and malnutrition. About half of the women were taken to death pits like the one at Samawa.

Forced deportation, typically accompanied by the razing of villages, was also a common feature of the Anfals. By the end of the campaigns, 1.5 million Kurds had been forcibly resettled. This was part of an overall scheme by Saddam to rearrange Kurdistan in northern Iraq, placing more key areas under Arab control. So unlike discreet acts of genocide undertaken in places like Srebrenica where Bosnian Muslim men were singled out and shot at or large-scale genocidal assaults like that which occurred at the sharp end of a machete in Rwanda, the genocide of Iraq's Kurds came in multiple waves. It was protracted as opposed to sudden. Another distinguishing feature of the Anfals is that the genocide was effectuated through a variety of methods and was followed by a general amnesty put in place by the same regime that undertook the atrocities. Yet genocide it was.

The Gassing of Halabja

Halabja lies roughly ten miles inside Iraq from the Iranian border in southern Kurdistan—about 150 miles northeast of Baghdad. The town's Kurdish residents speak the Hewrami and Sorani dialects. They are Sunni Muslims—the same religion as Saddam's and his Arab regime but not of the same ethnicity. The population of Halabja in 1988 was 40,000, but this was enlarged by another 20,000 Kurds from surrounding villages who were fleeing the war.

On March 13, 1988, Iranian forces began shelling Iraqi military positions in and around Halabja, and by March 15th Iranian advance forces were already on the streets of the city. Local Kurds did not resist the Iranian advance and the Patriotic Union of Kurdistan's (PUK) *peshmerga* in fact facilitated it. Saddam's forces counterattacked the next day, first with napalm—stripping away huge swaths of the city and citizens with massive firestorms—then with conventional bombs and artillery, and finally with gas.

Although it occurred at the beginning of the Anfal campaign, the attack on Halabja was not considered part of the Anfals because, in the bureaucratic mindset of the Iraqi government, Halabja was a city. The Anfals were undertaken specifically to deal with the Kurdish rural population—wiping out the villages, eradicating the PUK and Kurdistan Democratic Party (KDP), and displacing the Kurds entirely from strategic locations.

Nevertheless, the gassing of Halabja is widely considered the single most horrific incident during this notorious period, accounting for approximately 5,000 of the deaths suffered by the Kurds in the Anfals. Another 7,000 Kurds were wounded, crippled, blinded, or suffered other injuries related either to the conventional or chemical bombings of the city. Consequently, Halabja has become

emblematic of the Kurdish genocide, much as Srebrenica is for the Bosnian genocide or Auschwitz for the Jewish Holocaust.

According to a 2002 U.S. State Department report, General al-Majid's coldly
diabolical approach can be discerned from his methodology of extermination.
Knowing that the gasses he intended to use were heavier than air and would thus
sink, he opened the March 16 attack on Halabja with a conventional artillery
bombardment for several hours, setting off the air raid sirens. This drove the local
Kurdish population down into tunnels, cellars, and basements.

Those underground shelters became gas chambers as al-Majid unleashed
his bombardment of poison. Aboveground, animals died and birds dropped out
of trees. Belowground, humans met their end, trapped. Those who managed to
scramble to the surface emerged into thick clouds of chemical gas:

> Dead bodies—human and animal—littered the streets, huddled in doorways, slumped
> over the steering wheels of their cars. Survivors stumbled around, laughing hysterically,
> before collapsing. . . . Those who had been directly exposed to the gas found that their
> symptoms worsened as the night wore on. Many children died along the way and were
> abandoned where they fell.[1]

Agiza, who was eight years old and out in the fields when her village near
Bahdinan was gassed, remembered seeing the planes come in and drop bombs.
She recalled an experience similar to those recounted by survivors of Halabja:

> It made smoke, yellowish-white smoke. It had a bad smell like DDT, the powder they
> kill insects with. It had a bitter taste. . . . I saw my parents fall down with my brother
> after the attack, and they told me they were dead. I looked at their skin and it was
> black and they weren't moving. And I was scared and crying and I did not know
> what to do. I saw their skin turn dark and blood coming out from their mouths and
> from their noses. I wanted to touch them but they stopped me and I started crying
> again.[2]

Aras Abed Akra was twenty-two years old at the time of the gassing. He
recounted his story to a Financial Times reporter in 2002: "We could smell something strange like apples. Down in our shelter we felt short of breath. A soldier
went out and next door he saw that the caged birds of our neighbour were all
dead. We stayed in the shelter until evening, but then I just wanted to escape. We
wrapped our faces in wet towels. It was hard to breathe. One friend became blind
immediately when he removed his towel. We got confused and lost, couldn't see
more than a metre ahead."[3]

Medical camps were quickly set up across the border in Iran, which had
experience dealing with the aftereffects of poison gas that Saddam had used on
Iranian soldiers earlier in the war. Survivors who were strong enough streamed into
Iran. Kaveh Golestan, a Pulitzer Prize winning Iranian photographer, witnessed

the Iraqi MiG-26 sortie from outside Halabja, noting, "It was not as big as a nuclear mushroom cloud, but several smaller ones: thick smoke." Golestan, then entered the city after the bombing with a gas mask and protective suit to cover the story via military helicopter:

> It was life frozen. Life had stopped, like watching a film and suddenly it hangs on one frame. It was a new kind of death to me. You went into a room, a kitchen and you saw the body of a woman holding a knife where she had been cutting a carrot.
>
> The aftermath was worse. Victims were still being brought in. Some villagers came to our chopper. They had 15 or 16 beautiful children, begging us to take them to hospital. So all the press sat there and we were each handed a child to carry. As we took off, fluid came out of my little girl's mouth and she died in my arms.[4]

Once the gassings were complete, an effectiveness evaluation by Iraqi authorities began. According to Dr. Christine Gosden, a British professor of medical genetics at Liverpool University who treated Halabja survivors, "Iraqi government troops would be surrounding the attack site and they would have chem-bio suits on . . . included would be doctors and interested observers . . . they would go in and find out how many people were dead . . . and how many survived. What ages . . . did men, women or children or the elderly suffer more? From there they would shoot the survivors and burn the bodies. . . ."[5]

As photos (Figure 3.1) of dead children crumpled on steps or lying contorted and bleached in the streets reached the world, an outcry arose at last from the human rights community.

Despite the notice garnered in nongovernmental circles, the response to the attack on Halabja from other states was muted silence. None could offer much beyond platitudes, as they all had backed Saddam during the Iran–Iraq War with arms and financing. Indeed, Germany is widely considered to have been the industrial origin of the gas used by al-Majid during the Anfal campaign, and Kurdish leaders have long accused France, Italy, and the Netherlands of providing assistance to Saddam's chemical weapons program.[6]

The United States was also implicated, as noted by James Tuite in his background note to a 1992 Senate Banking, Housing and Urban Affairs Committee staff report assessing the use of chemical weapons by Saddam against American troops in the first Gulf War:

> [A]n inquiry was initiated by the Committee into the contributions that exports from the United States played in the weapons of mass destruction programs that have flourished under the direction of Iraqi President Saddam Hussein.
>
> On October 27, 1992, the Committee on Banking, Housing and Urban Affairs held hearings that revealed that the United States had exported chemical, biological, nuclear, and missile-system equipment to Iraq that was converted to military use in Iraq's chemical, biological, and nuclear weapons program.[7]

Figure 3.1. Kurdish father Omar Osman and his infant son, victims of the March 16, 1988 chemical gas attack on Halabja. *Source*: Iranian News Agency (IRNA), used with permission from the Kurdish Democratic Party.

Saddam tried to pass off the attack as coming from the Iranians, not Iraqi forces under General al-Majid. In fact, Iraqi troops were "sent into Halabja to carry away all the missile casings and unexploded projectiles." But journalists on the scene, like Christopher Hitchens, a British columnist for *Vanity Fair*, stumbled across remnants of evidence that was overlooked: "I still possess a photograph of myself, sitting queasily next to an undetonated chemical bomb with Iraqi air force markings. It was embedded in the basement of a ruined house, and had escaped the vigilance of the much-vaunted Republican Guard."[8]

The Reagan administration, which was then backing Saddam against the Ayatollah, initially bought Saddam's version of events. Intelligence collected by the Defense Intelligence Agency concurred with Saddam's claim (which was subsequently accepted and then refuted by the CIA). By then, the United States had restored formal diplomatic ties with Iraq, which had been severed since 1967. Donald Rumsfeld reopened diplomatic relations as President Reagan's special envoy for the Middle East. Although officially neutral during the war, billions of dollars in loan guarantees and other aid was flowing from Washington to Baghdad—Saddam was considered "unsavory" but the lesser of two evils.

President Reagan justified the U.S. position on national security grounds to maintain the steady flow of oil shipments through the Persian Gulf, as shown specifically in paragraph three of national security decision directive 114 (Figure 3.2), (see also other recently declassified documents pertaining to Washington's approach to Saddam in Appendix A).

The United States was also aware of chemical weapons possession and use by Saddam to counter insurgents within Iraq as well as the overwhelming numbers of Iranians coming across the frontlines in what were known as "human waves" (see Appendix B). The Reagan administration knew the Western origin of the chemical compounds. While Washington officially condemned the Baghdad regime for employing chemical weapons in violation of international law, it went on to block Iranian initiatives to condemn the acts before the U.N. Security Council.

Because the world was now on notice of Saddam's proclivity to use poison gas, the assertion that Iran was involved in the gassing of Halabja was no longer widely accepted. A thorough investigation by Dr. Jean Pascal Zanders, Chair of the Chemical and Biological Warfare Project at the Stockholm International Peace Research Institute, concluded that Iraqi forces had bombed Halabja, not Iran. Eventually, even the United States had to accept that Saddam had committed the attack.

Ultimately, Saddam admitted during the first half of the Anfal trial that he had used chemical weapons against Iran. He denied attacking the Iraqi Kurds— despite the introduction into evidence of a 1987 memo from Iraqi military intelligence requesting permission from the president to use mustard gas and Sarin against the Kurds and a reply document ordering the military to study the possibility of a sudden strike using those weapons against both Iranians and Kurds.

A decade after the horror that unfolded in Halabja, Dr. Gosden of the University of Liverpool, who initially treated the survivors decided to conduct a study assessing the aftermath and long-term effects of the gassings on the Kurdish population of Halabja. The multiple types of gas used by Saddam against the Kurds made her assessment of long-term effects particularly problematic. Nevertheless, Dr. Gosden was able to make the following findings.

LONG-TERM EFFECTS ON THE PEOPLE OF HALABJA

There had been no systematic and detailed research study carried out in Halabja in the ten years since the attack. The novel effects such as those on reproductive function, congenital malformations, long term neurological and neuropsychiatric effects, (especially on those who were very young at the time), and cancers in women and children are of special importance. There is no knowledge about the

Figure 3.2. National Security Decision Directive 114. *Source*: National Security Archives, George Washington University.

ways in which the serious and long-term damage caused by these weapons can be treated.

What we found is sobering, if not frightening. It must serve as a wakeup call about the need for improving our medical preparedness and national and international response plans to chemical weapons attack. For example, eye, respiratory, and neuropsychiatric problems do not appear to respond to conventional therapy. It may be necessary to develop new methods of research and treatment.

Severe respiratory problems. These require assessments of lung function, trials of drugs that may be of help and consideration of the possibility of lung transplants for the most severely affected.

Cancers. The cancer risks in this population are high and the people are dying very young of large, aggressive, rapidly metastasizing tumors. There is a need for improved diagnosis, surgery, pathology, and better imaging (CT, MR, and bone scans). Methods of chemotherapy and radiotherapy for these chemical weapons-induced cancers may be different from those of other cancers and require knowledge of the types of mutations that lead to these cancers.

Congenital malformations. The types and range of congenital malformation are extremely extensive, although certain major effects can be seen. These include congenital heart conditions, mental handicap, neural tube defects, and cleft lip and palate. There is a need for pediatric surgeons to repair heart defects, cleft palate, etc., improved diagnosis and imaging and many other forms of professional help (e.g., speech therapy, occupational therapy, and specialist teaching for the handicapped).

Neurological and psychiatric problems. These are among the most alarming of the effects of these weapons and are also the most difficult to quantify scientifically and diagnose. These are the problems that make the people feel extremely desperate. Many try to commit suicide and there are many examples of failed suicides, the surgeons frequently have to remove bullets from people who have unsuccessfully tried to shoot themselves. Conventional antidepressant drugs may have severe side effects on those with nerve gas or organophosphage poisoning.

Skin and eye problems. The effects of mustard gas burns may persist for life and cause much pain and suffering. Radical forms of therapy, such as corneal grafting for eye problems and skin grafting for severe skin burns, may be the only real forms of effective treatment.

Infertility miscarriages, stillbirths, neonatal, and infant deaths. Many of the people in Halabja have two or more major problems. The occurrences of genetic mutations and carcinogenesis in this population appear comparable with those who were one to two kilometers from ground zero in Hiroshima and Nagasaki, and show that the chemicals used in the attack have a general effect on the body similar to that of ionizing radiation.

All the people who were bombarded with this awful cocktail of weapons do not have identical problems. They received different doses; some were drenched in liquid mustard gas and nerve agents, others breathed in vapor; some people were outside, others were inside; and some were wrapped in clothing or wet sheets or washed off the chemicals quickly. It is important to note that people vary in their ability to detoxify and this is genetically determined. Finally, the DNA target for the mutagenesis is the whole of the human genome. Many different genes may be affected; in the body, conferring risks of cancer or disease; and, in eggs or sperm, causing congenital abnormalities or lethality in offspring.[9]

Proving that Saddam possessed specific intent to commit genocide against the Kurds would depend on the prosecution's ability to marshal its documentary and testimonial evidence. Such intent could have been established if eyewitness testimony like the following were presented:

> [W]e monitored . . . radio communications between the political and military leadership. . . . Saddam Hussein briefed the assembled commanders that there would be a chemical attack on Halabja and that soldiers should wear protective clothing. . . . I heard a telephone conversation between Saddam Hussein and Ali Hassan al-Majid. Saddam ordered him to form a working group. . . . After the meeting Ali Hassan al-Majid returned to the area HQ. . . . Aerial pictures of Halabja after the attack were shown to Saddam Hussein and other members of the Revolutionary Command Council.
>
> One of the President's bodyguards brought 30 prisoners out. They were Kurds. The President himself shot them one after another with a Browning pistol. Another 30 prisoners were brought and the process was repeated. Saddam Hussein was laughing and obviously enjoying himself. There was blood everywhere—it was like an abattoir. . . . Those who were still alive were eventually finished off by the security officers.[10]

Of course, Saddam was never tried for the gassing of Halabja, nor for the Anfal campaigns. He was executed for directing the massacre of 148 Shi'a in the village of Dujail before he could be fully held to account for the thousands of Kurds that were wiped out on his watch.

Part Two

The Two Gulf Wars

4

The 1991 Persian Gulf War

Following the stalemate of the Iran–Iraq War and the forceful subjugation of Iraq's restive Kurdish and Shi'ite population, Saddam turned his attention south to the small state of Kuwait, which is situated between Iraq and Saudi Arabia at the northeastern corner of the Persian Gulf. Like Iraq, Kuwait was controlled by the British following World War I. In 1961, it became the first Arab state on the Gulf to claim independence. Iraq challenged this declaration, asserting instead that Kuwait was an integral province of Iraq. The British dispatched troops to deter Iraq from enforcing this claim and nothing more came of it until 1990.

With 10 percent of the world's proven crude oil reserves and no military to speak of, Kuwait proved much too tempting an apple not to be picked by Saddam. With assurances from the American ambassador that the United States had no interest in involving itself in Arab–Arab relations, muted silence from Saudi Arabia, and Iran still licking its wounds from the devastating war with Iraq, Saddam calculated that no one that mattered would oppose his annexation of Kuwait based upon an historical claim.

Moreover, Saddam was simply not willing to pay his bills. Kuwait had heavily funded Iraq's war with Iran. When the fighting stopped, Iraq was in no position to repay the $14 billion it still owed to Kuwait, and the Kuwaitis were not willing to forgive the debt. Saddam attempted to raise revenue by increasing oil prices, but Kuwait offset this by increasing production. Not surprisingly, this infuriated the Iraqi leaders.

On August 2, 1990, Iraq launched a nighttime invasion of Kuwait at 2:00 A.M. with four Republican Guard divisions and Army Special Forces units in the vanguard with helicopter and fighter-bomber air support. Kuwait was caught unaware and its meager forces were overrun with ease. Kuwait's 35th Armored

Brigade fought a series of delaying actions east of the capital city as people departed for Saudi Arabia. The emir had already departed from the royal residence and took flight into the vast dark desert traveling west. 80 percent of Kuwait's small air force evacuated to bases in Bahrain and Saudi Arabia.

The war crimes committed by Saddam's forces during their seven-month long occupation of Kuwait were horrendous and caused much outrage in the international press. The United Nations condemned the invasion and ordered an immediate withdrawal of Iraqi forces which Saddam ignored. Western nations could not ignore that Saddam's capture of Kuwait meant a significant enlargement of known oil reserves under his control. Moreover, if Saddam annexed the Hama oil fields just across the border in eastern Saudi Arabia (which also only had a meager military), he would have the largest share of the world's oil supply, second only to Saudi Arabia itself.

Saddam's saber rattling in the direction of Riyadh shortly after his annexation of Kuwait made this seem a real possibility. Western nations and Japan, dependent on the region's oil, viewed this as a real economic threat that could not be left unchecked. Saddam then refused to pay back his war debt of $26 billion to the Saudis. Western fears became even more palpable as Saddam turned up the rhetoric against the House of Saud, referring to the royal family as corrupt, illegitimate guardians of the holy cities of Mecca and Medina. The condemnations from Baghdad grew louder as western troops began to pour into the country. Operation Desert Shield had begun.

In 1980, President Jimmy Carter stated what became known as the Carter Doctrine with respect to the security of the oil reserves in the Persian Gulf: "An attempt by any outside force to gain control of the Persian Gulf region will be regarded as an assault on the vital interests of the United States of America, and such assault will be repelled by any means necessary, including military force." President Ronald Reagan clarified this doctrine in 1981 to mean that the United States would specifically use force to protect Saudi Arabia.

Following those policy benchmarks, President George H.W. Bush launched what he termed a "wholly defensive" mission to prevent an Iraqi invasion of Saudi Arabia. Operation Desert Shield began on August 7, 1990, and quickly transported 500,000 troops to the region by air and sealift. U.S. F-15s were dispatched immediately to begin round-the-clock patrol of the eastern Saudi border. And two full carrier groups surrounding the U.S.S. Eisenhower and U.S.S. Independence steamed into the Gulf, including the recommissioned battleships U.S.S. Missouri and U.S.S. Wisconsin.

President Bush used the next four months to build an international coalition of thirty-four countries to contribute troops to the mission, secure financing of the operation from Japan and the Saudi's, persuade Israel to remain outside the conflict in a neutral posture, and gain the requisite authorizations to use force against the Iraqis in Kuwait from the U.S. Congress and the U.N. Security Council. After a final offer of peaceful resolution was rejected by Saddam, Operation Desert Shield became Operation Desert Storm. Iraqi forces were decisively defeated within three weeks.

The decision not to go to Baghdad and take out Saddam's regime turned out to be a fateful one for the long-suffering Kurds. President Bush and his administration followed the letter of the U.N. Security Council authorization to use force and ceased hostilities once Iraqi forces were removed from Kuwait and its sovereignty was restored. The coalition could not, it was believed, politically survive a direct strike at Saddam. Consequently, an effort was made to engineer an internal coup against the regime in Baghdad as quickly as possible to take advantage of the disarray in Saddam's forces following their humiliating defeat.

As U.S. forces departed Iraq for bases in Kuwait and Saudi Arabia, American radio broadcasts and CIA operatives in Iraq began inciting the Shi'a and Kurds in Iraq to rise up against their dictator. The Shi'a in the south were the first to mount an insurrection against Saddam. The rebellion began in early March 1991 in the town of al-Zubair on the outskirts of Basra. Together with mutinous Army conscripts, the Shi'a took control of the entire Tigris-Euphrates river valley from al-Zubair north to Karbala. Reprisals were swiftly dealt against local Ba'athist party and government officials.

Saddam's elite Republican Guard, however, responded immediately to the southern insurrection. Within two weeks, the rebellion was crushed. Over 6,000 Shi'a lay dead and another 10,000 to 20,000 wounded. Large swaths of Najaf, Karbala, Kufa, and Hilla were demolished. Over 10,000 Shi'a fled, some behind U.S. cease-fire lines, others into neighboring Iran.

In the north, Kurdish *peshmerga* led their own uprising while Saddam's forces were tied down in the south. They easily defeated the disorganized Iraqi regular Army, took over main population centers such as Rania and held them for about three weeks. By the end of March, Saddam's forces had finished with the Shi'a and had turned northward. Kurdish fighters abandoned the towns in the face of Saddam's superior firepower and his ruthless use of napalm and chemical weapons that his Foreign Minister, Tariq Aziz, characterized as designed to merely frighten the population. The Kurdish fighters retreated to the mountains in a futile attempt to establish defensive positions.

The overwhelming majority of the Kurdish civilian population fled the towns to avoid the advancing Iraqi troops—approximately 2.3 million people fled. One million Kurdish refugees had already entered Iran by mid-April and another 450,000 were camped on the roads leading to the Iranian border checkpoints. Another 500,000 had fled to Turkey and 350,000 more were fleeing into the mountains along the border. With the memory of the Anfal campaigns and the brutal gassing of Halabja fresh in their minds, the Kurds were convinced that Saddam had arrived to finish the job.

Turkey and Iran categorically refused to absorb any more Kurds. Their own restless Kurdish populations had been swollen with Iraqi Kurdish refugees to the point of becoming unmanageable. Kurds stuck in camps along the borders began quickly dying of exposure and disease. It was still winter in the mountains and there were no supplies of food, water, or shelter going to the transient Kurds. Augmented tragedy seemed all but assured.

American forces failed to support both the Shi'a and Kurdish uprisings, although they were instigated by the United States. The Kurds had been betrayed by the West again, just as they were almost seventy years earlier when the West allowed the collapse of the Treaty of Sèvres promising them a homeland. Although President Bush and Allied leaders had vowed not to become enmeshed in Iraq's internal struggles, the mass human suffering and the desperate refugee situation demanded international attention. To the surprise of many, the solution was a military one.

Operation Provide Comfort came in two phases. The first phase was the stabilization of the border region between northern Iraq and Turkey. U.S. forces moved to deliver humanitarian relief and to manage the border situation, as neither Turkey nor Iran wanted more Kurds flowing into their countries and swelling the ranks of their own restless Kurdish populations. From April to September 1991, U.S. forces flew over 40,000 sorties, relocated over 700,000 refugees, and rebuilt 70–80 percent of the Kurdish villages previously destroyed by the Iraqis. The task force airdropped 6,154 tons of supplies, flew in another 6,251 tons by helicopter, and delivered a further 4,416 tons by truck. Eventually, the Kurds were persuaded to move back to their homes under the protection of Allied aircraft, which began Phase II of the Operation.

The second phase established a joint-command military operation on July 24, 1991, to defend Kurds from retribution by Saddam's forces. A "No-Fly Zone" (see Figure 4.1) was established by the United States, the United Kingdom, and France north of the 36th parallel and was enforced by American, British, and French aircraft. Any of Saddam's aircraft, including helicopters that attempted to fly in the restricted area were to be shot down. Included in this effort was the delivery of humanitarian relief and military protection of the Kurds by a small Allied ground force based in Turkey.

While Operation Desert Shield and Operation Desert Storm were orchestrated by the U.S. Central Command in the United States, Operation Provide Comfort was run by U.S. European Command, headquartered in Germany. Humanitarian aid on the ground was provided by the U.S. Army's 353rd Civil Affairs Command and its subunits, the 432nd and 431st Civil Affairs battalions. These units were located in Turkey and Northern Iraq and established base camps for Kurdish refugees.

The operation ended on December 31, 1996, at the request of Turkey, which wanted to pursue improved relations with Iraq. On January 1, 1997, Operation Northern Watch picked up where Provide Comfort ended, and the United States and Britain continued to enforce the northern No-Fly Zone on a daily basis despite regular Iraqi antiaircraft fire. The No-Fly Zone ensured that Saddam's forces could not easily perpetrate further atrocities against the Kurds on the scale of the Anfal campaigns. Without air support, Saddam's only option was to deploy his entire military to physically penetrate the rugged mountains of Iraqi Kurdistan on foot. That would in turn have left him open to rebellion by the Shi'ites in the south with his army trapped in the northern mountains.

Figure 4.1. "No-Fly" Zones Patrolled over Iraq. *Source*: CIA, 1992.

Consequently, Operation Northern Watch restrained Saddam's forces from moving en masse against the Kurds. This allowed the Iraqi Kurds a period of autonomy unmatched by any in recent history and contributed to a renewed flourishing of Kurdish tradition and culture. Iraqi Kurdistan developed its own internal governing structures, albeit beset by internal political rivalries, and largely took care of its own educational and social services. The northern No-Fly Zone remained in effect until the Second Persian Gulf War, ending officially on May 1, 2003.

A southern No-Fly Zone was similarly created to protect the Shi'ite population south of Baghdad from Saddam's air force. Operation Southern Watch provided protection from August 27, 1992, until June 2002 when it transitioned to the more aggressive Operation Southern Focus in preparation for the March 2003 invasion of Iraq. Allied forces responded to Iraqi antiaircraft attacks by dropping over 600 bombs on almost 400 targets during the course of the operation.

5

Divided Loyalties (Internal Dissent within Kurdish Factions)

Despite a common goal of independent statehood, the 22 million Kurds living in Iraq, Iran, Syria, and Turkey are hardly unified. Several political factions exist that are not necessarily coterminous with current international frontiers. The political factions stem from groups of clans and tribes that banded together over time in the face of adversity from foreign rulers. Because of this structure, there is inherent rigidity among Kurdish political factions—very few people move between parties. Since they are driven by family allegiance, the parties crystallized long ago.

The Kurdish Democratic Party (KDP) was founded in 1945 from the Komala nationalist movement, a grouping of urban upper-class Kurds around Mahabad, Iran. Led by Mustafa Barzani, the KDP briefly established a Kurdish Republic in 1946 in northern Iran alongside the Azerbaijani Republic. The Western Allies viewed these new republics as extensions of Soviet influence and supported the Shah's military campaign against them. When Soviet troops withdrew from Iran in May, 1946, the Shah was free to renew Kurdish suppression.

Barzani fled to the USSR, where he remained in exile for eleven years. During this time, other KDP branches formed in Turkey, Iraq, and Syria, eventually absorbing elements of the original party. Most of the leaders were drawn from the educated Kurdish cadres and exhibited strong communist sympathies. Barzani came to head the Iraqi KDP in 1964 and consolidated his base of support there. Over the next ten years, Barzani garnered power among aristocratic loyalists, established the first *peshmerga* military forces, and engaged in brief struggles with Baghdad alternating with deals for more or less power—depending on the shifting political sands that year. Independence, however, remained elusive.

Frustrated at the lack of progress on nationalist issues, Jalal Talabani, one of the disgruntled members of Barzani's politburo, left with his supporters in 1975 to form the Patriot Union of Kurdistan (PUK). The PUK's initial purpose was to resume the armed struggle against Baghdad for Kurdish independence. Military success brought about three-fourths of Iraqi Kurdistan under the PUK influence. But progress against Baghdad ground to a standstill in the run-up to the Iran–Iraq War.

During the 1980s Iran and Iraq both sought to play the KDP and PUK against one another with some success. Saddam was effective in creating *jahsh* militias— small armed Kurdish groups loyal to Baghdad, that could be deployed in Kurdistan to undermine defenses, collect intelligence, cajole conscripts to fight in the south against Iran, and prepare the way for Iraqi military incursions. However, by July 1987, Tehran had convinced the PUK and KDP leadership to form a united front against Saddam in exchange for Iranian support.

Saddam responded shortly thereafter with his Anfal offensive to wipe out Kurdish resistance, consolidate Baghdad's control over the Iraqi Kurdistan, and Arabize certain strategic regions of the north. Chapter 2 details the Anfals and the destruction that reigned down on the Kurds during 1988.

Upon Saddam's defeat in the Persian Gulf War, both the PUK and the KDP moved to retake control of Iraqi Kurdistan, inviting *jahsh* militiamen back into the Kurdish ranks under a general amnesty. In the wake of Saddam's renewed suppression following the 1991 uprisings, the Kurds withdrew north of the 36th parallel, where the U.S. and British air contingents had established a no-fly zone to protect the Kurds from Saddam's planes.

From 1994–1998, the KDP, under the leadership of Massoud Barzani, and the PUK fought a bloody war for power over northern Iraq. The KDP controlled the northern portion of Iraqi Kurdistan, with its political base in Irbil, while the PUK controlled the southern portion, based out of Sulaymaniyah. However, after a U.S.-brokered deal in September 1998 that brought both parties together, the factions began focusing on developing their respective portions of the Kurdish economy and opening cross-border links with their Kurdish cousins in Iran and Turkey.

After the 2003 invasion and occupation of Iraq, Kurds were able to shift their regional government into a strong bargaining position relative to the defeated Sunni Arab and newly liberated Shi'a Arab elements. Although the political logistics proved challenging, the ultimate bargain put both PUK and KDP members into a Kurdish regional assembly under an Alliance List (a form of unity government), appointed the KDP's leader Massoud Barzani as head of the regional government, and sent the PUK's leader Jalal Talabani to Baghdad as president of the national government.

No significant opposition parties have formed to challenge the status quo between the PUK and the KDP. A small group known as Kurdish Islamic Union (KIU), led by Salahuddin Muhammad Bahauddin, was formed as Kurds were wrestling with the establishment of the Kurdish regional government. But that party's headquarters was torched in December 2005, and the KIU accused regional KDP officials of orchestrating the attacks; KDP denied any involvement.

The story of Kurdish political infighting in Iran is similar to that in Iraq. The KDP's struggles in Iraq during the 1960s and 1970s were the focus of Barzani's efforts. In a deal with Tehran for support to destabilize northern Iraq, Barzani commanded the remnants of the Iranian KDP (KDPI) to cease their struggle within Iran so that the Iraq front could be developed. Most followed these orders, but a splinter group broke off and formed the KDP in Iran Revolutionary Committee (KDPI/RC). This group was crushed by the Shah's forces in collusion with Barzani.

Subsequently a new group was formed, the Revolutionary Order of Toilers (Komala), which organized the peasantry and women. Since the 1980s, Komala has offered itself as an alternative to the elitist KDPI and continuous battles have been fought since then. Although both groups work for more autonomy within Iran, these efforts fall short of a call for complete independence.

In Turkey, the Kurdish nationalist movement has a distinctly militaristic bent. The Kurds have waged a guerrilla insurgency in southeastern Turkey since the 1920s. By 1939, the Turkish government had forced down a series of revolts and thousands of "problem Kurds" were shipped to western Turkey. Things were quiet until the 1960s when Kurds in Turkey, emboldened by the Kurdish uprisings in Iran and Iraq, took up arms once again. Cycles of repression followed as unstable governments rose and fell during a period of coups in Ankara for the following two decades.

In 1980, the Kurdish Workers Party (PKK) was formed by Abdullah Ocalan, a young radical, who began to stir up nationalist sentiment. By the mid-1980s the PKK carried out military attacks with support from the government in Syria—a government which sought to keep Turkey destabilized. There are no other Kurdish factions within Turkey to challenge the authority of the PKK; thus, their situation is unlike the divided Kurdish political base in Iran and Iraq.

Ocalan led the PKK's insurgent operations until his capture in 1999. He was ejected from his base in Syria the year before under intense pressure and the threat of invasion by Turkey. He fled to Russia, which refused to harbor him, then to Greece, which had supported his movement within Turkey, but was not allowed to stay. From there he flew to Italy and was held by Italian authorities after Turkey formally requested his extradition. However, Italian law forbade extradition of individuals to countries like Turkey that had the death penalty. Consequently, since Ocalan could not be extradited to Turkey under Italian law, he was released and then disappeared. The Turks were infuriated and protested vehemently.

Eventually, Ocalan ended up in Africa, hidden by the Greek government in its Kenyan embassy. This was not the best hiding place as U.S. intelligence agents were everywhere in Nairobi, investigating the al-Qaeda bombing of their embassy. U.S. agents tipped off Mossad (Israeli intelligence) of Ocalan's whereabouts and this was relayed to Turkey, Israel's military ally in the Middle East. Turkish agents then picked up Ocalan as he was being transported from the Greek embassy to the Nairobi airport on February 15, 1999.

Ocalan is currently incarcerated as the only inmate in a Turkish prison on the island of Imrali in the Sea of Mamara. The PKK quieted its military struggle during the ensuring years under pleas from Ocalan—induced by the Turkish government. Although Ocalan received the death penalty for his part in the insurgency, he most likely will not be executed due to a moratorium on capital punishment issued by the Turkish government, which is a candidate for membership in the European Union, where execution is banned.

Over the years, tensions have flared between the PKK and Barzani's KDP faction, which controls the Turkey–Iraq border. Barzani has criticized the PKK for establishing military bases inside Iraqi-Kurd territory to launch attacks into Turkey. On a policy basis, the PKK rejected the KDP/PUK decision to seek regional self-government within a federal Iraq. The PKK believes any independent Kurdish state should be a homeland for all Kurds.

Unity in purpose but disunity in methodology, has stymied Kurdish efforts to build a homeland since the post—World War I settlement of the 1920s dividing them as minorities in disparate states. Whether a consolidated effort within Iraq can achieve a gravitational center for Kurdish aspirations remains to be seen. Neither Turkey and Syria nor Iran wishes to see an independent Kurdish state emerge from the chaos in Iraq. Consequently, those states will likely seek to keep the Kurdish political factions as disunited as possible for the foreseeable future.

The 2003 Iraq War

Saddam, once a friend and ally of the United States, forfeited that position when he invaded Kuwait in 1990, justifying his invasion as a forcible reincorporation of a renegade province. This strategic miscalculation cost him dearly. Saudi Arabia, the Arab states of the Gulf, and the United States viewed Kuwait's occupation as a threat to the world's oil supply and surmised that his aggression would not stop with Kuwait. Thus, a coalition was formed and was duly authorized by the U.N. Security Council to invade Kuwait and repel the Iraqi army.

Although the coalition forces successfully repelled the Iraqis in January 1991, they stopped short of invading and occupying Iraq completely, which would have gone beyond the coalition's U.N. Security Council mandate of restoring Kuwaiti sovereignty. Subsequently, the United States and Britain jointly established "no-fly zones" in the north and south of Iraq that were patrolled over the ensuing decade by jet fighters and reconnaissance planes. These zones were created ostensibly to protect the Kurds in the north and the Shi'a in the south, and were patrolled throughout the remainder of the first Bush presidency, the Clinton presidency, and the pre-Iraq War second Bush presidency.[1]

America and the world were largely satisfied with this policy of containment coupled with economic sanctions imposed upon Saddam's regime to keep him weak and to defuse his ability to threaten his neighbors. After the terrorist attacks suffered by the United States on September 11, 2001, at the hands of Islamist Arab Osama bin Laden and his fundamentalist al Qaeda network, the United States shifted its policy position with regard to terrorism from one of deterrence to one of preemption and active prevention.[2] President Bush promised to hunt down terrorists wherever they were hiding and bring down the regimes of states that harbored them. This policy was extended to include states pursuing the development of weapons of mass destruction (WMD).[3]

Based on what turned out to be faulty intelligence, President Bush was convinced that Saddam had retooled his ability to pursue WMD and was close to perfecting a nuclear weapon. Logically, mere containment could no be an option. With the backing of U.S. Congress, the President sought out the United Nations to secure new resolutions to resume weapons inspections in Iraq to find and destroy that capability. Security Council Resolution 1441 required Saddam to produce 12,000 pages of documents disclosing his WMD programs. The resulting document production was rejected by both the United States and chief U.N. weapons inspector Hans Blix as incomplete.[4]

Secretary of State Colin Powell personally appeared before the Security Council and made an elaborate case for invasion based upon Saddam's refusal to comply with prior resolutions. The accusations leveled at Iraq included the continued production and possession of biological weapons, chemical weapons, and the pursuit of nuclear weapons coupled with new longer-range missile technology. Following (see Figures 6.1–6.5) are a few of the slides shown to the Security Council during Secretary Powell's presentation.

Despite the presentation made by the United States and backed by Great Britain, which urged the Security Council to authorize military action for the noncompliance, the rest of the Security Council members remained skeptical. France, Germany, and Russia blocked military action until the inspectors could complete their work. Fearful that such delay would allow Saddam another year to develop weapons, Britain and the United States formed a new coalition of forty nations, albeit much smaller ones than those, which participated in the U.N.-sanctioned Persian Gulf War, to invade Iraq and forcibly remove Saddam from power.

Since a military campaign season in the desert cannot endure the full summer heat, the coalition lost no time in pulling together its ground troops as a significant aerial bombardment of Baghdad and Iraqi military installations was initiated. Approximately 300,000 troops were massed, 98 percent of which were American and British. When the ground war began, Iraqi forces were quickly overwhelmed, and Baghdad fell on April 9, 2003. Kurdish *peshmerga* troops joined the fighting on the side of the coalition, attacking from the north. By April 15th major combat operations were over and the occupation of Iraq was underway.

The Coalition Provisional Authority (CPA) was established by the United States and its allies to govern Iraq during the occupation, and the military was redeployed throughout the country to hunt down the suspected WMD and capture Saddam and other Ba'athist leaders who had all fled Baghdad during the fighting. In December 2003, Saddam was captured hiding in an underground "spider hole" outside of Tikrit. Taken into custody and held by coalition forces, he was accorded prisoner of war status as a military leader.[5]

The CPA functioned as the governing authority of Iraq until June 2004 when the Iraqi Interim Government was appointed by the CPA. The Interim Government was in turn replaced by the Iraqi Transitional Government, elected on January 31,

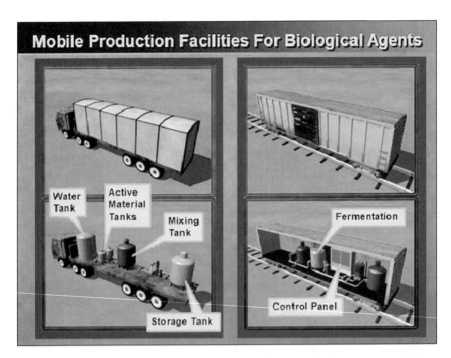

Figure 6.1. Iraq's Biological Agent Program/Slide 20. *Source*: U.S. Department of State, February 2003.

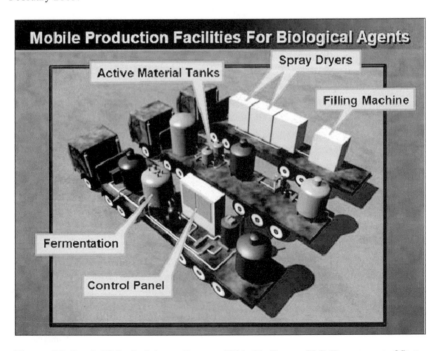

Figure 6.2. Iraq's Biological Agent Program/Slide 21. *Source*: U.S. Department of State, February 2003.

Figure 6.3. Chemical Weapons in Iraq/Slide 25. *Source*: U.S. Department of State, Feb. 2003.

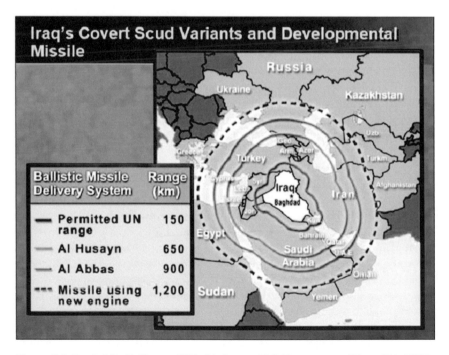

Figure 6.4. Iraq's Missile Ranges/Slide 34. *Source*: U.S. Department of State, Feb. 2003.

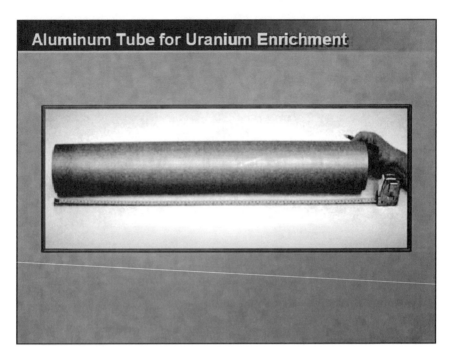

Figure 6.5. Equipment Used for Enrichment/Slide 31. *Source*: U.S. Department of State, Feb. 2003.

2005, and charged with drafting a permanent Iraqi constitution. The permanent Iraqi government under the new constitution took office in May 2006.

The CPA drafted the statute of the Iraqi Special Tribunal (IST), which was designed to try Saddam and his henchmen for major atrocities committed during their reign. The IST was then approved by successive governments, including the elected government, which renamed it the Iraqi High Tribunal (IHT). The original CPA drafters did not take into account when naming the tribunal that the term "special" was a sobriquet attached to courts under Saddam's regime known for their particular brutality.

Shortly after the cessation of formal warfare in April 2003, mass looting occurred, especially in Baghdad. Insufficient coalition forces had been deployed to secure Iraq after the quick defeat of its armed forces. But it was not simply commercial enterprises, markets, museums, and antiquities that were looted. According to the U.S. Department of Defense, approximately 250,000 tons of ordnance was looted during this period—about one-third of total ordnance available. This would become the initial source of weaponry for the insurgency that would follow.

From 2004 to 2008, the insurgency undertaken to resist the coalition occupation grew from a small Sunni-led resistance to a sprawling hit-and-run terrorist campaign. Without enough troops to secure the borders, foreign terrorist elements infiltrated Iraq, building an al Qaeda network within the Sunni community while Iranian agents boosted the Shi'ite community. Eventually these forces collided, turning from a combined resistance effort into a sectarian Sunni–Shi'a civil war with coalition forces caught in the middle. Kurdish forces largely remained in the north.

The intensity of the fighting, mounting casualties, and general fatigue depleted the coalition, which was shrinking each month with more nations calling their troops home. The United States eventually shouldered the burden and effectuated a temporary surge of 20,000 additional troops in the summer of 2007 together with more financial resources to tamp down on the violence and buy off both sides. By co-opting the Sunni sheiks in Anbar province to turn on al Qaeda agents and the Shi'a mullahs in Baghdad and the south to reign in their militias in exchange for political participation, violence began to drop in early 2008.

Part Three _____

Saddam on Trial

Creation of the Iraqi High Tribunal

Even before Saddam's capture, the Coalition Provisional Authority (CPA) and its adjunct Iraqi Governing Council were faced with the question of trial venues for captured war criminals. As the following table (see Table 7.1) indicates, the trial options were many and varied, but one in particular presented itself as a method for retaining the most control over events while simultaneously conferring maximum legitimacy on the proceedings from the perspective of Iraqis—establishment of a domestic special criminal tribunal.

A truth commission was never a realistic option, from either the domestic American or Iraqi political perspective. Retribution ranks high on the list of criminal justice goals in both cultures and justice systems. Accordingly, taking the truth commission option would be viewed in both societies as "letting Saddam off the hook." Likewise, an international tribunal presented a false option primarily due to the fact that one would have to be created from scratch; moreover, the Bush administration amply demonstrated its disdain for working with international bodies.

While the Pentagon was convening military tribunals to try captured al Qaeda and Taliban in the U.S.-led war on terror, no Iraqis unaffiliated with those groups were specifically being singled out for trial by military commission. Saddam would be no exception. Such tribunals are regarded as necessarily operating in a vacuum—which Iraq, unlike Afghanistan, is not—and part of the stated goal for liberating Iraq was to re-imbue it with democratic rule-of-law institutions. Thus, taking war crimes trials away from the Iraqis would be seen as denying them the opportunity to let justice take its course within Iraq. The same justification would apply for not trying Saddam in American federal courts.

Table 7.1   Options for the Trial of Saddam Hussein

Venue Option	Rationale/Accompanying Issues
Truth Commission	This option calls for no trial at all. South Africa successfully employed a truth and reconciliation commission that exchanged amnesty for criminal conduct for testimony and acknowledgment of acts committed in furtherance of Apartheid.
International Tribunal	The U.N. Security Council would have to create an ad hoc International Iraqi War Crimes Tribunal. Currently, there is no international court that could hear Saddam's case. The International Court of Justice only has definitive jurisdiction over states; the new International Criminal Court only has prospective jurisdiction over crimes committed after July 2002; and the existing tribunals for Yugoslavia, Rwanda, and Sierra Leone only have jurisdiction over the criminal events that unfolded in those particular conflicts. Possible Models: Yugoslav Model: Purely international (location away from country of crime and international judges and prosecutors only). Sierra Leone Model: Both international and domestic (location in country of crime and both international and domestic judges and prosecutors).
Military Tribunal	Under international law, the United States had the option to try Saddam before an American military tribunal. However, his status as a POW would bring all the protections of the Third Geneva Convention into play.
U.S. Federal Court	Just as Article III federal courts successfully tried Manuel Noriega after the American invasion of Panama, U.S. federal courts could conceivably try Saddam since genocide is criminalized by federal statute and the crime is accorded universal jurisdiction.
Special Iraqi Domestic Court	The Iraqi Special Tribunal (IST) was created by the Iraqi Governing Council to try war criminals such as Saddam. The IST would have jurisdiction over Saddam and his henchmen for genocide, war crimes, and crimes against humanity.

Yet another, perhaps more powerful reason for not trying Saddam in a military tribunal or a U.S. federal court is the perspective of the Arab street. From their vantage point rooted in the Arabic-Islamic honor code, Osama bin Laden could legitimately be tried in the United States because he struck the United States first. Saddam is another matter, however, because he was toppled from power after a full-scale invasion and occupation. From the Arab perspective, therefore, Saddam should be subjected to Arabic justice.

For these reasons, the domestically constituted IST was viewed as the most realistic venue option for trying Saddam. Promulgated just a few days before his capture and designed for trying the Ba'athist henchmen already arrested, the IST was to consist of Iraqi judges and prosecutors dispensing Iraqi justice against Iraqi defendants. Although the statute establishing the IST carefully contained all the accoutrements that allowed it to be described as domestic justice, international "guidance" was encouraged and, in some cases, required.

When the CPA drafted the statute of the IST, it specifically sought to avoid many of the problems associated with the Milosevic trial in The Hague. A major difference is that the IST was to be a domestic Iraqi court that existed within the Iraqi judicial system under the authority of the Iraqi government. Article 1 of the statute limits the IST's temporal jurisdiction to crimes committed in Iraq or elsewhere between the Ba'athists' assumption of power on July 17, 1968, and their deposition on May 1, 2003. It specifically incorporates liability for crimes committed during the wars with Iran and Kuwait and for crimes committed against Iraqi ethnic or religious groups, whether during armed conflict or not. The IST also was given adjudicatory power only over people, not parties or corporate entities.[1]

The IST's subject matter jurisdiction was limited as well. It could undertake prosecutions only for genocide, war crimes, crimes against humanity as defined largely by international law, and a small set of domestic Iraqi violations, including invading other Arab countries, wasting natural resources, abusing power, squandering public funds and assets, and attempting to manipulate the judiciary. Judges were appointed by the Iraqi government to trial chambers and a nine-member appellate body, which may include non-Iraqi nationals at the government's discretion. Provision was also made for the creation of a twenty-member body of permanent "investigative judges," who would issue subpoenas, arrest warrants, and indictments, as well as collect and evaluate evidence. The role of investigative judge parallels that which is used in inquisitorial criminal justice systems common in civil law countries: work as a disinterested third party to build the case for trial in court.

Each investigative judge was considered a separate organ and independent from the tribunal judges. Interestingly, the chief investigative judge was required to appoint non-Iraqi foreign "advisors" to act in an assistant or observer capacity while also monitoring the work of the Iraqi investigative judges to ensure that general due process standards were observed. Similarly, up to twenty prosecutors would be appointed by the government and accompanied by international advisors.

Borrowing from the statutes establishing the International Criminal Tribunal for the Former Yugoslavia (ICTY) and the International Criminal Tribunal for Rwanda (ICTR), the statute of the IST also did away with the defenses of sovereign immunity and superior orders while building in a command responsibility basis for criminal liability. The IST was also determined to learn from the mistakes of the Milosevic trial in order to maintain a formal and fair decorum with the defendant, impose counsel when necessary, and limit the prosecution's introduction of evidence so as not to unduly prolong the trial.

Following his appointment as the head administrator of the IST in early 2004, Salem Chalabi led a delegation of Iraqi judges and prosecutors to The Hague in

April 2004 to meet with jurists from the ICTY and the new International Criminal Court. Hoping to draw on their experiences, Chalabi said, "We do not want this tribunal to be the . . . ultimate historian of the atrocities of the previous regime. We want it to be about justice. And so we need to make sure the cases are properly prepared, that they're scrutinized appropriately, and the trials are fair. And this will take some time."[2]

During the spring of 2004, U.S. Department of Justice (DOJ) personnel began providing support to the new IST in the form of logistics and evidence collection. To this end, a DOJ Regime Crimes Liaison Office was established in Baghdad and given a budget of $75 million. The pivotal challenge faced by the staff attempting to marshal incriminating evidence was the deteriorating local security situation. For example, to exhume a mass grave—a process that takes two months—earth-moving equipment must be transported to the site, the local population must be kept at bay, and a significant military contingent must be present around the clock, diverted away from other patrols and duties.[3]

Gregory Kehoe, a U.S. government attorney and formerly a prosecutor with the Yugoslav war crimes tribunal in The Hague, was put in charge of the DOJ extension office. Kehoe noted:

> We are purely, again, in a support role as a liaison. What the problem in Iraq with the Saddam regime is that an infrastructure wasn't present to assist in these investigations. What we are attempting to do is gather information from various quarters, not only in the United States, but throughout the world, and provide the Iraqis with that informa-tion. And they then will develop that information through their investigative judges to decide what charges should be brought and against whom.[4]

Political instability within Iraq took its toll early on the IST. Salem Chalabi was deposed as head of the tribunal in September 2004 when murder charges were brought against him (the charges were later dropped), and replaced by Amer Bakri. Chalabi contended that he was pushed aside for political reasons because his uncle, Ahmed Chalabi—leader of the Iraqi National Congress and a rival of the prime minister—fell out of favor with the United States after it became known that he was spying for Iran.[5]

When it decided to create a domestic tribunal filled with Iraqi judges and prosecutors, the CPA may not have weighed the negative impact of local poli-tics on the new IST. Then again, under intense political pressure from the Bush administration in Washington to transfer sovereignty to Iraq on schedule at the end of June 2004, the CPA may not have had the time to fully consider all the alternatives.

High-level Iraqi judges who served during Saddam's reign were excluded from serving, as were Iraqis who were in exile during that period. The judges who were selected were typically low-level Ba'athists, not deemed sufficiently high enough in the party to have owed any allegiance to Saddam. This in turn exposed the judges to challenge by the defense that they were not qualified to oversee cases involving crimes of genocide, aggression, war crimes, and crimes against humanity. Preventatively, the judges underwent training by international experts in Dubai and London on how to handle these very crimes and those accused of committing them.

The IST became the Iraqi High Tribunal (IHT) when it was formally embraced by the elected Iraqi parliament via statute in 2006. The underlying structure, statute, and staffing, however, remained largely unchanged. (see Appendix D) New language was added to include a Court of Cassation and the requirement of non-Iraqi advisors was scaled back to an option that could be employed by the Chief Investigative Judge, prosecutors, and the president of the court. The backing of the democratically elected government was seen as essential to the legitimacy of the tribunal, which was originally designed by the occupying power.

At the end of June 2004, Saddam was stripped of his POW status, transferred to the new Iraqi government, and accorded the status of Iraqi criminal detainee to be tried domestically before the IHT.[6] As such, he was able to hire counsel before he underwent formal arraignment, although his counsel was not present for those initial charging proceedings.

The Dujail Trial

Saddam visited the predominantly Shi'ite village Dujail, northwest of Baghdad in 1982 during the Iran–Iraq War. A government cameraman videotaped the trip (later produced at trial), showing the Iraqi president speaking to people from the local Ba'ath Party headquarters. As Saddam's convoy left the village, it was ambushed by men hiding in orchard groves along the roadside. Saddam was not injured in the assassination attempt; he turned his convoy around, went back into Dujail, and announced that he would find and punish those responsible.

Saddam was filmed personally interrogating several villagers. Thousands of people were later arrested, questioned, tortured, and interned in the south. One hundred and forty-eight people were executed. The surrounding orchards, a major part of the local economy, were destroyed and the village itself was leveled and later rebuilt. Saddam's brutality and swift response to the attempt on his life was in keeping with both his reputation and character.

Twenty-three years later, on Wednesday, October 19, 2005, former Iraqi dictator Saddam Hussein and seven codefendants began their defense in Baghdad on charges that they ordered the summary execution of 148 Iraqi Shi'ites in 1982 in the town of Dujail. Among the accused were Saddam's former intelligence chief Barzan Ibrahim al-Tikriti; Vice-President Taha Yassin Ramadan; former chief judge of the Iraqi revolutionary court, Awad Hamad al-Bandar; and three Dujail Ba'ath Party bureaucrats: Abdulla Kadhem Ruaid, Mohammed Azawi Ali, and Mizher Abdullah Ruaid, and Ali Daeem Ali, a former mayor and gardener who worked in one of the government's departments.

On that Wednesday, all eight defendants were ushered into the defendant docks near the center of the Iraqi High Tribunal's Trial Chamber. Before pleading not guilty to the charges, Saddam defied the authority of the court by challenging,

"Who are you? What is all this?" He further quarreled with Kurdish Chief Judge Rizgar Mohammed Amin: "I preserve my constitutional rights as the president of Iraq. I do not recognize the body that has authorized you and I don't recognize this aggression."

Following adjournment after three hours, Saddam scuffled with guards who tried to restrain his arms while exiting the court. The trial was set to resume six weeks later. When it did resume, the prosecution introduced the recorded testimony of Waddah al-Sheikh, an intelligence officer in Saddam's regime who took part in an investigation of the 1982 assassination attempt on Saddam's motorcade in Dujail. Saddam raised the attempt on his life as justification for detaining 400 Shi'ite citizens—including women, children, and elderly men. According to al-Sheikh, "Saddam's personal bodyguards took part in killing people." He further claimed he did not "know why so many people were arrested," and that Barzan Ibrahim al-Tikriti "was the one directly giving the orders." Al-Sheikh revealed that intelligence officers who participated in the operation were later decorated by Saddam.

Saddam's litany of complaints against the court continued during the trial proceedings. He even protested that guards had confiscated his pen, which prevented him from signing court papers. At the completion of a second chaotic day in court, the trial adjourned until December 5 due to the absence of four defense lawyers and so the defense could replace two of its lawyers who had been murdered.

On Monday, December 5, 2005, the first live witness testified in court. Ahmad Hassan Mohammed recounted the torture of women and children and the abandonment of murdered babies in the streets by Iraqi security forces. According to Mohammed, "People who were arrested were taken to prison and most of them were killed there. The scene was frightening. Even women and babies were arrested."

Mohammed further recalled that Iraqi forces used a mincing machine to gruesomely murder and torture live victims. His statements also included an account of the torture and execution of one of his friends. According to Mohammed, soldiers fired shots at his friend's feet and broke his limbs before killing him. Mohammed's testimony was regularly interrupted by Saddam and his half-brother, Barzan Ibrahim al-Tikriti. During one outburst, Saddam defiantly declared to the court that he was unafraid of execution. The day also included the suspension of trial proceedings for over an hour when defense lawyers walked out of court in protest of the chief judge's refusal to allow an in-court challenge of the legitimacy and lawfulness of the proceedings.

On Tuesday, December 6, three witnesses from Dujail testified in court. All three spoke behind a curtain to conceal their identity. One woman, her voice disguised, claimed an Iraqi security agent had stripped, beaten, and tortured her by electric shock. She testified that she had been detained for four years at the infamous Abu Ghraib prison. She blamed Saddam and his leadership for her suffering, though she could not identify any of the defendants as her specific assailant.

A male witness averred he was captured by security forces and held in Abu Ghraib with two sisters and his parents for eleven months. While in prison, he said his father died from blows to the head and that guards "used to bring men to the women's room and ask them to bark like dogs." After the judge ordered the trial to continue the next day, Saddam advised him to "go to hell" and complained of exhaustion.

On Wednesday, December 7, Saddam refused to appear, which resulted in hours of disagreement over how to continue the trial. The argument ended and the trial resumed in his absence with testimony from two anonymous witnesses regarding torture.

Witness "F," speaking anonymously behind a screen, detailed his more than two-month-long experience in an intelligence prison and subsequent eighteen-month confinement in Abu Ghraib prison. He recounted beatings in the presence of Barzan Ibrahim al-Tikriti, Saddam's half-brother, admitting, however, that he was blindfolded when beaten and only informed of al-Tikriti's identity and attendance by other prisoners. The witness testified that sleep deprivation, days of uninterrupted standing, and starvation were daily torture techniques used in Abu Ghraib. Following testimony, the judge adjourned until December 21.

On the 21st, two witnesses presented more testimonies of torture by Iraqi security servicemen as Saddam sat in passive silence. First, Ali Mohammed Hassan al-Haydari testified that all forty-three members of his family were tortured, culminating in the shooting deaths of some of his brothers. Only fourteen years old at the time, he claimed, "I saw my brother being tortured in front of my eyes."

Another witness testified anonymously that day, giving an account of how Barzan Ibrahim al-Tikriti made appearances at the detention center during his imprisonment. He stated, "When I was being tortured, Barzan was sitting and eating grapes." Al-Tikriti responded by shouting, "My hand is clean!" and appealing to the judge that he was a politician and not a criminal. Saddam, attempting to turn the tables away from the merits of the trial against him, accused U.S. troops of abuse. He said, "I have been beaten on every place of my body, and the signs are all over my body!" The prosecution responded to his claims of mistreatment with derision.

On December 22, a litany of egregious torture allegations was again leveled against Saddam and his codefendants by three anonymous witnesses. One witness, stating he was eight years old at the time of the Dujail retaliation, said that all his male relatives permanently disappeared after being tortured along with his grandmother. Saddam tried to discredit the testimony by claiming the witness was too young at the time of the alleged crimes to remember accurately.

Saddam also declared that it pained him to hear the stories of torture and said, "When I hear that any Iraqi has been hurt, it hurts me too." The day was punctuated by angry retorts from Saddam and Barzan Ibrahim al-Tikriti. Saddam condemned the United States and accused it of lying about weapons of mass destruction and whether American guards had physically assaulted him. Al-Tikriti protested that authorities edited the televised trial before broadcasting it. Following the testimony, the judge adjourned until January 24, 2006.

The trial, however, did not resume on January 24th. The court failed to convene allegedly due to the absence of witnesses who had not yet returned from the Hajj pilgrimage. Chief Judge Rizgar Amin resigned prior to the scheduled resumption of the trial, citing Iraqi officials' criticism that he was not harsh enough with the defendants. Rumors of an argument among remaining judges over who would replace Mr. Amin also surfaced. On January 23, Judge Raouf Abdul Rahman was appointed successor to Mr. Amin.

Six days later, the new chief judge asserted his authority and removed Barzan Ibrahim al-Tikriti from court for persistently complaining of inadequate medical treatment for his cancer. Chief Judge Rahman next charged that defense lawyers were encouraging the defendants to disrespect the court and subsequently ejected one lawyer from the defense team. Other defense lawyers left the courtroom in protest. Saddam was also removed after arguing vehemently with the chief judge.

Four substitute lawyers were immediately appointed to the defense team. When two defendants, Taha Yassin Ramadan and Awad Hamad al-Bandar, protested and eventually left the chamber because they disapproved of the appointments; the judge adjourned until February 1. When the trial resumed, Chief Judge Rahman declared he would proceed with or without Saddam in the courtroom. Objecting to a refusal by authorities to remove the chief judge due to claims of bias, five of the defendants along with their lawyers did not appear. The court appointed a new defense team to serve in their stead.

Five witnesses for the prosecution testified without further incident. One woman recounted how she was arrested, stripped, hung upside down, and kicked in the chest repeatedly by defendant Barzan Ibrahim al-Tikriti. The next day, all eight defendants failed to appear. The three defendants who had shown up the previous day were refused entry by the chief judge for what he referred to as disorderly behavior and chaos.

One witness testified anonymously about how Iraqi security forces tortured his family. "They tortured us severely. Even one of my sisters, they took her clothes off and beat her up in front of me. They hanged me from the ceiling and subjected me to electric shocks," he said. Following the testimony of another witness, the chief judge adjourned until February 13.

Ten days later, guards forcibly escorted all eight defendants into court. Chief Judge Rahman defended his decision to compel the defendants' appearance, declaring, "The law states that if the defendants refuse to appear before the court, he will be forced to appear." Saddam hurled insults at the United States and the new chief judge and demanded Rahman's removal based on accusations of bias. "This is not a court, this is a game," he barked.

Two of Saddam's former officials testified, though they claimed they were given no choice. Ahmed Khudayir, formerly in charge of Saddam's office, denied recollection of a document displaying his apparent signature, which revealed Saddam had authorized murders in Dujail in 1984. "I don't remember. I don't remember anything at all," he said. The other witness was former foreign intelligence chief, Hassan al-Obeidi.

February 14th again began with a raucous. Saddam declared that he and his codefendants were on a hunger strike, and had been for three days previously, to object to the court's handling of the case. Barzan Ibrahim al-Tikriti wore long underwear into court for the second consecutive day to signify his defiance of the court's procedure. More of Saddam's former dignitaries testified. One spoke behind a curtain to conceal his identity; another, ex-intelligence official Fadil Mohammed al-Azzawi, adamantly maintained he was forced to appear and had no knowledge to impart regarding the Dujail atrocities. He claimed he had mistakenly signed a witness statement due to poor eyesight.

Saddam's former personal assistant and culture minister, Hamed Youssef Hamadi, also offered evidence. He identified handwriting on a document proposing rewards for six officials who took part in the Dujail apprehensions as Saddam's writing. "It looks like President Saddam's," he said.

Barzan Ibrahim al-Tikriti defended himself vigorously. He insisted, "I released all the detainees inside the hall—more than 80 persons. I swear to God I said goodbye to them one by one and apologized." He further claimed he had no responsibility for any killings and that he personally commanded the prisoners' release.

On February 28, defense attorneys decided to return to court for the first time in a month, since accusing the chief judge of bias and protesting through their absence. The defense again demanded postponement of the trial and removal of the chief judge and prosecutor. After their demands were rejected, two of the defense team's top lawyers again left the court. Subsequent proceedings progressed in relative calm.

Jaafar al-Moussawi, chief prosecutor, produced a memo dated June 16, 1984, claiming Saddam's signature appeared on the document and approved the killing of 148 Shi'ite citizens of Dujail. A second document dated two days before the pronounced death sentences, allegedly signed by Awad al-Bandar (Saddam's codefendant) was admitted into evidence.

On March 1st, all defendants filed quietly into court. Only one defense lawyer failed to appear. The prosecution presented evidence for a second day, which included more allegedly damning letters and documents connected to the defendants. Close to 100 death certificates of Dujail citizens along with transfer orders banishing victim families to the desert and seizing their property, were admitted.

The submitted letters included one revealing the mistaken execution of four accused villagers and the accidental release of two others. A second documented the death of fifty victims during interrogation prior to their planned hanging. At the close of evidence, Saddam unexpectedly acknowledged sole responsibility for his regime's actions and declared that none of his codefendants had any responsibility. He confessed that he had the dead victims' farms destroyed but maintained he had committed no crimes.

March 12 was another day involving an unyielding defense against witness accusations. Two defendants, former Ba'ath Party bureaucrats Mizher Abdullah Ruaid and Ali Daeem Ali, entered the witness stand and denied responsibility for the Dujail violence. Ruaid contested testimony accusing him of aiding the capture of Dujail villagers and razing their property.

The following day, Awad Hamad al-Bandar, former chief judge of the Iraqi revolutionary court, admitted sentencing 148 Dujail Shi'ites to death. However, he defended his action, saying the killings complied with Iraqi law. He claimed all the executed parties had been fairly tried after they admitted the attempt to assassinate Saddam pursuant to an Iranian directive. At the time, Iraq was engaged in a bitter war with Iran. The prosecution scoffed at the suggestion that the victims had received a proper trial. Another codefendant and Ba'ath Party official from the region of Dujail rebuffed accusations he had imprisoned Dujail citizens.

Three days later. Saddam began once again assailing the court's credibility, referring to it as a "comedy." He also denounced sectarian violence in favor of the uprising against the U.S. military occupation. The judge responded by excluding the press from the remainder of the hearing after Saddam ignored warnings not to use the court for political diatribes.

Barzan Ibrahim al-Tikriti defended himself against evidence that included a letter purportedly bearing his signature and requested commendation of intelligence officials who organized the Dujail assault. Al-Tikriti claimed the signature was forged and that he had stopped in Dujail only once after the assassination attempt, during which time he reprimanded security officials for indiscriminate arrests. He further claimed he arranged for the release of numerous captives. Claiming he was unconnected with the government agencies in charge of the security crackdown in Dujail, he flatly denied responsibility for any killings. The judge adjourned until April 5.

When the Iraqi High Tribunal (IHT) reconvened, the prosecution opened with a vigorous cross-examination of Saddam. It submitted twenty-eight identification cards of Dujail villagers under eighteen years old, implying that Saddam approved of the execution of the cardholders despite the fact that Iraqi law prohibited the execution of minors at that time.

Saddam called the evidence fake, pointing out that ID cards are routinely forged. He claimed the trial judge was afraid of the interior minister and accused the prosecution of coaching and bribing witnesses. To support his claims of deliberate fabrication, he proposed that an international body scrutinize the signatures on documents authorizing executions in response to the assassination attempt. Later that day, the chief judge ordered the removal a female defense attorney for submitting photos of Iraqis tortured in prisons the United States maintained.

On April 17, 2006, the prosecution cited handwriting experts who confirmed that Saddam signed death warrants condemning 148 Dujail Shi'ites to death. The prosecution read the verification into evidence from an expert report. The defense countered that the supposed experts were influenced by the Iraqi interior ministry. Defense attorneys requested that the handwriting be analyzed by neutral international experts.

Barzan Ibrahim al-Tikriti again renounced the prosecution's efforts to connect him to the Dujail slayings, maintaining any proffered signatures were forgeries.

The judge adjourned until April 19 to increase time for handwriting experts to inspect the signatures.

On Wednesday, April 19, the judge stated that handwriting experts had reaffirmed that Saddam's authentic signature appeared on the documents in evidence, specifically those condemning the Dujail citizens to death. The experts had also agreed on the authenticity of Barzan Ibrahim al-Tikriti's signature on similar documents. Al-Tikriti charged that the prosecution was fabricating evidence and "using any means to make the accused guilty."

Monday, April 24th, produced more damning corroborative evidence. Prosecutors played a recorded phone conversation relaying a dialogue between Saddam and then Vice-President Taha Yassin Ramadan. The recording included a discussion of the obliteration of Dujail farmland. Another report from handwriting experts again confirmed signatures of Saddam and six other defendants on documents implicating the defendants in the Dujail massacre. The experts could not, however, verify the signature of Mizher Abdullah Ruaid. Barzan Ibrahim al-Tikriti summarily dismissed the evidence. He maintained that the prosecution was simply trying to ruin the reputation of the defendants through false data.

Monday, May 15, was the day formal charges were read against Saddam, signaling that the prosecution had completed the presentation of its case. Saddam declined to plead on the charges. He said to the judge, "I can't just say yes or no to this. I am the president of Iraq according to the will of the Iraqis and I am still the president up to this moment."

The charges against Saddam and Barzan Ibrahim al-Tikriti, his half-brother, included ordering the killing of 148 people in Dujail. The charges also included the preliminary retaliatory slaying of nine people in Dujail. Finally, the two were charged with illegally arresting 399 people, torturing women and children, and destroying farmland. Other charges were leveled against all eight defendants. Each pleaded not guilty or refused to plead.

Tuesday, May 16, three witnesses testified in defense of Dujail Ba'ath Party officials Abdulla Kadhem Ruaid, Mizher Abdullah Ruaid, and Mohmmed Azawi Ali. The other five defendants did not appear. Some of the witnesses were relatives of the three defendants and testified anonymously behind a curtain.

The evidence included testimony that the Ruaid family members were victims of the Dujail crackdown rather than the perpetrators. According to two witnesses, the Ruaids ranked low in the Ba'ath Party hierarchy and had farmland destroyed along with other victims. Another witness, a member of the Ruaid family, recounted that Mizher Abdullah Ruaid was forced to continue his duties at the Dujail telephone exchange during the attacks rather than participate in the retaliatory assaults. "He was on night shift for the government, how would he have been able to take on another task?" the witness stated. A second family member pleaded with the court, "My father is a tribal sheikh and people loved him for his love and fairness towards people. . . . It's a crime to bring him here."

All eight defendants were in court when the trial resumed the following day. Testimony was again offered in defense of four lower ranking defendants.

The witnesses anonymously recalled that these four defendants were insignificant Ba'ath Party members who were above suspicion in the Dujail incidents. Chief Judge Rahman approved the defense's request that Saddam and Barzan Ibrahim al-Tikriti also testify in defense of one of the lower ranking defendants—Taha Yassin Ramadan.

On Monday, May 22, defense attorney Bushra Khalil quarreled with Chief Judge Rahman, attempting to disrupt the proceedings. She was later barred from the courtroom and reprimanded for interrupting the trial. Saddam was also silenced when he objected to the removal.

One of Saddam's half-brothers, Sabawi Ibrahim al-Tikriti, testified in defense of Barzan Ibrahim al-Tikriti. A second witness also testified for al-Tikriti, screened from view. Finally, an employee of the Iraqi revolutionary court gave testimony for the defense regarding the impartiality and fairness of the trials preceding the execution of the 148 Dujail Shi'ites.

Two days later, Tariq Aziz, Iraqi Foreign Minister and Deputy Prime Minister under the Ba'ath Party, defended Saddam. He referred to Saddam as a "colleague and comrade for decades" and cited the ex-president's right to take retributive action in response to the 1982 assassination attempt. Abed Hamid Mahmud, Saddam's former personal security director, articulated the details of the attempt on the former dictator's life. Also that day, Barzan Ibrahim al-Tikriti accused Chief Judge Rahman of "insulting a woman" by expelling Bushra Khalil of the defense team the previous Monday.

More defense witnesses testified on Monday, May 29, regarding the neutrality of the hearings held before the killing of the 148 Dujail villagers. A former lawyer for the revolutionary court stated that defendant Awad al-Bandar, chief judge on the court, respected the rights of accused by granting them a full and fair opportunity to defend themselves. A former defendant before the revolutionary court also vouched for the court's impartiality in all its trials.

An unidentified defense witness testified the next day, claiming 23 of the alleged 148 executed Dujail citizens were still alive. The witness, in his teens at the time of the Dujail massacre, volunteered to provide the names of unexecuted villagers. He recounted that these survivors dispersed abroad after they were released and only returned after Saddam's ouster in 2003. The chief judge instructed the defense team to call a limited number of witnesses to corroborate this testimony and stressed that the testimony's quality was of paramount concern.

On Wednesday, May 31, defense lawyers again asserted the prosecution was manufacturing false evidence and urged the judge to postpone the trial pending further investigation of the accusations. A witness for the defense claimed the chief prosecutor, Jaafar al-Moussawi, paid him a $500 bribe to fabricate testimony and made threats against his family. The prosecutor responded by threatening legal action against the witness.

Defense attorneys offered video recordings to impeach a central witness for the prosecution. The video depicted Ali al-Haidari, governor of the Baghdad Governate, approving of the attempt on Saddam's life in Dujail. Al-Haidari was assassinated in 2005. The witness had testified earlier that no such assassination attempt had ever occurred. Chief Judge Rahman again exercised his authority by having Barzan Ibrahim al-Tikriti thrown out for disrupting the trial.

The trial resumed on Monday, June 5. The defense team stubbornly disputed the genuineness of documents proffered by the prosecution and insisted that the chief judge postpone the trial for further inquiry. The arrest of four defense witnesses amid allegations of false testimony also provoked criticism from defense attorneys.

The defense then called witnesses to speak on behalf of defendant Ali Daeem Ali. These witnesses assured the court that Ali was innocent and "ha[d] never hurt anyone." Defendant Ali, himself a former Ba'ath Party official and Dujail mayor, was charged with supplying security forces with the names of people who later became victims in the Dujail massacre.

Following up on prior testimony, the defense team recited the names of 15 people from the 148 supposedly executed Dujail victims. These names, according to the defense, identified ten people from that list of those executed who were still living and another five who either died naturally or in the Iran–Iraq war. Chief Judge Rahman demanded that manuscripts be produced to support the defense's assertion. At the end of the proceedings, the judge adjourned until June 12.

On the 12th, animosity between the defense and judges erupted into heated exchanges. Security escorted Barzan Ibrahim al-Tikriti from the court for quarrelling with the chief judge. Curtis Doebbler, one of several Western lawyers retained by the defense, requested more time to prepare the defense's case, claiming the conduct of the trial put the defense "at a serious disadvantage." He pointed out that prosecutors consumed over five months in presenting its case, contrasted with the urging of judges that the defense rush to present its evidence in a matter of weeks.

Chief Judge Rahman announced to the court that the four witnesses accusing the prosecution of bribery in exchange for false testimony had confessed. He said, "We reached a decision that these witnesses were lying and we took action against them." He read confessions of perjury made by the arrested witnesses. The disputed testimony involved whether any of the 148 said to have been executed in Dujail were still alive, which, according to the defense, discredited the prosecution's entire case.

Tuesday, June 14, was the last day Chief Judge Rahman permitted for presentation of the defense's case. He scolded the defense for spouting "endless rhetoric" and lectured, "You've presented 62 witnesses. If that's not enough to present your case, then 100 won't work."

Barzan Ibrahim al-Tikriti was again tossed from court for referring to the judge as a "dictator" and repeatedly interrupting the proceedings. Former members of Saddam's security detail testified that Saddam had commanded them to hold their fire to save innocent people immediately following the 1982 assassination attempt. The trial was adjourned and closing arguments were scheduled for June 19.

During closing arguments, chief prosecutor Jaafar al-Mussawi recommended execution for Saddam, Barzan Ibrahim al-Tikriti, and Taha Yassin Ramadan. "They were spreading corruption on Earth . . . and even the trees were not saved from their oppression." The prosecution requested the release of Mohammed Azzam Azzawi, former Ba'ath Party official, recommending the charges against him be dropped. With the defense set to deliver its closing argument on July 10, the judge adjourned.

The argument from Saddam's lawyers, however, did not take place as scheduled on July 10. Instead, Saddam sent a letter to Chief Judge Rahman declaring his boycott of the trial. In the letter, Saddam wrote that the proceedings were motivated by the "malicious" aims of the United States which made a charade of Iraqi and international law.

Defense lawyers representing Saddam, Barzan Ibrahim al-Tikriti, Taha Yassin Ramadan, and Awad Hamad al-Bandar, also announced that they would not attend further proceedings until their security detail was enhanced and other demands were satisfied. The kidnapping and murder of Khamis al Obeidi, a lawyer defending Saddam, in the prior month prompted the protest. Obeidi was the third lawyer on the defense team murdered since the preceding October. The lawyers for former Dujail Ba'ath Party officials Ali Daeem Ali and Mohammed Azawi Ali nevertheless completed their closing statements.

The next day, Chief Judge Rahman warned defense lawyers that they would be replaced by other appointed lawyers if they did not return to court. He further advised that the defendants would be prejudiced if they did not relent. Out of all the defendants, only Abdullah Kazim Ruaid and his son, Mizhar Abdullah Ruaid, appeared. The lawyers for these two defendants made their closing arguments. Chief Judge Rahman adjourned the trial until July 24, ordering the defense to appear at that time.

On the 24th, the trial resumed. Saddam still did not appear because his hunger strike had caused him to be hospitalized. In addition, the defense team failed to heed the chief judge's warnings to return, maintaining the trial was unfair and that their demands were ignored. Defendant Barzan Ibrahim al-Tikriti did appear and was condemned by the chief judge for his role in the Dujail crackdown. The judge then adjourned the trial for one day hoping defense lawyers would present their final statements on Wednesday.

On July 26, Saddam appeared in court claiming he was forced into the chamber from his hospital bed. In the event of a guilty verdict, he asked that he be executed by firing squad rather than by hanging in honor of his military background. Noticeably thinner due to his hunger strike, it was reported that he had begun taking food once again. The court appointed defense lawyers to replace those who continued to boycott despite Saddam's vigorous objections.

The following day, former vice president Taha Yassin Ramadan and Awad Hamad al-Bandar appeared for summations. Ramadan refused representation from the court-appointed lawyer. Saddam did not appear at the final session and the chief judge adjourned until October 16 when the five-judge panel would deliver a verdict.

The verdict was not delivered on October 16, however. On October 29, chief prosecutor Jaafar al Moussawi announced that the verdict, now set for November 5, might be further delayed in light of judicial "checks." Zalmay Khalilzad, U.S. ambassador to Iraq, rebuffed suggestions that the Bush administration was pressing the court to deliver its verdict before the November 7 mid-term elections in the United States.

On Sunday, November 5, Saddam Hussein was convicted of crimes against humanity. He was sentenced to be hanged for the murder of 148 Shi'ite Dujail villagers. Death sentences were also meted out to Barzan Ibrahim al-Tikriti, Saddam's half-brother, and Awad Hamed al-Bandar, former chief judge of the Iraqi revolutionary court. The defense team was given one month to file an appeal, which it did on December 3.

The trial court's opinion was long and detailed. Ranging over 200 pages, the IHT began with an acknowledgment of the importance of balancing basic human rights against the interests of efficient administration of justice. Chief Judge Rahman noted that Iraq's laws, as of April 16, 2003, remained in effect unless otherwise changed by the government and, therefore, the death penalty was a legal option currently in force under the Iraqi penal code.

The opinion went on to recite and define the charges of murder, unlawful arrest, destruction of property, and other crimes against humanity that had been filed against the eight defendants: Saddam Hussein, Barzan Ibrahim al-Tikriti, Taha Yassin Ramadan, Awad Hamad al-Bandar, Abdulla Kadhem Ruaid, Ali Daeem Ali, Mohammed Azawi Ali, and Mizher Abdullah Ruaid.

The crux of the IHT's judgment began with an attack on the defense. The court addressed what it called "false testimony of defense witnesses," concluding that the defense team had compromised its integrity by recruiting witnesses and persuading them to testify through threats and coaching.

The court noted that the attacks on Dujail civilians were not random but appeared ordered, systematic, and deliberate—calculated to intimidate and terrorize the villagers of Dujail in purported violation of Iraqi laws in force at the time. Many of the 148 victims were summarily tried and condemned to death. The court listed the names of many who were tortured to death, those who died while being held in Abu Ghraib prison, and those who died subsequently in desert camps.

Continuing its harangue of the defense, the IHT noted the "offensive" behavior of foreign defense attorneys before the court, specifically identifying U.S. attorneys Ramsey Clark and Curtis Doebbler along with Mr. al-Armouti of Jordan and Ms. Bushra Khalil of Lebanon. According to the court, "the attorneys boycotted the sessions using false claims the sole purpose of which was nothing but publicity and advertisement." Regret was expressed regarding the murder of a defense attorney, but the court insisted such events did not hamper the credibility or transparency of the proceedings. The court claimed it followed applicable penal law procedures with regard to expelling the defendants and portrayed an attitude of tolerance toward the defendants' antics throughout the trial.

The court's opinion in fact blamed defense attorneys for their own lack of security, stating the defense team declined to accept the court's offer of heightened security and repeatedly risked their security by appearing on television and disseminating information on the Internet.

Shifting to a more defensive tone, the court next addressed the defense team's petitions for security, removal of the chief judge, postponement of the trial, and a finding of no jurisdiction. The IHT dedicated numerous paragraphs to defending its legitimacy pursuant to the laws of the democratically elected Iraqi government. In addition, it swiftly disposed of any claim of immunity on the part of Saddam Hussein based on his acts as the leader of Iraq, citing the Nuremburg trials and other international law as precedent.

The court stated the defendants' retribution on the village of Dujail violated both customary international law and domestic Iraqi law simultaneously. It reasoned that even if no Iraqi national laws proscribed such actions at the time, international law undeniably categorized such actions as crimes against humanity in 1982. Nevertheless, the court stated that, if proven, the defendants' acts violated both the Baghdad penal code of 1969 and the Iraqi military penal code of 1940. Therefore, no notice issue existed regarding retroactivity of the alleged crimes or punishments.

A fairly methodical and pedantic structure then followed. The court explained its method of analysis and how it would apply the method to the charges against individual defendants. The opinion set forth the specific charges, evidence, defenses, and legal analysis separately with regard to each defendant.

Saddam Hussein was first in the court's verdict. The charges against him included crimes against humanity encompassing murder, removal of a population or the compulsory transfer of a population, imprisonment or the strict denial of any type of physical freedoms in a way that contradicts basic principles of international law, torture, compulsory concealment of people, and other inhumane acts of a similar nature which deliberately cause great suffering or serious harm to the body or mental or physical health.

The IHT next had to connect Saddam to the actions of his agents in the field. After disposing of the case against Barzan Ibrahim al-Tikriti, the court set forth the elements of aiding, abetting, and agency under which Saddam could be held responsible for the Dujail atrocities. It proceeded to recite the evidence, testimony, and accusations leveled against the deposed leader.

The court also set forth some of the statements Saddam made during the trial and investigation of the case. According to the IHT, when asked about his apparent signature on documents admitted into evidence, Saddam stated, "If the signature and the handwriting were mine and it is known to be mine then I hold full responsibility for my handwriting and signature which is well known." The court noted Saddam's assent that if the expert matching of any signature "proved [the signature] to be mine, then it is mine." If such evidence were produced, Saddam stated, "I alone hold full responsibility and not the members of the Revolutionary Council Leadership."

Regarding Saddam's testimony in general, the court expressed dissatisfaction when Saddam said, "I remember when I want to remember and I don't remember when I don't want to remember." The court also noted Saddam's general denial when he claimed, "I did not and I shall not give an order to kill civilians."

Addressing the charge of deliberate killing as a crime against humanity, the court declared that Saddam knew the nature of the crime and nevertheless plotted in a way that satisfied every element. The court could find "no legal, or legitimate, or human justification that can be accepted for arresting and detaining hundreds of women, children, old men and young men of the inhabitants of Dujail." Further, the opinion emphatically rejected Saddam's denial that he commanded soldiers to fire at Dujail farmers, stating no subordinates would have dared commit such acts without orders from their supreme leader. The court therefore concluded that the killing of so many Dujail citizens occurred under either direct or indirect orders from Saddam.

Under applicable Iraqi law, the court stated the party who orders the commission of a crime is deemed a principal offender who is more dangerous than those who carry out the physical acts. Despite admitting a lack of direct evidence showing Saddam had issued the orders to execute Dujail villagers, the court determined the circumstances were sufficient to infer complicity. Further, the opinion concluded all accomplices to such crimes are liable for its results regardless of the actual role each participant assumed.

Finding yet another route to liability, the court determined that Saddam's position as commander-in-chief required him to prevent the crime or punish those who committed it in light of his apparent knowledge. Failure to do so caused him to be liable for the crimes of those under his command. Finally, the court turned to religious creeds to justify its judgment by citing to the Qur'an: "God, to Whom be ascribed all perfection and majesty, says [in the Qur'an], 'And do not kill anyone whose killing God has forbidden, except for a just cause. And whoever is killed wrongfully, We have given his heir the authority. But let him not exceed limits in the matter of taking life. Verily, he is helped (by the Islamic law).' (Al-Isra', verse 33)."

With regard to the crimes of displacement, forced removal of citizens, and unlawful imprisonment, the court again found the circumstantial evidence sufficient to convict Saddam with knowledge of the acts despite his denials. The opinion noted specifically that the operation undertaken by the director of Iraqi intelligence was highly unlikely to have occurred without Saddam's knowledge and authorization.

The torture allegations perhaps commanded the most detailed attention from the court—including a litany of torture accounts relayed by witnesses. Again, the court repeated its conviction that Saddam was accountable based on his clearly inferable knowledge of the events and his subsequent failure to halt, investigate, or punish the inhumane deeds.

The IHT abruptly dismissed charges of coercive disappearance against all the defendants, including Saddam. The opinion cited lack of evidence needed to hold the defendants accountable under international law. In the court's estimation, the prosecution submitted no proof that any of the victims' relatives inquired regarding the whereabouts of their kin.

Finally, the court condemned Saddam for ordering the farms and gardens of the villagers of Dujail destroyed. It noted the extreme suffering produced by confiscations and the uprooting of produce-bearing trees that were the lifeblood of Dujail. The court conclusively announced that the prosecution had proven all the charges, save coercive disappearance, beyond a reasonable doubt. The five-judge panel unanimously found Saddam and his codefendants guilty of "a large scale systematic and programmed attack with the aim of punishment and intimidation," stressing that Saddam was chiefly liable due to his position as former president and military leader.

It sentenced Saddam Hussein, along with Barzan Ibrahim al-Tikriti and Awad Hamad al-Bandar, to death by hanging for the crime of deliberately killing Dujail villagers. Saddam was sentenced to an additional ten years in prison for forced displacement of Dujail citizens, five years in prison for unlawful imprisonment and extreme deprivation of the freedom of the victims, ten years in prison for acts of torture, and seven years in prison for other inhumane acts including the destruction and confiscation of land. The other defendants, also found guilty of assorted crimes, were sentenced to varying prison terms as well.

The court noted it had informed the convicted defendants that transcripts would automatically be sent to the appellate court to facilitate discrete review of the sentence if the defendants chose to appeal within thirty days.

The Anfal Trial and Saddam's Execution

It should be noted that only a handful of former despots have ever been charged with genocide. Thus, charging Saddam with this crime in the Anfal trial was not an insignificant move for the Iraqi High Tribunal (IHT). Indeed, the tribunal had not encountered this crime in the previous Dujail trial.

As one of the most heinous crimes, universal jurisdiction can be invoked by courts empowered to do so over genocide. However, no international court has asserted jurisdiction over the Anfal genocide. The ad hoc U.N.-backed International Criminal Tribunals for Yugoslavia, Rwanda, Sierra Leonne, and Cambodia are restrained by limited geographic and temporal jurisdiction over crimes occurring in those respective territories. The newly created International Criminal Court is only empowered with prospective jurisdiction from 2002 onward (the Anfals occurred in 1988). And the International Court of Justice only has jurisdiction granted to it by states seeking to litigate their claims against other states. However, a domestic national court has weighed in on the Anfal.

A Dutch court in The Hague found that the Anfal campaigns were in fact genocide, as the Kurds had consistently claimed. The judgment came in the case of a Dutch trader named Frans van Anraat, who was found guilty of complicity in the 1988 chemical attack that killed 5,000 Kurds in the Iraqi town of Halabja. Van Anraat supplied thousands of tons of raw materials for chemical weapons to the Saddam Hussein regime during the Iran–Iraq war, some of which were redirected toward decimating the Iraqi Kurdish population.

The court determined that it "has no other conclusion than that these attacks were committed with the intent to destroy the Kurdish population of Iraq." And it said Van Anraat's role "facilitated the attacks. He cannot counter with the argument that this would have happened even without his contribution." Van Anraat is serving a fifteen-year sentence.[1]

Saddam Hussein's trial before the IHT on charges relating to the 1987–1988 Anfal military campaign against Iraqi Kurds in northern Iraq began on Monday, August 21, 2006. Six codefendants also faced charges in the Anfal trial, including:

- Ali Hassan al-Majid (a.k.a. "Chemical Ali")
- Sultan Hashem Ahmed, a former military commander
- Saber Abdel Aziz, military intelligence director during the Anfal
- Hussein Rashid, former Iraqi deputy of armed forces operations
- Taher Ani, ex-governor of the Iraqi city of Mosul
- Farhan Jubouri, military intelligence leader in northern Iraq during the campaign.

Each defendant faced charges of war crimes and crimes against humanity for orchestrating the brutal Anfal attacks. Saddam and General al-Majid faced separate charges of genocide. The genocide charge raised the evidentiary bar for the prosecution, as genocide is much more difficult to prove than the other crimes.

Estimates from international organizations suggest around 100,000 Kurds were killed in the military campaign, most of them civilians. About one-fifth of Iraq's population is Kurdish. As in the Dujail trial, Saddam faced the death penalty if convicted. The chemical attack on Halabja was to be tried separately at a later date. Just as Saddam's military considered the Halabja attack to be a separate military campaign, the IHT also considered it a separate crime.

THE TRIAL

The Anfal trial focused on the eight campaigns waged under General al-Majid's direction against the Kurds in 1988. The following description of the Anfal trial up to the point of Saddam's execution contains testimony and quotes from trial participants derived from news sources cited in the bibliography.

The opening court session on August 21, 2006, lasted five hours. For most of that time, Saddam listened expressionlessly as prosecutors explained the eight stages of the Anfal campaign, aimed at purging the Kurds from their native mountains in northern Iraq. The trial was broadcast throughout the Middle East by satellite.

Saddam refused to plead in the case along with his codefendant and cousin, General al-Majid. Represented by the same counsel as in the Dujail case, Saddam again disputed the IHT's legality and authority only to be summarily rebuffed by the judge. The chief defense lawyer for Saddam, Khalil al-Dulaimi, refused to address the Anfal charges and cited the Geneva Conventions as authority for the proposition that the existence of the IHT violated international law.

When asked to state his name and residence along with the other defendants, Saddam rejoined in a raspy voice, "I won't give you my name because all the Iraqis know my name." When further asked whether he respected Iraqi law, he replied, "You're sitting there in the name of the occupation and not the name of Iraq." Finally relenting, he called himself "the president of the republic of Iraq and commander in chief of the heroic Iraqi armed forces."

The chief prosecutor in the trial was Minqith al-Faroon. He alleged the Anfal campaign, which means "spoils of war" when translated into English, resulted in the deaths of 182,000 people. According to the chief prosecutor, the deaths occurred from the use of poisonous gas, the flattening of entire villages, and the subjection of women and children to horrid detention camp conditions. "It is difficult to fathom the barbarity of such acts," he emphasized.

According to observers, al-Faroon's concise and poignant arguments were in stark contrast to the disconnected ramblings of the Dujail trial's chief prosecutor, Jaafar al-Mousawi. Al-Faroon blatantly accused Saddam of genocide and showed the court photos of mass graves in the northern Iraqi town of Hatra and the southern desert near Samawa. More than 9,000 documents supported their accusations, prosecutors maintained.

When Saddam faced accusations that detained women were raped during the campaign, he irately asserted, "I can never accept the claim that an Iraqi woman was raped while Saddam was president!" The following day, the prosecution called its first two witnesses. The witnesses, speaking in Kurdish, described the carnage of chemical weapons attacks in their villages. They testified smoke with a foul odor induced vomiting and blinded victims. One of the two recalled witnessing the death of many Kurds from the harmful symptoms.

The first witness, Ali Mostafa Hama, said villagers fled to mountainsides while Saddam's military helicopters maintained a barrage of bombs. Because Iraqi procedural law allows defendants to question witnesses along with defense lawyers, Saddam briefly challenged the witness: "Who taught him to say 'We were attacked because we were Kurds'?"

"Saddam Hussein used to say we were his people," said the second witness, Najiba Khider Ahmed. She wept during her testimony and sliced the air with her hand. "If we were his people, why did he strike us with all those weapons?" she questioned. "I had one son," Ahmed grieved. "They Anfalized him. My nephew was also Anfalized. My brother was also Anfalized."

In response to this evidence, two defendants, who were high-ranking Iraqi officials during the campaign, claimed the attacks were targeted strictly at Iranian troops and the Kurdish *peshmerga* fighters who supported them. Commander Sultan Hashem Ahmed, who oversaw the Anfal attacks, claimed civilians were evacuated prior to the operations.

More damning testimony from Kurdish witnesses was given on Wednesday, August 23. Adiba Oula Bayez, the wife of a witness who had testified earlier, recalled warplanes had bombed her village of Balisan in 1987. The bombs, she explained, emitted smoke with the smell of "rotten apples." When her entire family became ill and blind for days following the attack, she suspected the smoke was a poisonous chemical.

She testified further: "On the fifth day, I slightly opened my eyes. And it was a terrible scene. My children and my skin had turned black." The attacks, she contended, resulted in the death of one of her children and her miscarriage of two pregnancies. Another female witness from the same village, Badriya Said Khider, alleged the 1987 attacks caused the death of her parents, husband, son, and other relatives. She told the court she was still suffering from the chemicals' side effects.

A third female witness, dressed in traditional black garb, as were the first two, said she was trapped in her village for a day after the attacks. In order to soothe burning throats, she explained, "We drank milk, and when we vomited it was like cheese."

Saddam's defense strategy became clear after this third day of testimony. Rather than impeaching witnesses' claims about the attacks, defense attorneys suggested the deaths were an unfortunate consequence of legitimate efforts to force Iranian troops from the area. Questioning focused on whether witnesses had observed Iranian-supported troop movement in the attacked villages. However, each witness responded with a similar denial: "No, no, never," said Bayez. "I never saw anyone like this."

Finally, Moussa Abdullah Moussa, a Kurdish *peshmerga* fighter at the time, claimed he had witnessed multiple military operations throughout 1987 and 1988. He described discovering his brother and son dead but still embracing each other. Moussa also recalled seeing some victims' eyes fall from their sockets.

When accused of treasonous activity in Iraq, Moussa explained, "Nobody asked me to participate in a military operation. I was a guard in the First Brigade headquarters." When further pressed about prisoners and the rebel fighters' cause, he said, "Sure, there were war prisoners. They were released. One goal [of our operations] was liberation, to have Kurdish identity, democracy and peace." The judge adjourned the trial until September 11, 2006.

When the trial resumed, more Kurdish witnesses appeared. Saddam denied any disdain for the Kurds, citing his acceptance of Kurdish fighters in key branches of the Iraqi military. In addition, Saddam derided Kurdish leader Massoud Barzani for stating the Iraqi flag should not fly over government buildings in northern Iraq's Kurdish areas. Regarding the national debate sparked by the statements, Saddam asserted, "We inherited [the flag], I did not establish it."

Dr. Katrin Elias, a former Kurdish guerilla fighter who now lives in the United States, gave an account of a chemical weapon attack she witnessed in June of 1987. She described bombs, dropped from planes, with a subdued detonation, which brought on weeks of vomiting and blindness. Dr. Elias condemned "all the international organisations or companies which provided the Iraqi regime with these weapons." Other civilian Kurds also detailed their forced removal from homes, arrests, and torture along with the deaths of family members.

The next day, Kurdish men testified before the court about the loss of family members in the Anfal campaign. Ghafour Hassan Abdullah lamented he discovered the location of his mother and two sisters after their identity cards were exhumed from a mass grave fifteen years after the attacks. He lashed out at Saddam, saying, "Congratulations Saddam Hussein. You are now in a cage!"

Saddam insisted evidence from mass graves be examined in a third-party neutral country "like Switzerland" and accused the court of betrayal, exclaiming, "You are agents of Iran and Zionism. We will crush your heads!" Losing his cool when a lawyer labeled Kurdish *peshmerga* guerillas "freedom fighters," Saddam said any country would mobilize its military to quash such a rebellion.

On September 13, a Kurdish witness named Majeed Amad from the village of Sargalow testified his town had been bombed for twenty days, causing villagers to flee to Iran. "When the villagers returned to Iraq," he explained, "they surrendered to the Iraqi army and were imprisoned." He claimed, "We have not heard from them since then." Omar Othman Muhammad testified planes dropped chemical-filled balloons followed by missiles to effect the spread of poisonous gas.

The chief prosecutor al-Faroon accused the chief judge Abdullah al-Amiri of favoring Saddam and asked him to recuse himself. In addition, he blamed the judge for allowing the defendants to threaten witnesses and engage in political rants. However, Chief Judge al-Amiri refused to step down, citing his twenty-five years of experience and his fair-mindedness.

In an exchange with a Kurdish witness the following day, former president Saddam inquired why the witness had sought a meeting with him to locate his family members. "Why did you try to meet me when you knew I was a dictator?" he asked the witness. Fueling the prosecutor's accusations of the previous day, Chief Judge al-Amiri interrupted, claiming Saddam was no dictator. "You were not a dictator," al-Amiri defended, "People around you made you [look like] a dictator."

"Thank you," Saddam replied, smiling in appreciation.

The witness, Abdullah Mohammed Hussain, testified he confronted Saddam following the arrest of family members in the Anfal campaign. In response to his questioning, Hussain recalled Saddam replied, "Shut up. Your family is gone in the Anfal." The witness relayed that his relatives' bodies were found in a mass grave two years prior to the trial.

During the five days before the trial's resumption, Chief Judge al-Amiri was replaced amid charges of bias from the government of Iraq. According to a cabinet spokesperson, Amiri's lack of "neutrality" caused the Prime Minister, Mr. Maliki, and the cabinet to request his removal and to appoint Chief Judge Mohammad al-Khalifa in his stead. This meddling by the government in the affairs of the tribunal was deeply resented by many of the judges.

Bassam al-Husseini, an aide to the prime minister explained, "There was pressure from the Iraqi people in Kurdistan because their feelings were hurt. The government had to respond to this pressure." He defended the decision, stating Iraqi prime ministers could lawfully remove judges from the court.

Human rights groups criticized the move. "It's not clear whether the proper procedure was used or not," said the director of the Human Rights Watch international justice program, Richard Dicker. Despite the expressed concerns over al-Amiri's bias, Human Rights Watch called the request for removal a "blatant violation" of judicial independence.

On September 19, witness Iskandar Mahmoud Abdul Rahman recollected a 1988 attack on his village involving chemical weapons. Rahman testified, "We took the floor; white smoke covered us, it smelled awful. My heartbeat increased. I started to vomit. I felt dizzy. My eyes burned and I couldn't stand on my feet." Rahman took off his shirt to reveal dark scars to court reporters. He claimed the scars formed when surgeons from Iran had cut off his burned skin.

In an abrupt change of ambiance, the new chief judge, al-Khalifa, had Saddam removed from the courtroom for failing to acknowledge him as al-Amiri's replacement. Al-Khalifa, a Shi'ite Arab and former deputy chief judge, ordered Saddam out of court for refusing to sit down. To protest, Saddam's lawyers also walked out and threatened to boycott the remaining proceedings if the government continued to meddle in the trial.

Five days later, Saddam was removed from court again for insisting he be freed from the caged witness box. Chief Judge al-Khalifa demanded Saddam show greater respect. He exclaimed, "I'm the presiding judge. I decide about your presence here. Get him out!"

Mohammed Rasul Mustafa appeared to testify about the bombing of a village near where he lived. A strange smell that caused him breathing difficulties radiated from the bombs, he explained. While jailed for five months, Mustafa recalled witnessing guards murdering a fellow prisoner with a steel cable. Another witness, Rifat Mohammed Said, imprisoned in the same Nugrat Salman camp as Mustafa, testified he saw children die of starvation and a guard named Hajaj rape and torture detainees.

The next day, Saddam was again ejected from the courtroom for continually refusing to keep silent. Chief Judge al-Khalifa reprimanded Saddam before having him tossed from the court: "You can defend yourself, question witnesses . . . and I am ready to allow you, but this is a court, not a political arena." Microphones were then turned off while the former dictator read a long prepared statement printed on a piece of paper.

After a two-week adjournment, the trial resumed with testimony from more Kurdish witnesses. A thirty-one-year-old woman remembered how Iraqi troops had arrested her and eight family members while raiding her village. Thirteen-years-old at the time, she claimed she had knowledge of relatives "buried alive" by soldiers. Recovered identity cards confirmed the death of five of her sisters in a Samawa mass grave in southern Iraq.

Another witness testified two of his sisters and their four children, his pregnant wife, two brothers, and his mother had all disappeared when his village was ransacked in 1988. He said he had not seen any of them since that time. Although all seven defendants appeared for the testimony, a defense team leader stated defense lawyers would persist in their boycott of the trial.

On October 10, another Kurdish woman testified anonymously behind a sheet regarding her imprisonment in camps under the Ba'ath Party regime. According to this witness, men in protective suits and masks sprayed prisoners with a substance "that caused the spread of lice and other diseases, like bronchial coughing." She recalled the practice brought on the death of numerous children. Even pregnant women were mistreated, she said. She told of one woman who gave birth on a toilet and had to cut the umbilical cord with a bottle shard.

Following this testimony, the chief judge again ordered Saddam out of the courtroom. To merit the ejection, Saddam had shouted a passage from the Quran. Another defendant, Hussein Rashid al-Tikriti, was escorted from the courtroom after he hit a bailiff who was trying to force him to sit.

The next day, Saddam verbally attacked the chief judge for turning off the microphone to silence his defense. Judge al-Khalifa defended his act as necessary to control the courtroom. Three more Kurdish witnesses testified before the trial was adjourned until October 17, 2006.

On that day, defense attorneys finally reappeared after a month-long absence. They heard evidence of more atrocities recounted in the testimonies of Kurdish witnesses. The witnesses told of the rounding up of thousands of Kurds during the Anfal campaign. Hundreds of these Kurds died in prison camps, according to the testimony. One survivor stated thirty-three relatives of his vanished during that time. Saddam disparaged the witnesses for supporting "the Zionists" by encouraging division in Iraq. He claimed the testimony was adding to Iraqi sectarianism.

The following day, the prosecution continued its case with one Kurdish witness telling of the killing of fellow citizens in the Iraqi desert. In 1988, the witness stated, Saddam's military herded prisoners into the desert for execution and burial in mass graves. He remembered seeing mounds in the desert "that all had people buried underneath." Despite indications the defense team had ended its boycott, the team failed to appear for the day's testimony.

On October 19, another witness, Abdullah Saeed, divulged the horrors of chemical weapon use in more Kurdish areas of Iraq. He said government troops detonated chemical weapons in Kurdish villages during 1988. After attacks on two neighboring towns, he said, acrid smoke clouds wafted toward his home.

"[C]hildren, women and other persons infected with chemical weapons [were loaded] onto three trucks and fled to another village," he explained. He further recalled Iraqi troops stopped these lorries en route, arrested the passengers, and transported them to prisons in southern Iraq. Disease and malnutrition killed hundreds in the prison camps he and another witness said. The judge adjourned for Ramadan until the end of October.

After Ramadan, the chief defense lawyer and the judge exchanged harsh words that culminated in the lawyer's exit from the courtroom. The lawyer insisted the trial process was unfair. After the appointment of new defense attorneys, more Kurdish witnesses spoke of their experiences. Jamal Sulaiman Qadir said it was like "Doomsday" when he entered his town following chemical attacks. He described the bodies of children among piled corpses in the village, some of whom were "still clutching lollipops or Eid sweets because it was the last day of Ramadan." Fakhir Ali Hussein said the bombs emitted "a smell in the village like rotten apples." He produced a list with the names of thirty-five people he claimed were killed from attacks on his own and nearby villages.

On October 31, five more Kurdish witnesses testified. One anonymously stated he was among prisoners transported by bus to an execution site in April 1988. Once at the site in western Iraq, he explained, "[t]he guards took two prisoners at a time from the bus, shot them dead and dragged their bodies to a huge ditch." He said he was blindfolded, handcuffed, and forced to the ground where guards shot at him repeatedly. "We were pulled away by our legs," he said. "I pretended I was dead."

A forty-six-year-old housewife named Bafrin Fattah Ahmed described her blindness caused by the chemicals dropped from planes, after which her husband and son disappeared. The judge adjourned until November 7 to await the verdict from the Dujail trial.

Two days after Saddam's death sentence was handed down in the Dujail trial, the Anfal trial resumed. Uncharacteristically subdued, Saddam petitioned for unity in Iraq: "I call on all Iraqis, Arabs and Kurds, to forgive, reconcile and shake hands." Forty-eight hours earlier, he had expressed blind fury at the imposition of his death sentence in the Dujail trial. In stark contrast, Saddam's disposition changed to that of a polite deliberator once back at the Anfal trial.

During both the Dujail and Anfal trials, Saddam became known for mysterious and rapid mood shifts; one moment loudly provoking a continued Sunni resistance against American occupiers, and the next calmly conferring with judges, discussing legal issues, encouraging cross-examination, and occasionally directing defense lawyers to calm down.

Kurdish testimony continued that day, the 21st day of similar testimony. Witnesses from one village told the court about scores of men rounded up, promised pardons, and then abruptly shot by soldiers. One witness, Qahar Khalil Mohammed, said, "[The soldiers] led us out of the village, separated men from the women and children. A total of 37 men were separated, including myself." He described how they were lined up and shot. Thirty-three villagers died in the mass execution, he recounted, but he survived despite multiple wounds.

"There were 16 soldiers facing us, with two officers," Mohammed explained. "One of the officers said, 'Sit down,' and immediately the other one said, 'Shoot.' The soldiers all fired on us, and we collapsed on the ground. When they had finished the bullets in their Kalashnikovs they reloaded, and they did this three times. One of the officers asked an older soldier to administer the coup de grâce to all the bodies." Pointing to his scarred forehead, he said, "This is my coup de grâce."

Saddam, a student of the law in Cairo for three years during the 1960s, gestured for the judge's attention and suggested the court should require more specific testimony. "He said there were two officers involved," Saddam noted. "You should ask, 'What did they look like? What was their rank? What were their names?' The court should be able to find at least one of these officers. What we have here is a witness who takes us on a tour, but offers no details." He queried,

"Is this the way to get to the truth?" He calmly nodded to the judge, sat down, and said, "Thank you."

The chief judge quickly stopped the prosecution's response: "The defendant Saddam has raised a purely legal point. Under the law, the witness can say what he wants. But it is the court's responsibility to weigh the validity of witness testimony."

Abdul Karim Nayif corroborated Mohammed's testimony with a similar report. In addition, he produced a video for the court that showed a mass grave containing human remains near the execution site. Despite this corroboration, Saddam refuted the testimony, claiming there was no verification of the events. He quoted Jesus and the Quran in an oration about acceptance and mercy, making a subtle appeal for an end to factional infighting.

Though American and Iraqi officials had originally planned for Saddam to stand trial for multiple crimes, the escalating war was apparently raising concerns that Saddam continued to inspire Sunni insurgents. Instead, focus turned to the pending automatic appellate review of the Dujail sentence by a nine-judge court.

The Anfal trial resumed on Monday, November 27, 2006. Another survivor of an Anfal firing squad execution testified. Taimor Abdallah Rokhza described the killing of Kurdish villagers. "There was a trench there and we were lined up and a soldier was shooting at us," he said. A defense lawyer, Bedia Araf, said a Canadian or American had appeared at his house and handed him a list of thirty witnesses they recommended he call to testify. According to Araf, the surprise visitor claimed he could control whether Saddam was convicted or acquitted. Losing patience, the chief judge expressed frustration at the defense's delay in producing its proposed witness lists.

The next day, a forensic scientist from the United States, Dr. Clyde Snow, testified about evidence of mass graves where the bodies of Kurds killed in 1988 were discovered. Dr. Snow recalled his travels to northern Iraq and a town called Koreme with a team of physicians in 1992. He displayed a slide show of twenty-seven men and boys killed by Iraqi soldiers in that village and exhumed by he and his colleagues. The slide show revealed skeletal remains. Some bodies were found with prayer beads or Kurdish belts still worn. Dr. Snow explained evidence regarding over eighty gunshot wounds discovered in the corpses. Saddam objected that Dr. Snow's testimony should be disallowed due to his bias as an American; his petition was rejected. He also proposed the remains could have been gathered from multiple locations for burial in the grave.

On Wednesday, November 29, more forensic experts from the United States testified regarding mass graves containing the bodies of Kurdish citizens killed in 1988. Douglas Scott, a forensic archaeologist, explained gun casings and shells discovered around bodies in a grave in Koreme, a Kurdish village, suggested "firing-squad type organisation." He believed at least seven executioners used Russian Kalashnikov assault rifles to fire 124 bullets at the victims.

A U.S. physician, Asfandiar Shukri, reported his examination of Kurdish refugees near Iraq's border with Turkey suggested the Iraqi government had exposed them to mustard gas. He described the mustard gas as "similar to what was used by the Nazis in the Second World War."

The chief judge ordered one of Saddam's lawyers, Badia Araf, removed from the proceedings for "insulting the court" when he referred to the prosecutor as "brother." The days of expert forensic testimony were characterized by observers as "the most chilling testimony in the 14 months since Saddam Hussein and his associates first went on trial." According to the experts, 301 victims, nearly 80 percent women and children under thirteen, were herded to desert sites where they were gunned down and buried in machine-dug pits.

The experts testified about three particular mass grave sites out of more than 200 discovered after the 2003 invasion of Iraq. The evidence revealed a recurring pattern of methodical butchery designed to kill secretly and efficiently, according to the testimony. Their technological savvy revealed an atypically comprehensive story of how the mass killings were accomplished.

Throughout the testimony, the sixty-nine-year-old Saddam remained inexpressive, taking occasional notes and expressing no shame or sympathy. Demanding coordinates of the graves and their location in relation to highways, he cautioned his questioning did not imply he had any knowledge of the killing.

Following expert testimony, Saddam insinuated his impending execution was on his mind by referring to the accelerated trial process. He also prefaced his rebuttal to testimony with a Muslim recitation: "Praise be to Allah, the most merciful, the most compassionate. May he grant that we all die as Muslims."

Michael K. Trimble, a civilian Army Corps of Engineers employee and forensic archaeologist, was the foremost expert witness discussing forensic evidence. According to Trimble, tangled bodies filled the grave, many bound together, blindfolded and grasping one another. One female victim was found still cradling a baby, both with single gunshot wounds to the head. A pregnant victim was found with the bones of her unborn child inside her decomposed body, still enveloped in her dress.

Trimble went on to describe the method of execution: men divided from women and children and driven into wedged pits; others knelt on the lip of graves before being shot in the back of the head; children, some as young as five, sprayed with machine gun fire, protectively raising their arms and "twisting and turning and trying to get away."

In the graves near Hatra, he said, around a quarter of the 123 women and children buried mysteriously had no gunshot wounds, implying they were buried alive. Of those who were shot, Trimble explained, the pattern of fire was consistent with that found in other mass graves throughout the world: The killers first squatted to shoot the victim's legs out. "And there's a reason," he stated. "When you shoot people in the legs, and bring them down, it's much easier to dispatch them."

The defense team continued to suggest the killings were mere collateral losses during the Iraqi war against Iran. Saddam himself also attacked the forensic testimony. A new expert should be recruited, he explained, one who would search "other mass graves that I hear have not been dug up," in order to present evidence

American sources had not compromised. "I suggest this because those who hear that this expert is an American, especially Iraqis, will have every reason to be suspicious about his findings," Saddam reflected.

Chief Judge al-Khalifa cut off the defendant's questions, citing reports that contained their answers that were in the possession of defense attorneys. In response, al-Majid complained, "I have every right to defend myself. But, of course, if your honor court deems it right to deprive me of my rights, then I will not trouble the court any further." The court heard more testimony from Kurdish witnesses on Monday, December 4. Abdel Qadar Abdullah, the next to last witness and a Kurdish chemistry teacher, testified gas attacks caused the loss of twenty of his relatives.

The prosecution requested its case conclude after testimony from around seventy witnesses. The judge agreed to the request. It was expected the prosecution would proceed to introduce documents linking the defendants to the Kurdish deaths.

The following day, Saddam petitioned the court to excuse his presence from the remainder of the trial because he claimed the proceedings were a charade. He submitted a letter written in his own handwriting in which he charged the chief judge and prosecutors had insulted him. He wrote, "I wasn't given the chance to speak when I tried to clarify the truth by raising my hand three times."

Despite his threatened boycott, Saddam reappeared in court on December 6 with a grin. The prosecution's final witness, a Kurdish medical worker, told of caring for Kurdish victims of Iraqi military gas attacks in 1987. This was Saddam's final day in court. A recess in the Anfal trial was called for twenty-one days. Resuming on Monday, January 8, 2007, the chief judge immediately dropped all charges against Saddam, who had been executed by hanging on December 30, 2006.

EXECUTION

Saddam's execution by hanging occurred at 6:00 A.M. local time at Camp Justice, at an Iraqi Army base in Kazimain, a northeastern Baghdad suburb. None of Saddam's lawyers were present.

The scene of the hanging was chaotic. Cheers and jeers commingled with shouting by Shi'a captors surrounded Saddam as he ascended the scaffolding to meet his fate. Saddam refused to wear the traditional black hood over his head. According to Mowaffak al-Rubaie, a final exchange occurred between Saddam and one of his guards:

> "You have destroyed us. You have killed us. You have made us live in destitution."
> "I have saved you from destitution and misery and destroyed your enemies, the Persian and Americans," Saddam responded.
> "God damn you," the guard said.
> "God damn you," responded Saddam.[2]

Saddam Hussein was then hung. A guard cut the taught rope after a short time and Saddam's lifeless body tumbled to the floor. Dancing broke out among the Shi'a around the corpse. Videos of the tumultuous and amateurish hanging were broadcast around the globe to horrified reaction from foreign governments and nongovernmental organizations. The unseemly display, in fact, appeared to confirm the worst fears of those who had argued that the trial proceedings were unjust.

Larry Cox, head of the U.S. national section of Amnesty International, observed: "The rushed execution of Saddam Hussein is simply wrong. It signifies justice denied for countless victims who endured unspeakable suffering during his regime and now have been denied their right to see justice served. It is a failed opportunity to establish the rule of law in Iraq."[3]

When asked about Saddam's chaotic execution at a Creighton University lecture a year and a half later, Chief Investigative Judge Raid Juhi al-Saedi pointed out that the execution of Saddam was an executive function, not a judicial function. Thus, the IHT had no control over how the sentence was carried out, by whom, and under what conditions.

Within Iraq, political and judicial reaction was varied. Prime Minister Nouri al-Maliki said, "Your generous and pure land has got rid—and for ever—of the filth of the dictator and a black page of Iraq's history has been turned and the tyrant has died."[4] However, Judge Rizgar Mohammed Amin, the initial chief judge in Saddam's Dujail trial, said the execution was illegal as it occurred at the beginning of the Eid al-Adha festival commemorating Abraham's offering of Ishmael to God. Executions are banned during this religious week. Prime Minister al-Maliki, however, got a clerical ruling that allowed the execution before dawn of the holiday.

The reaction from Iraqi citizens was also varied. The Sunni were resigned and stoic. Although U.S. and Iraqi troops were prepared for a backlash—none materialized. Iraq's Shi'a were jubilant, firing off rifle rounds in the streets of southern Iraqi cities.

The Kurdish reaction was decidedly negative. Mahmoud Osman, an Iraqi Kurdish politician noted the unfinished business left by Saddam's death: "Of course, Saddam has committed too many crimes. He deserves for those crimes capital punishment. But so quickly done, so quickly executed . . . and only in one case—it would leave the other cases and leave a lot of secrets without being known."[5] *The Washington Post* also noted, "Many Kurds were disappointed that Hussein was executed for the Dujail killings, widely viewed as a test case for the larger Anfal genocide trial."[6]

Kurdishmedia, an English-language Web site designed to allow interaction among Iraqi, Iranian, Syrian, and Turkish Kurds as well as those throughout the world, catalogued widespread feelings of dismay alongside a complete lack of surprise that their needs were not taken into account. Dr. Fereydun Hilmi's response was a common one: "[M]any of us feel cheated once again by the leaders who said nothing and did nothing to expose the truth about the claims of Halabja, Anfal and the Kurdish rights to justice. . . . I myself never expected a different behaviour but most still believed their leaders would do something in this direction."[7]

Disaffected blog entries on the Web site from Kurds concerning the execution asserted many foreign and ethnic conspiracies together with harsh words for the Kurdish political leadership, but were unified in the determination that Saddam's death was detrimental to having their story told in court. Here are three representative sentiments:

Does Saddam's execution for Shi'a of Dujail stipulate incapability of Kurdish leadership?

> "Saddam's execution was not in the interest of the Kurdish people. It was a slap to the face of the Kurdish people. Now Anfal trial means nothing, because Saddam is dead and he can't be convicted for his crimes against Kurdish people. This shows how Kurdish leadership is weak and has no influence over any policy in Baghdad. Kurdish People have many questions for Saddam but unfortunately these questions would go unanswered. It's a shame and a disgrace for the Kurdish people. Saddam was hanged for killing 148 Arabs and never convicted for Genocide against Kurdish people. This Execution should have been postponed until Saddam was tried for all of his crimes against innocent Kurdish People. We are victims and no one cares about us our leadership was not able to do anything. We have weak policy and we would not able to achieve anything anymore."

The unfinished business: Saddam Hussein's trial was it just a Shi'a justice?

> "Most of the free world fails to understand how/why there is so little revealed about the trial of Saddam Hussein, and indeed why he was not fully hold in account for his crime in Kurdistan not to forget loss of one million human during Iran/Iraq war and occupation of Kuwait.
>
>   It's clear that Saddam was not allowed to divulge top secrets of how the US and the West armed his regime and gave him the political and military means to keep his opponents at bay. Some of the crimes against Kurds that he was found guilty of had the blessings of the Americans at the time, and there was not any demand for justice from the Washington when it happened."

The execution of Saddam Hussein without judgment on the Anfal Genocide

> "The Arab-dominated Iraqi high tribunal made a mistake by ignoring the interests of the Kurdish victims and the Kurdish nation as a whole. This undermines the future attempts for true reconciliation. The laws of the tribunal and the priority given to a small case such as the Dujail case reveal the biased procedure of this Iraqi court."[8]

Because Saddam was executed before the Anfal trial was completed, his culpability in the genocide of the Iraqi Kurds was neither fully explored nor defended. His codefendants continued in the dock to finish the trial, chief among them was General al-Majid, who ultimately drew the death penalty himself.

POSTHUMOUS PROSECUTION

Had Saddam's trial for the Anfal campaigns been continued posthumously, as was strenuously argued by this author and many other international legal scholars and groups, it is likely that Saddam still would have been found guilty of genocide. Following is an overview of how the genocide portion of the trial against Saddam would have unfolded and what the arguments on either side would have entailed.

Formally outlawed in 1948, genocide has existed in practice from time immemorial. Indeed, multiple biblical references discuss its use as a war tactic against ethnically or religiously distinct cultures. It was known in the ancient world as a legitimate practice, used most famously by the Romans against Carthage. Throughout the Middle Ages and into the modern era, genocide was regularly practiced until the slaughter of the Armenians by the Ottoman Turks during World War I. International outrage at the atrocity shifted world opinion toward condemning genocide, culminating in the adoption of the Convention for the Prevention and Punishment of Genocide ("Genocide Convention") in 1948 after World War II and the Holocaust.

The Genocide Convention provides the definition of genocide that exists intact in many subsequent international and domestic statutes, texts, and resolutions, including the statute establishing the IHT:

> [G]enocide means any of the following acts committed with intent to destroy, in whole or in part, a national, ethnical, racial or religious group, as such:
> (a) Killing members of the group;
> (b) Causing serious bodily or mental harm to members of the group;
> (c) Deliberately inflicting on the group conditions of life calculated to bring about its physical destruction in whole or in part;
> (d) Imposing measures intended to prevent births within the group;
> (e) Forcibly transferring children of the group to another group.[9]

The elasticity of the definition is deceptive. While many fact patterns may fit into the two required objective slots, namely, a protected group (e.g., racial) and an act of destruction (e.g., killing), the definition is silent as to just how widespread the acts must be. For example, do the acts have to be pervasive enough to constitute widespread destruction as required for a crime against humanity? Furthermore, most perpetrators go free on the prosecution's inability to prove the subjective element of intent.

Judicial and legal authorities have interpreted the intent required for genocide to be specific rather than general.[10] Varying rationales exist for this conclusion, but the higher threshold means more proof—proof that is almost invariably difficult to come by in the form of intercepted conversations, correspondence, or documents that demonstrate the perpetrator's state of mind at the time the genocide was carried out. Not all *genocidaires*, as genocide perpetrators are known, meticulously catalogue, index, and document their activities in excruciating detail as the Nazis did when carrying out Hitler's Final Solution.

However, the International Criminal Tribunal for Rwanda (ICTR) determined in the 1999 case *Akayesu* that specific intent to commit genocide can be successfully inferred through context, thereby easing the way for this showing somewhat:

> [I]t is possible to deduce the genocidal intent inherent in a particular act charged from the general context of the perpetration of other culpable acts systematically directed against that same group, whether these acts were committed by the same offender or by others. Other factors, such as the scale of atrocities committed, their general nature, in a region or a country, or furthermore, the fact of deliberately and systematically targeting victims on account of their membership of a particular group, while excluding the members of other groups, can enable the Chamber to infer the genocidal intent of a particular act.[11]

Charges of genocide against General Radislav Krstic at the International Criminal Tribunal for the Former Yugoslavia (ICTY) failed precisely because of the specific intent requirement. Krstic was convicted for the 1995 genocide that targeted and killed 8,000 Bosnian Muslims in Srebrenica, on a theory of joint criminal enterprise.[12] However, his conviction was overturned by the Appellate Chamber, which concluded that, although the Srebrenica genocide had occurred and others in the joint criminal enterprise shared a specific intent to carry it through, the evidence did not support the inference that Krstic had the required specific intent to destroy, rather than mere knowledge.[13]

It is because of this very high hurdle that Slobodan Milosevic was likely to have been found guilty of only complicity in genocide as opposed to genocide proper. Complicity only requires a showing of knowledge. Milosevic, however, died before his trial could be completed and sentence passed. With a history of heart troubles, Milosevic's repeated requests to be treated in Russia were denied on the basis that he would likely not return to complete his trial. Thus, Milosevic was secretly withholding his medications to make himself sicker and his case for transfer to Russia stronger. Eventually, he withheld too much and killed himself. As for Saddam Hussein, he probably would have been found guilty of genocide proper, not just complicity in genocide, had he survived to be sentenced in the Anfal case.[14]

Unlike Milosevic who acted as his own attorney at The Hague, Saddam was represented by attorneys who could have deployed multiple strategies in an attempt to slip the genocide noose. Jacques Verges, a seventy-eight-year-old French criminal defense lawyer who famously represented Carlos the Jackal twenty years ago, noted that Saddam could turn the tables on the United States and try to make the American complicity in Saddam's crimes the subject of the trial:

> During the Reagan administration... [Donald] Rumsfeld himself was in charge of some key relations with the Iraqi authorities.... Western countries sold weapons to Saddam. Western countries encouraged the war against Iran. Western countries were present in Iraq through diplomatic delegations. They weren't blind.... Obviously, in the course of a trial, the fundamental element will be: "you treat me like a pariah, but

I was your friend. What we did, we did together. I fired the bullet, but you're the one who gave me the gun—you even pointed out the enemy."[15]

Saddam's version of this defensive tactic may have actually opted to admit that he was a monster and seek to pin accomplice liability on the West. One lawyer from his rather amorphous twenty-member defense team immediately sought to challenge the court's legitimacy by suggesting publicly that Saddam could not receive a fair trial before an Iraqi national tribunal. Instead, the lawyer demanded moving the case to an international tribunal because of the magnitude of the crimes.[16]

Another of Saddam's attorneys argued that the Geneva Conventions prohibited an occupying power from dissolving domestic courts and creating its own, but there is clear provision in the treaty for creation of military commissions that follow the strictures of due process.[17] Moreover, the CPA was careful to clothe creation of the IHT as an extension of the Iraqi Governing Authority. Although that CPA-appointed body was close to the occupying power, it was not close enough to support this aspect of the defense's challenge to the IHT's legitimacy. In any case, the newly elected Iraqi assembly blessed the IHT (indeed renaming it), extending its own representative legitimacy to the tribunal.[18]

It is important to note that Saddam faced genocide charges not only with respect to the Kurds annihilated during the Anfal campaigns, but also with respect to separate trials for the attack on Halabja and for the genocide of the Marsh Arabs in southern Iraq. Indeed, the fact that Saddam brought up the subject of Halabja on his own during the arraignment indicated that the atrocity there was at least on his mind.[19]

For the prosecution, the case for genocide of the Kurds was much easier to make than the case for genocide of the Marsh Arabs would be. The Kurds are an ethnic group distinct from their Sunni Arab persecutors. They suffered from systematic persecution over a long period that included direct group killing, razing of villages, gassing of civilians, and internment in a network of camps and detention centers controlled from a central bureaucracy that orchestrated this destruction at the national, regional, and local levels. The portion of the genocide convention definition implicated here is "destroyed in whole or in part."

The case for genocide of the Marsh Arabs would be more tenuous, however. The Marsh Arabs are a cultural and religious group also distinct from their Sunni Arab persecutors, but their partial destruction was the result of a more indirect method—draining the southern Iraqi marshes on which they relied for subsistence. The portion of the genocide definition implicated here is "deliberately inflicting on the group conditions of life calculated to bring about its physical destruction in whole or in part." Moreover, documentary evidence of coordinated state policy to commit genocide against the Marsh Arabs was not as abundant as the evidence used to support the Kurdish genocide charge.

Typically, proof that genocide occurred is easier to produce than proof of intent to commit the crime. Prosecutors in the Anfal trial show physical acts that characterized genocide with abundant witness testimony, documentary evidence, and grizzly physical evidence as mass graves were unearthed. Indeed, before it was even over, the U.S. Senate recognized the Anfal campaign as genocide as it was unfolding. Foreign Relations Committee Chairman, Claiborne Pell, speaking at a 1992 hearing, recounted the committee's actions:

> It was just 4 years ago that I introduced, and the Senate passed, legislation imposing comprehensive financial and economic sanctions against Iraq.
> Our legislation was entitled "The Prevention of Genocide Act of 1988." In the relevant part, the act said the Iraqi army has undertaken a campaign to depopulate the Kurdish regions of Iraq by destroying Kurdish villages in much of northern Iraq and by killing the civilian population.
> Iraq's campaign against the Kurdish people appeared to constitute an act of genocide. At the time, both the Reagan administration and the House conferees vehemently objected to characterizing Iraqi conduct in Kurdistan as genocide. We now know that that description was very apt.
> In 1987, Iraq initiated a campaign to depopulate Iraqi Kurdistan. The military operation, code named the Al-Anfal campaign, encompassed the systematic destruction of every village in Kurdistan, the massive use of chemical weapons against defenseless villagers, and the deportation and execution of tens of thousands of men, women, and children.
> In all, at least 180,000 people died in the Al-Anfal campaign; about 5 percent of the population of Iraqi Kurdistan. Had the gulf war not intervened, it is likely that Iraq's Kurdish population would have been exterminated.
> There was, in 1987 and 1988, clear evidence of Iraq's conduct. In 1987, the Foreign Relations Committee published a staff report revealing the systematic destruction of Kurdish villages. In 1988, our committee published another staff report documenting the extent of use of chemical weapons against Kurdish civilians.
> That report, which is the only published American Government documentation on the actual use of chemical weapons since World War I, described Iraqi actions as having many of the characteristics of genocide. It also described the machinegun killing of Kurdish civilians and burials in mass graves.[20]

Beyond proving that the acts constituted genocide, the prosecution had to prove the mental element—the specific intent on the part of the perpetrators that destruction of the target population was the goal. As in the Milosevic trial, the toughest hurdle for the prosecution to overcome would have been proving Saddam's specific intent. Saddam's lawyers would not have made this job easy; they would have argued alternative multiple intents. Saddam would have contended that it was never his intent to destroy them. Rather, his primary intent could have been to impose greater central control over the oilfields underlying traditionally populated Kurdish areas in the north, and his secondary intent could have been to combat Kurdish forces assisting Iran during the Iran–Iraq War.

For proof of the primary intent, Saddam would have pointed to national security concerns associated with allowing a restive, potentially breakaway population to remain in control of the country's largest oil reserves. He would have argued that his draconian forced migration policies were geared to this end, and that to the extent that large numbers of Kurds died, it was because they resisted. To break this resistance, harsh methods like use of concentration camps and gas had to be employed—but not to kill them as a group, only to frighten them into compliance.

In fact, the economic security theme would have been a strong one in Saddam's defense. Saddam's attorneys may have used it as an underlying point, not only to escape conviction for the Kurdish genocide, but also to escape conviction for the Marsh Arab genocide and for the war crimes, aggression, and crimes against humanity charges in connection with the occupation of Kuwait. If the defense attorneys could have convinced the judge that Saddam's intent was to secure Iraq's economic wealth by invading Kuwait and depopulating the Kurdish and Marsh Arab areas—thereby securing the oilfields in all three—then the prosecution's showing of intent would have become much harder. Saddam, at the top of the policy food chain in Iraq, would have been the key decision maker with enough panoramic perspective to see and coordinate national-scale economic policy. The prosecutor, then, would not only have had to show the requisite evil intent, but also demonstrate that the alternative intent was not plausible.

For proof of the secondary intent, namely, the intent to combat Kurdish forces assisting Iran in its war against Iraq, Saddam would have produced evidence of collusion between Kurdish and Iranian forces during the Iran–Iraq War. For Saddam's attorneys there was plenty of this evidence to introduce. He would have argued that fighting the Iranians and fighting the Iraqi Kurds were one and the same thing from the Iraqi perspective. That Kurdish forces took Halabja in 1988 with support from Iranian forces as they crossed into northern Iraq legitimized the attack by Iraqi forces on that city as a military necessity. Saddam would have contended that while it was unfortunate that 5,000 Iraqi Kurds died during combat, his intent was not to kill civilians outright but to retake a strategically important area.

The prosecution would have been required to blunt these alternative intent theories. Geography helps them to undermine the secondary alternative intent theory for the Anfal campaign—that Saddam was combating Kurds colluding with Iranian forces during wartime. The majority of Kurdish villages gassed or destroyed during the Anfals were either on the border with Turkey, not Iran, or some distance inland from the Iranian border where most of the military incursions were taking place.[21] Moreover, those targeted by the Anfals were civilians, not military forces or armed Kurds.

The prosecution could have chosen to admit the logic of counterinsurgency as the underlying idea for creation of the Anfal and to argue that the counterinsurgency nonetheless evolved into genocide. As one genocide researcher for Human Rights Watch noted, "The fact that Anfal was, by the narrowest definition, a counterinsurgency, does nothing to diminish the fact that it was also an act of genocide. There is nothing mutually exclusive about counterinsurgency and genocide. Indeed, one may be the instrument used to consummate the other."[22]

The economic rationale of the primary alternative intent theory would have been harder to attack, but with some reverse engineering the prosecution would likely have been able to undermine it as well. For example, in a damning quote drawn from one of many audio tapes captured by the United States and translated by the Canadian Broadcasting Corporation, al-Majid discusses the Anfals: "Tell him I will strike. I will strike with chemicals and kill them all. What is the international community going to say? The hell with them and the hell with any other country in the world that objects."[23] If that evident genocidal intent could have been imputed back up the chain of command to Saddam, then Saddam's alternative explanations would have likely collapsed.

The prosecution would have been helped considerably by the fact that so many survivors of Saddam's genocidal policies volunteered to present evidence against him and, indeed, did testify in droves against General al-Majid. In relation to the attack on Halabja, a female student at that time was rounded up with other students and paraded before Saddam at military headquarters in Suleimaniyeh. She saw him on a green telephone and heard him distinctly give the order to bombard the city. "I would like to testify that I saw him make that phone call that day. I think the matter has come alive again, and now we will see justice." An Arab Iraqi from Baghdad who witnessed planes loaded with "unusual" weapons at the Arbil airfield that morning also wanted to tell his story in court.[24]

Lack of knowledge would have been another defense for Saddam to raise—which also would go to the establishment of specific intent. As Milosevic had done before at his trial in The Hague, and as Hermann Goering had done at Nuremberg, Saddam would claim that he was unaware of the activities of his subordinates. This defense would fail, however, as it had in prior trials, if the prosecution properly asserted the command responsibility doctrine that imputes knowledge up the chain of command to leaders who reasonably should have known what was happening.

Moreover, the *tu quoque* ("you too") defense would likely have failed. To the extent that this defense was raised to a genocide charge, it would involve the United States and the West's supplying Saddam the means and assistance to carry out his actions (helicopters and chemical weapons). It could also have been raised in the later trial against Saddam for aggression against Kuwait, arguing that the American-led invasion of Iraq was a clear-cut case of aggression. *Tu quoque* would lose its force in a domestic tribunal, however, and an argument that Iran used chemical weapons first—which is itself disputed—would similarly be lost on an Iraqi court. *Tu quoque* was dismissed altogether by the ICTY in the Milosevic case.[25]

The sovereign immunity defense was one that was raised in the Dujail trial to little effect. To have succeeded Saddam would have had to show that the American-led invasion of Iraq was illegal under international law, and therefore, by extension, Saddam was still legally the head of state. The flurry of activity surrounding the mounting of this particular defense after Saddam's capture was indicative of its very weakness:

> Arab lawyers representing deposed Iraqi dictator Saddam Hussein plan to appeal to UN Secretary-General Kofi Annan to take action to end their client's "illegal detention" and bring him back to power.

Annan's recent declaration that the liberation of Iraq by the US-led coalition was "illegal" has been welcomed by Saddam's lawyers, who believe the secretary-general should make "the necessary moves" to restore their client as president of Iraq.

"It is now clear that the occupation . . . lacks any legal, ethical, or religious authority," says Hussein Megalli, president of the Jordanian Bar Association and one of Saddam's lawyers. "Saddam is still the legitimate president of Iraq and cannot be tried by an illegal body."

. . . .

Saddam's lawyers say that since Annan implicitly recognizes Saddam as head of the Iraqi state, the logical next step for the UN is to seek measures to "efface the traces of American aggression."

The lawyers are not clear as to what form Annan's intervention to secure Saddam's release should take. But they point to the precedents of Haiti and Sierra Leone when the UN intervened to restore "illegally deposed presidents" to power.[26]

Putting the American-led invasion on trial would have been a clever, if ultimately doomed, approach in that it could have shored up the ancillary illegitimacy argument against the IHT. Such a politically charged position has been raised before in other tribunals. In response to the charge of illegitimate "victor's justice" leveled against the International Military Tribunal (IMT) at Nuremberg by the Nazi defendants, the tribunal reiterated the sources of its own legitimacy:

The jurisdiction of the Tribunal is defined in the Agreement and Charter, and the crimes coming within the jurisdiction of the Tribunal, for which there shall be individual responsibility, are set out in Article 6. The law of the Charter is decisive, and binding upon the Tribunal.

The making of the Charter was the exercise of the sovereign legislative power by the countries to which the German Reich unconditionally surrendered; and the undoubted right of these countries to legislate for the occupied territories has been recognised by the civilised world. The Charter is not an arbitrary exercise of power on the part of the victorious nations, but in the view of the Tribunal, as will be shown, it is the expression of international law existing at the time of its creation; and to that extent is itself a contribution to international law.

The Signatory Powers created this Tribunal, defined the law it was to administer, and made regulations for the proper conduct of the Trial. In doing so, they have done together what any one of them might have done singly; for it is not to be doubted that any nation has the right thus to set up special courts to administer law. With regard to the constitution of the court, all that the defendants are entitled to ask is to receive a fair trial on the facts and law. . . .

But it is argued that the [Kellogg-Briand] Pact does not expressly enact that such [aggressive] wars are crimes, or set up courts to try those who make such wars. To that extent the same is true with regard to the laws of war contained in the Hague Convention. The Hague Convention of 1907 prohibited resort to certain methods of waging war. These included the inhumane treatment of prisoners, the employment of poisoned weapons, the improper use of flags of truce, and similar matters. Many of these prohibitions had been enforced long before the date of the Convention; but since 1907 they have certainly been crimes, punishable as offences against the laws of war; yet the Hague Convention nowhere designates such practices as criminal, nor is any sentence prescribed, nor any mention made of a court to try and punish offenders. For many years past, however, military tribunals have tried and punished individuals guilty of violating the rules of land warfare laid down by this Convention. In the opinion of the Tribunal, those who wage aggressive war are doing that which is equally illegal, and of much greater moment than a breach of one of the rules of the Hague Convention. In interpreting the words of the Pact, it must be remembered that international law is not the product of an international legislature, and that such international agreements as the Pact have to deal with general principles of law, and not with administrative matters of procedure. The law of war is to be found not only in treaties, but in the customs and practices of states which gradually obtained universal recognition, and from the general principles of justice applied by jurists and practiced by military courts. This law is not static, but by continual adaptation follows the needs of a changing world. Indeed, in many cases treaties do no more than express and define for more accurate reference the principles of law already existing.[27]

Milosevic likewise challenged the legitimacy of the ICTY. On the opening day of his trial, Milosevic declared, "I consider this tribunal false [a] tribunal and [the] indictments false indictments. It is illegal, being not appointed by UN General Assembly, so I have no need to appoint counsel to illegal organ.... This trial's aim is to produce false justification for the war crimes of NATO committed in Yugoslavia."[28]

The ICTY, in fact, had already addressed this issue in the *Tadic* case six years prior to Milosevic's challenge. There, the tribunal similarly relied on, among other bases of legitimacy, the authority of the U.N. Security Council acting under U.N. Charter provisions:

The attack on the competence of the International Tribunal in this case is based on a number of grounds, some of which may be subsumed under one general heading: that the action of the Security Council in establishing the International Tribunal and in adopting the Statute under which it functions is beyond power; hence the International Tribunal is not duly established by law and cannot try the accused.

It is said that, to be duly established by law, the International Tribunal should have been created either by treaty, the consensual act of nations, or by amendment of the Charter of the United Nations, not by resolution of the Security Council. Called in aid of this general proposition are a number of considerations: that before the creation of the International Tribunal in 1993 it was never envisaged that such an ad hoc criminal tribunal might be set up; that the General Assembly, whose participation would at least have guaranteed full representation of the international community, was not involved in its creation; that it was never intended by the Charter that the Security Council should, under Chapter VII, establish a judicial body, let alone a criminal tribunal; that the Security Council had been inconsistent in creating this tribunal while not taking a similar step in the case of other areas of conflict in which violations of international humanitarian law may have occurred; that the establishment of the International Tribunal had neither promoted, nor was capable of promoting, international peace, as the current situation in the former Yugoslavia demonstrates;

that the Security Council could not, in any event, create criminal liability on the part of individuals and that this is what the creation of the International Tribunal did; that there existed and exists now no such international emergency as would justify the action of the Security Council; that no political organ such as the Security Council is capable of establishing an independent and impartial tribunal; that there is an inherent defect in the creation, after the event, of ad hoc tribunals to try particular types of offences and, finally, that to give the International Tribunal primacy over national courts is, in any event and in itself, inherently wrong. . . .

The force of criminal law draws its efficacy, in part, from the fact that it reflects a consensus on what is demanded of human behaviour. But it is of equal importance that a body that judges the criminality of this behaviour should be viewed as legitimate. This is the first time that the international community has created a court with criminal jurisdiction. The establishment of the International Tribunal has now spawned the creation of an ad hoc Tribunal for Rwanda. Each of these ad hoc Tribunals represents an important step towards the establishment of a permanent international criminal tribunal. In this context, the Trial Chamber considers that it would be inappropriate to dismiss without comment the accused's contentions that the establishment of the International Tribunal by the Security Council was beyond power and an ill-founded political action, not reasonably aimed at restoring and maintaining peace, and that the International Tribunal is not duly established by law.

Any discussion of this matter must begin with the Charter of the United Nations. Article 24 (1) provides that the Members of the United Nations:

confer on the Security Council primary responsibility for the maintenance of international peace and security, and agree that in carrying out its duties under this responsibility the Security Council acts on their behalf.

The powers of the Security Council to discharge its primary responsibility for the maintenance of international peace and security are set out in Chapters VI, VII, VIII and XII of the Charter. The International Tribunal was established under Chapter VII. The Security Council has broad discretion in exercising its authority under Chapter VII and there are few limits on the exercise of that power. As indicated by the *travaux préparatoires*:

Wide freedom of judgment is left as regards the moment [the Security Council] may choose to intervene and the means to be applied, with sole reserve that it should act 'in accordance with the purposes and principles of the [United Nations].'

The broad discretion given to the Security Council in the exercise of its Chapter VII authority itself suggests that decisions taken under this head are not reviewable. . . .

Although it is not for this Trial Chamber to judge the reasonableness of the acts of the Security Council, it is without doubt that, with respect to the former Yugoslavia, the Security Council did not act arbitrarily. To the contrary, the Security Council's establishment of the International Tribunal represents its informed judgment, after great deliberation, that violations of international humanitarian law were occurring in the former Yugoslavia and that such violations created a threat to the peace. . . .

The Security Council established the International Tribunal as an enforcement measure under Chapter VII of the United Nations Charter after finding that the violations of international humanitarian law in the former Yugoslavia constituted a threat to the peace. In making this finding, the Security Council acted under Article 39 of the Charter, which provides:

> The Security Council shall determine the existence of any threat to peace, breach of peace, or act of aggression and shall make recommendations, or decide what measures shall be taken in accordance with Articles 41 and 42, to maintain or restore international peace and security.

When, in resolution 827, the Security Council stated that it was "convinced" that, in the "particular circumstances of the former Yugoslavia," the establishment of the International Tribunal would contribute to the restoration and maintenance of peace, the course it took was novel only in the means adopted but not in the object sought to be attained.[29]

The IHT in Saddam's Dujail case responded to the assertion of the tribunal's illegitimacy (arguing that the IHT was merely an extension of U.S. military power) by tracing the IHT's legal evolution from its formation under the Coalition Provisional Authority through the Transitional Government to the fully elected Iraqi government and under the auspices of the U.N. Security Council throughout:

> The court noted that it received four preliminary petitions from the defense team during the course of trials.... The second petition was submitted on December 21, 2005 relating to the legality of the High Iraqi Tribunal 'a plea to the legality of the court....' And in light of the two resolutions of the security council concerning re-establishing the country's establishments and the entity of rule in Iraq after the complete collapse of the authority's establishments....
>
> The Interim Coalition Authority exercises the powers of the government temporarily for effectively managing the affairs of Iraq during the transitional period for the purpose of regaining stability and security and forming the conditions that may enable the Iraqi people to determine its political future freely, also to assume the development and enhancement of the exerted efforts to rebuild and re-establish the national establishments to represent the denominations of the people and facilitating the exerted efforts to revive the economy, rebuild and secure continual development.
>
> It is also stated in paragraph (9) of the decision: "It is favored for the Iraqi people to help the authority by cooperating with the special representative in establishing a temporary Iraqi administration described as a transitional administration, and where the Interim Coalition Authority was a transitional authority for the purpose of having complete sovereignty and in light of the relevant decisions of the security council and the formation of an authority in coordination with Iraqi personalities dated December 10, 2003, it announced the establishing of a government council in Iraq comprising national Iraqi personalities and the acknowledgment of the security council for the government council according to decision n° 2031511 dated October 16, 2003."
>
> And in light of the U.N. resolution referred to, the government council published on March 8, 2004 a temporary constitution and by virtue of this constitution to "establish a road plan for the establishment or formation of a permanent Iraqi government."
>
> The terms confirmed the establishment of an Iraqi criminal court specialized in crimes against humanity committed during the former government according to

the several complaints submitted to the governing council in this respect and upon the issuance of the law for establishing the Iraqi criminal court specialized in crimes against humanity n° 1 of 2003 and the rules of the procedures issued in accordance with the provisions of article 16 thereof. In light of this law, the judicial and administrative personnel of this court were formed. And on June 28 the occupation of Iraq ended and a "sovereign Iraqi government" undertook the ruling of Iraq pursuant to the powers it was granted by virtue of the temporary constitution.

And on May 3, 2005 a new elected government replaced the temporary government in light of the Security Council relevant decisions referred to in the preamble of this decision. And on October 18, 2005 the law n° 10 of 2005 published the law of the High Iraqi criminal court where it is stated that the obligatory reasons of the law "for the demonstrating the crimes committed in Iraq since July 7, 1968 until May 1, 2003 for the purpose of establishing the rules and penalties that condemn the perpetrators of these crimes in a fair court and for the purpose of forming a High National Criminal Iraqi tribunal consisting of competent Iraqi judges for the legislation of this law."

In light of the aforementioned, and disregarding any suspicions or further claims in this respect, the court wishes to clarify that on December 10, 2003, the government council acknowledged by the international security council decision n° 1511 that it "embodies the sovereignty of Iraq during the transitional period until a representative government is formed adopted internationally, to undertake the responsibilities of the authority" to publish the Special Iraqi court of law that preceded the High Iraqi Tribunal which owns the judicial power to judge any citizen whether Iraqi or residing in Iraq accused by committing extermination or war crimes or crimes against humanity or other crimes committed between June 17, 1968 till the first of May 2003, which was independent from the remaining courts in Iraq and any other governmental authority. And pursuant to the provisions of article 16 of the law, the rules and procedures were issued and the evidences pertaining to the High Criminal Iraqi tribunal. . . .

The Interim Government continued financing and supporting the special criminal court until a permanent Iraqi government elected on May 20, 2006 assumed power. And on October 18, 2005, it cancelled the special Iraqi court of law and law n° 10 of 2005 was published "High Iraqi criminal court" keeping all the personnel of the court including the judges and public prosecutors, and it was confirmed that every decision or order issued by the "Special Iraqi Court" pursuant to its aw is a legal order of obligatory compliance and the High Iraqi Tribunal will put it into effect.

Therefore, in pleading the petition of the attorney of the accused (Awad Hamad Al Bandar) concerning the legality of this court and the law issued by its virtue, the court refuses the pleading legally and definitely for the law n° 10 of 2005 was issued by a legal government elected by 78% of the Iraqis and it ratified the Iraqi law by a national questionnaire three days before issuing this law n° 10 of 2005 by virtue of article 131 of this constitution:

The court "continues its activities as an independent judicial body and considers the crimes of the former regime and its main personalities." Accordingly, and in light of the apparent constitutional and legal facts, the plea of the attorney Badr Awad al-Bandar concerning the legality of the court is a false and refused pleading and is not conforming to the law.[30]

Thus, while many procedural, jurisdictional, and substantive defenses would have been thrown in the court's direction, Saddam would still likely have been found guilty of genocide in the Anfal case had his trial been allowed to continue. The witness testimony and documentary evidence against his codefendants was more than enough to convict them, and their close association with Saddam would have provided critical linkage for the prosecution.

International Law—The Road Not Taken

Just as international law was cast aside with respect to the U.S.-led invasion of Iraq in 2003, so too were arguments for an international criminal tribunal to try Saddam and his henchmen ignored. The Coalition Provisional Authority, under the direction of American ambassador L. Paul Bremmer, created a domestic tribunal within Iraq designed to try Iraqis under Iraqi law. The perils of this path were equally obvious, but also stubbornly ignored. However, none of the justice choices available to the occupying force were easy.

On the heels of de-Ba'athification, the Iraqi judiciary had been largely stripped of its capacity to deliver justice. Military courts were not allowed under the terms of the Geneva Conventions. There was no existing international tribunal that could take Saddam's case: the International Court of Justice only heard cases between states, the new International Criminal Court only had prospective jurisdiction over crimes occuring after July 2002—not retroactive jurisdiction over the crimes Saddam had committed, and the existing U.N.-backed tribunals for the former Yugoslavia, Rwanda, and Sierra Leone were geographically and temporally limited to crimes in those countries respectively. Thus, to try Saddam internationally, a new international tribunal would had to have been created by the U.N. Security Council along the lines of the tribunal created in 2007 to handle the case of the assassinated Lebanese prime minister, Hariri.

Not wanting to involve the United Nations, and unsure of what level of support there would be for international justice from the vast majority of members that had opposed the invasion in the first place, the domestic tribunal option was selected even though the war was continuing. The precarious security situation worked quickly to undermine the proceedings, leading to the assassination of three defense counsel in the Dujail trial. Politics also intervened, leading to the resignation of the presiding judge after government interference in the Dujail case. The trials that followed alternated wildly between the chaotic and the mundane— depending on the day. Ultimately, Saddam swung from the gallows in a rushed and amateurish execution carried out in vengeful hatred—an unsurprising end to a marred effort at justice.

Could justice have been better served? Probably. But one key component mitigating against international justice for Islamic states is the disconnect between international criminal law and criminal law guided by Islam. The crimes for which Saddam was tried (war crimes, crimes against humanity, and genocide) are all international crimes that were transposed into the jurisdiction of the Iraqi High Tribunal (IHT). These crimes are the bedrock jurisdictional ground of most international criminal tribunals.

It is a truism that there are multiple levels of incongruency between Islamic societies and Western societies. Some of these differences are obvious, like those concerning the treatment of women, recognition of civil liberties, degree of so- cietal religious adherence/tolerance, and the seriousness with which pluralistic liberal representative democratic institutions are supported. Others less so. Many differences are based on values, tradition, and the continued existence of a vi- brant tribal life, especially in Arab and African societies that predate Islam but today exist under the veil of Islam. Do these incongruencies rise to the level of incompatibility?

Women's rights advocate, Ayaan Hirsi Ali, a Somali woman and Dutch par- liamentarian who is a former Muslim, reinforces this message of incompatibility everywhere she goes: "The 21st century began with a battle of ideas, and this battle is about the values of the West versus those of Islam . . . Islam and liberal democracy are incompatible . . . Islam unreformed, as a set of beliefs, is hostile to everything Western."[1]

In the wake of 9/11, many were moved to give renewed credence to Harvard political scientist Samuel Huntington's dire prediction of civilizational warfare[2] in the context of pitting Islamic society against Western society. Figure 10.1 graphically depicts this diametric opposition of Islam to the West.

Huntington first floated his thesis to the general public in a 1993 *Foreign Affairs* article, in which he asserted:

> The great divisions among humankind and the dominating source of conflict will be cultural. Nation states will remain the most powerful actors in world affairs, but the principal conflicts of global politics will occur between nations and groups of different civilizations. The clash of civilizations will dominate global politics. The fault lines between civilizations will be the battle lines of the future.[3]

While Huntington demurred on the question of whether a clash of civilizations was actually occurring after 9/11, he left that possibility open, noting: "Clearly, Osama bin Laden wants [9/11] to be a clash of civilisations (sic) between Islam and the West. The first priority for our government is to try to prevent it from becoming

"Emerging alignments" of civilizations, per Samuel Huntinton's theory in *The Clash of Civilizations* (1996).

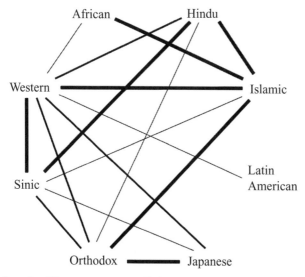

Greater line thickness represents more conflict in the civilizational relationship.

Figure 10.1. Illustration derived from Samuel Huntington, *The Clash of Civilizations* (1996), Christopher Parham.

one. But there is a danger it could move in that direction. The administration has acted exactly the right way in attempting to rally support among Muslim governments. But there are pressures here in the US to attack other terrorist groups and states that support terrorist groups. And that, it seems to me, could broaden it into a clash of civilizations."[4]

Corollary to this supposition of societal incompatibility, which is no doubt true in some degree, is the general observation that most international criminal law structures are based upon Western models. Thus, the argument that such legal norms and institutions are also largely incongruent with Islamic societies should come as no surprise. The trial of Saddam Hussein by Muslim judges attempting to use a Western-style judicial institution is a case in point.

The IHT was conceived and constructed by Western attorneys working for the Coalition Provisional Authority. The statute of the IHT grafted important Western concepts like due process, defense protections, and evidentiary standards—which would be found in most international criminal tribunals   onto a domestic criminal court within the postwar Iraqi legal system. That Saddam's trial was a chaotic affair, beset by difficulties from the beginning, evinces the failure of this graft to take. Muslim Iraqi judges, operating within an Islamic society, attempted valiantly to operate the Western machinery, but to little avail. The Saddam trial and its aftermath have been roundly condemned in the international community as such a failure that the case would not be cited as authority by any subsequent international judicial body.[5]

What is it about Islamic states that creates such a fundamental disconnect? First of all, no single Islamic state is identical to another. Key diversity factors revolve around geography, ethnicity, and cultural differentiation. Degree and type of tribalism in each state also come into play. Yet one might generalize that all Islamic societies tend to be more socially conservative than non-Islamic societies. However, it remains axiomatic that conservative Islamic African values ≠ conservative Islamic Arab values ≠ conservative Islamic Persian values ≠ conservative Islamic South Asian values.

The societies in which Islam thrives today color the type of Islam practiced within those states as assuredly as North American, Latin American, European, or African value systems color the type of Catholicism practiced—which is not exactly as Rome proscribes, much to the consternation of the Pope. Nevertheless, Islamic tradition can sometimes be similar worldwide—as in the case of the relatively poor treatment of women. Whether this is a function of the pre-Islamic tribal society or of Islam itself is a better question, and one that is better answered by a sociologist, not by an international law specialist.

Diversity within the Muslim world also comes by way of political organization. Not all Islamic states are Islamic republics, monarchies, theocracies, or secular states. For instance, Libya is a secular dictatorship, Morocco a constitutional monarchy, Brunei a religious sultanate, Turkey a secular republic, and Saudi Arabia a religious monarchy. The political systems adopted vary widely in the Muslim world, which directly impact the character of criminal law in those states and therefore can affect the acceptance and use of international criminal law.

Examples of Islamic Republics include Pakistan, Afghanistan, Mauritania, and Iran—which has a very high degree of religiosity mixed with state apparatus. This is emphasized in key provisions of Iran's constitution, which glosses the law with heavy religious overtones—including identifying God as the supreme source of legislation:

> Article 2—The Islamic Republic is a system based on belief in:
> 1. The One God, His exclusive sovereignty and the right to legislate, and the necessity of submission to His commands;
> 2. Divine revelation and its fundamental role in setting forth the laws;
> 3. The return to God in the Hereafter, and the constructive role of this belief in the course of man's ascent towards God;
> 4. The justice of God in creation and legislation; . . . .
>
> Article 4—All civil, penal, financial, economic, administrative, cultural, military, political, and other laws and regulations must be based on Islamic criteria. This principle applies absolutely and generally to all articles of the Constitution as well as to all other laws and regulations, and the fuqaha' of the Guardian Council are judges in this matter.

By comparison, the tone of similar provisions in Turkey's secular constitution, reveals the degree of political diversity within the Muslim state—especially as that relates to the underlying character of the laws in those countries:

> Article 2—The Republic of Turkey is a democratic, secular and social state governed by the rule of law; bearing in mind the concepts of public peace, national solidarity and justice; respecting human rights; loyal to the nationalism of Atatürk, and based on the fundamental tenets set forth in the Preamble. Article 12—Everyone possesses inherent fundamental rights and freedoms which are inviolable and inalienable.…
>
> Article 13—Fundamental rights and freedoms may be restricted only by law and in conformity with the reasons mentioned in the relevant articles of the Constitution without infringing upon their essence. These restrictions shall not be in conflict with the letter and spirit of the Constitution and the requirements of the democratic order of the society and the secular Republic and the principle of proportionality.

Religious overtones in the law have significant consequences for how populations connect the law with the state. Iran, unlike Turkey, operates on the basis of Islamic law reigning supreme and the clerics controlling the laws that are promulgated and enforced.[6]

This raises the question, what is Islamic law? The origins of Islamic law date to the seventh-century founding of the religion. Shari'a (root: shara'a شرع) is a term used to denote divinely inspired Islamic law, which means "the way" as used in the Qur'an 45:18—"Then We put thee on the (right) Way of Religion: so follow thou that (Way), and follow not the desires of those who know not."[7] The sources of Shari'a are:

- *The Qur'an*, which is infallible;
- *The Sunnah*: ancient traditional interpretive guides to the Qur'an functioning as a living example of Muhammad;
- *The Fiqh*: the body of Islamic jurisprudence including the rulings of judges and Islamic scholars that direct and apply Shari'a to individual Muslims in their daily lives— inclusive of:
- *The Qiyas*: analogical reasoning of jurists;
- *The Ijma*: consensus[8]

As with any legal system, there is a divergence of Shari'a interpretation even within the predominantly Muslim states that utilize it. Every Muslim agrees on the authority of the Qur'an as the word of God. Sunni and Shi'a Muslims disagree about which aspects of the Sunnah to follow depending upon which ancient scholar authored portions of the Sunnah: Sunni Muslims tend to follow all of it while Shi'a Muslims typically do not follow that written by Umar, the second Sunni Caliph.[9]

Some Muslim scholars challenge the inclusion of the Fiqh as it inappropriately blends revealed and unrevealed truth. They argue that the Qur'an and Sunnah should be kept separate as a Basic Law from the Fiqh, which is a constantly evolving body of law.[10]

The Fiqh is not subject to codification; it is an evolving body of jurisprudence as determined by Islamic scholars. But it is much less ascertainable than the evolving law in common law Western jurisdictions. The Fiqh is subdivided into schools of thought (four Sunni schools and one Shi'ite), which further fracture it:

- Malikites (most conservative): Northern African states
- Hanafites (more emphasis on custom): Afghanistan, Turkey, Pakistan, Egypt
- Shafi'ites (rationalists): Indonesia, Eastern African states
- Hanbalites (Wahhabi traditionalists): Saudi Arabia
- Shi'ites (subdivides into three branches): Imamiya is followed in Iran[11]

Despite diverging opinions on Shari'a, the religious intonations persist no matter the school of interpretation. Such intonations are therefore included in the criminal aspects of Islamic law. Western criminal law also originally shared religious intonations, but long ago abandoned these for the secularized bearing of today.

The divergence of Shari'a from Western law varies with which aspects of Islamic law are at issue. The civil, especially commercial (financial and contractual) aspects of Shari'a, largely comport with generalized Western law. The personal (family law) and criminal aspects of Shari'a however diverge significantly from generalized Western law.

Western law, especially the civil code iteration, has formed the basis for international criminal law and the foundation for international criminal tribunals, infusing international criminal process with Western predilections.

Thus, the more a predominantly Islamic state has incorporated the criminal aspects of Shari'a, the less likely that state is to participate in international criminal law processes. Criminal Islamic law (Shari'a) divides itself into two categories: Crimes against Men (homicide and wounding) and Crimes against God, which include theft, banditry, unlawful sexual intercourse, unfounded accusation of unlawful sexual intercourse (slander), drinking alcohol, and apostasy. Crimes against God are those mentioned in the Qur'an and have fixed punishments that may not be altered. These are known as *hadd* crimes, and examples of the punishments mandated for such crimes include:

- Theft: Amputation of one or both hands
- Banditry: Crucifixion
- Adultery: Death by stoning
- Fornication: Flogging
- Slander: Flogging
- Public Intoxication: Flogging[12]

Deterrence is the key goal for these infractions, thus the harshness of the punishment. The Saudis have long claimed that the low crime rate within the Kingdom compared to that in other predominantly Muslim states that do not wholly incorporate Shari'a is irrefutable proof that deterrence works in their society—a claim that has gained some salience with even Western social scientists.

Moreover, *hadd* punishments must be administered sequentially, so if a person is convicted of theft, slander, and drinking alcohol, the punishments follow in sequence: amputation, flogging, and additional flogging. Because *hadd* punishments are harsh, the evidentiary standard is high. Only confessions made in court are valid, witness testimony must come from a minimum of two Muslim men of good standing (or one Muslim man and two Muslim women), and circumstantial evidence is not admitted if retaliation is demanded. Since these are crimes against God, repentance, if proved, can exculpate one being tried for a *hadd* crime. "By showing his repentance, the offender actually proves that he has already been reformed and does not need to be punished anymore."[13]

That said, there remains interpretive flexibility, so judges rarely inflict these punishments. If a person cannot be sentenced to a fixed punishment for a *hadd* offense because of lack of evidence, although it is otherwise plausible that he is guilty, he may be sentenced to discretionary punishment. For such sentences, the strict rules of evidence do not apply. Circumstantial evidence is allowed, especially assumptions based on a person's reputation. Yet, while crimes are circumscribed under Islamic law, elements of crimes are often not codified. Consequently, the criminal justice system is ripe for abuse due to the prosecutor's inherently lower threshold of proof.

How homicide is treated under classic Shari'a provides one with a glimpse into this system. The objectives for homicide prosecution include a combination of retribution and retaliation. Retaliation is only allowed "if the victim's bloodprice is the same as or higher than the offender's."[14] In comparison, in the United States, financial compensation for murder is handled on the civil side of the ledger, not the criminal side, as was famously demonstrated in the California state trials of the American football star O.J. Simpson in the 1990s.

Prosecution is a decidedly victim-driven endeavor, as opposed to criminal prosecution in Western societies where victims play no role other than possibly as witnesses to the crime. In Shari'a societies, the victim's surviving family serves as the prosecution in an adversarial process. Continuance of the prosecution is dependent upon the will of the victim's family—they can withdraw at any time. The killer may be pardoned by the victim's family.

If a defendant's guilt is proven, the victim's family may demand retaliation or blood money. Financial compensation varies with the victim's sex, religion, and legal status (for example, the blood price of a woman is half that of a man). Retaliation is allowed if killing was intentional, otherwise the victim's family is entitled to financial compensation. Retaliation involves inflicting the same wounds on the perpetrator as the victim endured (eye for an eye; life for a life logic prevails here). The victim's family also may carry out the execution of a death sentence under the supervision of a state agent, but the potential executioner must demonstrate sufficient skill with a sword. If the victim has no next of kin, the state undertakes prosecution and punishment.

Only confessions and eyewitness testimony are admissible for homicide under classic Shariʿa; no circumstantial evidence is admitted. *Mens rea* concepts are also in play: "[An] offender must have had the power to commit or not to commit the act (*qudra*); must have known (*ʿilm*) that the act was an offence; and must have acted with intent (*qasd*)."[15] Generally, minors and the insane do not qualify as prosecutable perpetrators. Moreover, killing an attacker in defense of life, honor, or property of oneself or one's relatives is lawful if the act is proportional to the acts of the attacker.

The level of criminal Shariʿa utilized within a predominantly Islamic state varies. For example, Pakistan employs it very selectively and under a westernized respect for the rule of law, while Saudi Arabia uses it exclusively, enforcing Islamic law through a 5,000-member religious police force.

Many states with predominantly Muslim populations incorporate some degree of Shariʿa in commercial or family matters. Fewer use it for criminal law. Since 1972, seven states have readopted precolonial criminal aspects of Islamic law: Libya, Pakistan, Iran, Sudan, the Northern States of Nigeria, Egypt, and Saudi Arabia, where Shariʿa was never extinguished. The Egyptian Supreme Court endeavors to balance the mandate of Article 2 of the Egyptian constitution, requiring all legislation to conform to Shariʿa, with life in the modern world through creative judicial interpretation against the backdrop of an overall reconstruction of Islamic law.

On the other end of the spectrum, the strictest aspects of Shariʿa were in play under the Taliban government in Afghanistan, which was overthrown in 2001. Parts of Malaysia and the UAE are moving toward incorporating Shariʿa, with varying prospects for success. What is the attraction to reintroducing the criminal aspects of Shariʿa within a predominantly Muslim state? As Professor Rudolph Peters of Amsterdam University notes, it has multiple attractions for multiple constituencies:

> Muslims, in order to be good Muslims, must live in an Islamic state, a state which implements Shariʿa. It is not sufficient that that such a state gives Muslims the choice to follow or not to follow the Shariʿa, it must actually impose the Shariʿa on them, but implementing Islamic criminal law. . . . The establishment of an Islamic state is presented as a religious duty for all Muslims and as an endeavor that may bring Paradise within their reach. And there is another felicitous prospect connected with it: that of a pious and virtuous community on earth that enjoys God's favour and is actively aided by Him to overcome poverty and humiliation. . . . The reintroduction of Islamic criminal law is, from this perspective, a step towards salvation in the Hereafter as well as in this life. It is, therefore, much more than a merely technical reform of penal law. The notions connected with it make the project of enforcing Islamic criminal law attractive to both the ruling elite and large parts of the Muslim population.[16]

Although some reintroduction of Shari'a may be in play, that is not to say that the population or government would support a complete imposition of Islamic law for all aspects of the law. For example, the recent Red Mosque uprising in Islamabad centered on the Pakistani government's resistance to the imposition of the restrictive Taliban version of Shari'a concerning family law advocated by Islamists in Pakistan.

Furthermore, the level of Shari'a implementation may not be uniform even within a state. The Islamic regions of a large state that is not overwhelmingly Muslim may develop Islamic criminal law systems within the framework of the larger state. Nigeria is a recent example. States within Nigeria, like those within the United States, have the power to enact their own criminal law. Between January 2000 and April 2002, twelve northern Nigerian states had introduced the criminal aspects of Shari'a, set up Shari'a courts, and adopted Shari'a penal codes conforming to the Malikite school. As a result, Nigeria now has dual criminal justice systems that nevertheless feed ultimately into a single Supreme Court, albeit after passing through dual appellate processes en route.

The question then arises, if secular and Shari'a criminal justice systems can coexist within a federal polity, can Islamic criminal law coexist with international criminal law in a similar fashion? Such a duality is already arguably being achieved with respect to human rights, as discussed later in this chapter. Whether this offers a viable model is problematic.

The temporal nature of justice is another element of incongruity. Justice is swift in Muslim societies—especially in those that practice Shari'a. Criminal justice systems in the Muslim world tend to operate on shorter time horizons than they do in the West. This is especially true in Arab societies, where the cultural paradigm reflects a preference for quick rewards and punishments. This tension played out dramatically during the trial of Saddam Hussein in Baghdad, culminating in his hastily organized execution on December 30, 2006.

A case in point is Saudi Arabia. Criminal trials in Saudi Arabia are conducted rapidly, many turning on coerced confessions resulting from beatings and torture while in confinement. Punishment ensues shortly thereafter. Article 47 of the Saudi Rules of Procedure prohibits sitting on a case for more than a month. Article 27 of the Saudi Directives Concerning Review of Legal Judgments similarly prohibits consideration of appeals beyond a month: "No judgment should remain under consideration for purposes of review, ratification or comment for more than one month." Needless to say, these procedural rules keep the dockets manageable and the justice swift.

Criminal trials in Western states are more protracted in both common law and civil law societies. Such trials are often followed by extensive appeal opportunities, especially when the sentence is death. Modern international criminal tribunals follow the Western model in this regard, and trials can stretch into years, as evidenced by the five-year-long trial of Slobodan Milosevic in The Hague. Consequently, there is a wide divergence in time horizons for criminal process in

Islamic societies versus those in international criminal tribunals and other Western domestic bodies.

Many Islamic states that incorporate Shariʿa belong to treaties outlawing international crimes as well as human rights conventions. For instance, Saudi Arabia is a member of the Convention Against Torture, the Convention on the Rights of the Child, and the Convention on the Elimination of all forms of Discrimination Against Women, the Genocide Convention, and the Geneva Conventions. However, Saudi *interpretation* of rights contained therein is rather restrictive. No one would reasonably argue that the rights guaranteed to women are observed in Riyadh on the same basis as they are in Oslo, yet both Saudi Arabia and Norway are parties to the same convention. The same is true of torture.

Beyond interpretation, there is also a fundamental disagreement concerning the very package of human rights guaranteed Shariʿa. From the Islamic perspective, Islamic human rights are actually more universal than those prescribed by U.N. conventions because it extends to all individual's belief in God. The fallacy of such an argument is revealed in the collision of "individual liberty" with God's will which, in Islam, is always superior. Islam, moreover, stresses the duties of believers while international human rights law stresses the rights of man. For example, adultery is one of the gravest crimes in Islam but is not considered a serious crime under international law. Even Muslim defenders of an Islamic version of human rights admit this incongruency:

> The most significant difference between modern westernized attitudes towards human rights and their implementation and an Islamic perspective is the function of religion in general and the position of God in particular. Whereas God hardly finds his place anymore in Western lay societies, he is the seat of justice in the Muslim world. Islam sees God as the ultimate source of justice, which includes the Human Rights. The main goal of God's message to human kind is the attainment of Justice. At this point there is a strong connection between Justice and Islam.[17]

Thus, the Islamic view of human rights, especially in Shariʿa states, diverges from the Western view and also from the Universal Declaration on Human Rights (UDHR)—which Iran called a secular interpretation of the Judeo-Christian tradition which could not be followed by Muslims in good faith. This divergence led to the 1981 Universal Islamic Declaration of Human Rights and later the 1990 adoption by the Organization of the Islamic Conference (OIC) of the Cairo Declaration on Human Rights in Islam.

The Cairo Declaration was a direct Islamic response to the UDHR, and Shariʿa pervades the document. In fact, Shariʿa is the basis for the Cairo Declaration, which can only be interpreted to conform with Shariʿa. The Cairo Declaration departs substantively from the UDHR in key aspects: Article 6 qualifies rights of equality for women, Article 22 qualifies individual freedoms such as speech (must conform to Shariʿa), Article 5 leaves open the possibility of discrimination in marriage on the basis of religion, and Article 20 allows for corporal punishment—thereby undermining the human dignity keystone of all human rights law, as reflected in Article 5 of the UDHR with respect to torture: "No one shall be subjected to torture or to cruel, inhuman or degrading treatment."

The Western consensus on this Shariʿa-based alternative to human rights is that, in principle, the Muslim world should not be allowed to create a valid exception to international human rights norms. To do so denies the common humanity shared by all people.

The internationalization of criminal law, which began in earnest with the trial of Nazi leaders at Nuremberg in 1946, has gained traction since the end of the Cold War. A proliferation of international institutions has given rise to a variety of structural models available for the prosecution and adjudication of violations of international criminal law. Yet, very few Islamic jurists or Islamic states participate in the institutions that support the development of this international jurisprudence.

Ad hoc tribunals, created by the U.N. Security Council to address war crimes, crimes against humanity, and genocide in the former Yugoslavia and in Rwanda, were designed to be temporary in nature with narrowly prescribed territorial, subject matter and temporal jurisdiction. They were, and still are, staffed by international legal specialists drawn from outside the countries in which the atrocities took place, and the tribunals are physically removed from those states as well.

The International Criminal Tribunal for the Former Yugoslavia (ICTY) and the International Criminal Tribunal for Rwanda (ICTR) are both considered successful in that they added vital justice elements to the conflicts they are associated with, achieved a relatively high degree of interaction among the legal academy, and continue to produce complex legal opinions that further elucidate difficult elements of international criminal law. Nevertheless, the international community quickly came to recognize that a chief weakness to the ad hoc systems centered on a lack of involvement (and investment) by the local community. In short, the ad hoc tribunals became over-internationalized.

An attempt to remedy this central weakness was the creation of a hybridized model. Following conclusion of the civil war in Sierra Leone, the U.N. worked with the local government to create a tribunal that contained both local and international judges, prosecutors, and staff, and was physically located in the country where the crimes occurred. U.N. officials sought to create a similar model for Cambodia, as the government began to pursue surviving former members of the Khmer Rouge that participated in the 1975 genocide. That effort has not been as successful as the Sierra Leone effort due, in large part, to political issues on the Cambodian side of the equation.

In addition to the ad hoc and hybrid models, both intended to be temporary in nature, a permanent model has emerged with the creation of the International Criminal Court (ICC) in 2002. Located in the The Hague and staffed with international experts, the theory behind the ICC is that a venue will be available when local courts cannot or will not prosecute atrocities within their jurisdictions. Moreover, it is meant to be shielded from the potential for politicization and serve as a more viable deterrent to despotic conduct than previous institutions. Perhaps tellingly, all of the ICC's prosecutorial activity to date has concerned situations in Africa.

Few nationals from Islamic states participate in international tribunals, and the ones who do, tend to stem from the secularized traditions: The ICTY and ICTR each have one judge from Turkey and Pakistan. The hybrid tribunals for the Sierra Leone and Cambodia Special Courts have none, and neither does the International Criminal Court.

International criminal law has come to focus mainly on three types of atrocity: genocide, war crimes, and crimes against humanity. A fourth crime, aggression, was tried at Nuremberg and Tokyo, but has not been tried since. It is an inchoate, undefined crime within the Rome Statute for the ICC. Islamic states have largely signed treaties outlawing these types of crimes. Yet, Islamic states have not participated meaningfully in the institutions that investigate and prosecute them. Nevertheless, Islamic societies have had (or will have) some degree of interaction with these three crimes in the context of the following international and domestic tribunals:

- *Bosnia-Herzegovina's War Crimes Chamber* in Sarajevo (taking ICTY overload and locally initiated cases): International and Bosnian (Muslim) judges trying mostly Serbs
- *Kosovo's War Crimes Chamber*: Muslim, Serb, and international judge triumvirate trying mostly Serbs
- *Iraqi High Tribunal*: Prosecution of atrocities committed under Saddam: Muslims trying Muslims
- *East Timor's Hybrid Tribunal*: Mostly Catholics trying Catholics (Muslims are being tried in Jakarta by fellow Muslims)
- *International Criminal Court*: Investigation of genocide in Darfur, Sudan: Non-Muslims trying Muslims

The IHT is the only Arab nexus of these five tribunals, three of which are domestic courts, one is an analogue to a hybrid court, and one is a full-blown international tribunal. All of these tribunals, including the three domestic courts, were designed by Westerners with American and international expertise, not by Islamic legal scholars. All of the tribunals are code-based. All of the tribunals except the IHT experience chronic issues with asserting jurisdiction over defendants, collecting evidence, and administrative concerns with respect to staffing and expertise. The U.S.-led occupation of Iraq has allowed the Regime Crimes Liaison Office to render much of these support elements to the IHT.

There will also be interaction among Muslims and international criminal law in the context of the Hariri assassination. The International Criminal Tribunal for the Assassination of former Lebanese prime minister was created by the U.N. Security Council under Chapter VII of the U.N. Charter on June 10, 2007 without the approval from Lebanese parliament. The two Islamic states on the U.N. Security Council (Qatar and Indonesia) abstained. Syria, Hezbollah, and

Lebanon's president oppose the tribunal. The tribunal will exist outside Lebanon and be staffed by international personnel, including an international prosecutor assisted by a Lebanese deputy and a blend of international and Lebanese judges. The U.N. Commission conducting the investigation into the assassination is led by Belgian prosecutor Serge Brammertz, the ICC's deputy prosecutor. This will be the first international tribunal to depart from focusing on the three traditional international crimes, concentrating instead on terrorism and murder charges. The defendants will likely be Syrian and Lebanese Muslims, yet there will be little Islamic law influence in the process.

Despite a lack of participation on the institutional side of the equation, Islamic states have participated meaningfully in the development of international criminal law as it is to be applied. For example, many Arab states participated in negotiations leading to the creation of the ICC, including the final round of negotiations between 1996 and 1998. Most sought to exclude the designation of forced pregnancy as a crime against humanity and restrict the definition of sexual violence to rape only; a noninterference clause was finally inserted to protect national customs with regard to pregnancy. These states also pushed for the crime of aggression to be state-centered to allow for the coexistence of criminalized individual aggression and the duty on the individual to Jihad (the first meaning is personal struggle, but the secondary meaning is military struggle against Western hegemony—especially in the Arab world). This impasse remains—the crime of aggression was left undefined in the Rome Statute.

Very few Islamic states signed on to the Rome Statute. Of the 104 states parties, 20 are OIC members (all found in Africa). Fifteen of these have predominantly Muslim populations. Jordan is the only Arab state party. None of the Shariʿa-centered Islamic states are parties. Nigeria, which is not wholly Shariʿa, is the only state party to the Rome Statute with a partial Shariʿa system.

Why are Shariʿa-centered Islamic states less likely to participate in international criminal law than Western States? There are a number of factors that may help explain this disconnect:

- *Islamic law*: If the legal system is derived from religious authority rather than secular, participation is less likely
- *Level and type of Shariʿa practiced*: If only the commercial or nondivergent aspects of Islamic law are in play, participation is more likely; it become less likely if the criminal or more divergent aspects are in play
- *Cultural drawbacks*: The shape and extent of tribalism in the society that may disdain outside interference together with broad-based cultural expectations like speed in trial and sentencing and victim participation are factors that could come into play
- *Rule of Law factors*:
  - Independent judiciary (nonexistent in most Arab states)
  - Crimes in Shariʿa jurisdictions are not defined, can lead to abuse
- *Fractured nature of Shariʿa* and the various schools of Islamic law

- *Level of tailoring in tribunal design to accommodate Islamic traditions*: No war crimes tribunal to date, international or domestic but Western-designed, has been able to adequately accommodate Islamic interests
- *Level of antagonism by/with West*: International criminal law is a Western-driven process; the adoption of Shari'a itself in some states was a direct rejection of Western criminal codes incorporated during the colonial era that supplanted Shari'a; political antagonism will hobble efforts at greater participation

Some have proposed the development of a hybrid international/Islamic criminal court to encourage both the the the tradition of Shari'a and participation of Islamic states in international criminal law bodies. However, the diversity of predominantly Islamic states, cultures and traditions within predominantly Islamic states, degree of incorporation of Islamic law, adherence to varying schools of Islamic law, and disagreement over the content of criminal law mitigates against creating a sustainable centralized international criminal tribunal in the Muslim world. Nevertheless, the Muslim world is about where the Western world was sixty years ago in the development of international criminal law—agreeing on the broad outlines of the crimes but differing on the particulars. Such obstacles were eventually overcome in the West, beginning with Nuremberg.

Once, and if, internal differences concerning criminal law are surmounted within the Muslim world, differences between the Islamic and Western legal traditions must be addressed. This, if it materializes, will be a very long process. Eventually, creation of a hybrid International / Islamic Criminal Tribunal could be a first step in addressing the disconnect between Shari'a-centered Islamic states international criminal law and human rights. But, again, that does not appear to be on the horizon.

A different theory is offered by Professor Mashood Baderin of the University of London, who proposes reconstituting the Wilâyah al-Mazâlim, a grievance tribunal from the early days of the Islamic Empire. This ancient court was endowed with broad jurisdiction to address violations of individual rights by state officials. Baderin seeks to use this type of body to help bridge wide gaps between the Cairo Declaration and international human rights law. For instance, the International Covenant on Civil and Political Rights (ICCPR) provides guarantees against torture, forced labor, servitude, social/legal inequality, personal liberties, and freedom of thought, whereas many Islamic societies do not.

As envisioned by Baderin, a reconstituted Mazâlim court "would be composed of . . . Islamic jurists learned in Islamic jurisprudence, but also . . . international human rights law." The court would have compulsory jurisdiction across Islamic states, accommodate the views of all Islamic schools, and develop a jurisprudence that moves toward a common interpretation of Islamic law for human rights. While this notion is attractive, the lack of unity in the post-Caliphate world among Islamic states renders its viability a weak prospect.

Participation from Islamic states in the creation of international criminal law, and their support of international criminal law institutions, is spotty at best. The more a predominantly Islamic state adheres to a Shariʿa system, the less likely there is to be participation of any kind. To the extent this happens, as was the case with ICC negotiations, it is to blunt the incursion of international criminal law into the Islamic world, not to further the work of the field. Yet, as in the case of new judicial efforts in the Sudan, Bosnia, Indonesia, Kosovo, and the forthcoming Hariri tribunal, Muslims will increasingly be drawn into working with these institutions whether supported by their Islamic courts or not.

How can more meaningful participation from the Islamic world be achieved? A number of outstanding questions remain. Does creation of a separate legal system for Islamic versions of human rights and international criminal law undermine the "universality" of those immutable concepts? What place does cultural relativism have in this discourse? If secular and rule of law-centered Islamic states like Turkey and Pakistan can participate in international criminal law, can the incompatibility between Shariʿa-centered Islam and international criminal law be bridged in any way other than adopting a dualistic approach? How can the legitimacy of international criminal law and the tribunals that implement it be maximized for Islamic societies? Is legitimacy a separate question from compatibility?

Finally, can the Maslah (public interest) component of Islamic law be creatively invoked to get around the Shariʿa obstacle? Islamic law defers greatly to public interest as an overriding consideration that modernists can work with to argue that the traditional hard-line Islamic punishments to crime can only be imposed if they are in the public interest. Once this premise is accepted, then those seeking to bring Islamic law into the modern world can thereby connect it with international law and progressively redefine "public interest." While that might be a generational answer to this intractable problem, it might be the best answer out there.

Saddam's trial for the Dujail massacre underscored inherent problems in grafting western notions of justice onto traditional Islamic systems. This perhaps could have been avoided if an international trial could have been negotiated, although that was never attempted. And even if it were, the disconnect between Shariʿa and international criminal law would have been difficult to overcome, although the new Hariri Tribunal may prove that such a daunting task is not altogether insurmountable.

As more and more former despots are held accountable for their crimes, especially genocide, current despotic leaders should feel less secure. No longer will they find safe havens negotiated in exchange for their resignation and departure as Uganda's Idi Amin found in Saudi Arabia or Haiti's Baby Doc Duvalier found in the south of France. Nigeria's extradition of former Liberian dictator Charles Taylor from exile to the Special Court for Sierra Leone proved there is no safe haven—prompting Libya's Muammar Qaddafi to nervously observe, "This means that every head of state could meet a similar fate."[18] Indeed, shortly after the British House of Lords stripped former Chilean dictator Augusto Pinochet of sovereign immunity against charges of torture and pronounced him extraditable to Spain for trial, Congolese dictator Laurent Kabila sought assurances of his own immunity from prosecution before traveling to a conference of francophone African states in Marseilles.

If concern over international ramifications induces just one leader to refrain from committing atrocities, then such prosecutions have been well worth the trouble. Such international efforts are products of the late 1990s, and were organized well after the genocide of the Iraqi Kurds. Still, one wonders if Saddam would have thought twice about undertaking such horrors against the Kurds, as well as others in Iraq, if a real threat of international prosecution existed. Given his psychology—probably not.

Conclusion

It is not unusual for former despots standing trial before either international or domestic tribunals to die before the full trial process is completed. Indeed, one might consider it the norm. Hermann Goering committed suicide before his sentence was carried out at Nuremberg and Hideiki Tojo attempted to eviscerate himself according to Japanese custom during the proceedings of the International Military Tribunal at Tokyo. Slobodan Milosevic died from improper medication dosage before his trial was completed before the International Criminal Tribunal for the former Yugoslavia (ICTY) in The Hague. And Augusto Pinochet died of natural causes before the completion of his trial in Chile. Saddam Hussein's execution fits this pattern.

Saddam was convicted and sentenced for the massacre of 148 Shi'ites in Dujail, but did not complete the trial process for the genocide of thousands of Kurds in the Anfal trial or even begin the five other trials that awaited him, including a separate trial for the gassing of the Kurdish city of Halabja in 1988. The Iraqi High Tribunal (IHT), in a departure from the typical practice of rolling multiple crimes together in a single lengthy trial, opted to try Saddam and his cronies in seven distinct trials not running simultaneously, but seriatum.

The perception that survivors of the mass atrocities carried out by Saddam—that were scheduled to be the subject of the six other trials besides Dujail—might feel cheated if he were executed before those trials was, perhaps, forseeable. Nevertheless, the IHT hewed scrupulously to its execution schedule after Saddam drew the death sentence in the first trial, and that execution was quickly carried out after confirmation by the appellate court.

Not only were the judicial proceedings against Saddam for the Kurdish genocide not continued posthumously, they were terminated by the IHT and the charges against Saddam were dropped. And the Halabja trial did not even get underway. At least after Slobodan Milosevic's death, the ICTY simply terminated the proceedings; it did not drop the charges against him.[1]

Saddam Hussein's body was buried before dawn on December 31, 2006 (within 24 hours of his death) in al-Awja, a small village eight miles south of Tikrit on the western bank of the Tigris River. He was interred at 4:00 A.M. local time near the graves of his two sons, Uday and Qusay, who had been killed during the U.S.-led invasion of Iraq. American military presence was palpable both before and after Saddam's execution. He was handed over to Iraqi guards by his U.S. jailors for hanging, and his body was then flown by a U.S. military helicopter to Tikrit, where it was handed over to Sheikh Ali al-Nida for washing and burial according to Islamic customs.

It was here, near Tikrit, that Saddam Hussein was born in 1937. Tikrit was also the birthplace, 800 years earlier, in 1138, of one of the most famous Islamic warlords and statesmen—Saladin. Two very different men. Two very different stories. Saladin was a Kurd. Today, Saladin remains a figure of legendary and heroic porportions—a wise leader and brilliant military tactician who rid Muslim lands of the Crusaders. Saddam, by contrast, is destined for a more reviled memory—wrought with egomaniacal violence and crazed, despotic tendencies.

Perhaps by that measure, the Kurds won after all—at least with respect to history. But their promised "day in court" against Saddam Hussein evaporated just as their promised homeland did in the 1920s. Yet the Kurds persevere in the face of strife. As the mists lift after dawn in the mountains of Kurdistan, daily life must persist. The ghosts of Halbaja and the Anfals must remain restless for now.

Appendix A: Declassified U.S. Government Documents—Financial Backing for Iraq during Iran–Iraq War

Memo from Assistant Secretary of State Richard Murphy to Lawrence Eagleburger and letter from Eagleburger to William Draper urging the Export-Import Bank to provide Iraq with financial credits since Saddam had agreed to stop supporting terrorists and had expelled Abu Nidal from Iraq.

Department of State

8339263A

ACTION MEMORANDUM Under Secretary had seen.

DATE: DEC 24 1983

'83 DEC 22 P 7:5?

2 2 DEC 1983

TO: P - Mr. Eagleburger

FROM: NEA - Richard W. Murphy

SUBJECT: EXIM Bank Financing for Iraq

Issue:

Whether to sign a letter to EXIM President Draper recommending that EXIM approve financing for Iraq.

Essential Factors:

EXIM currently opposes loans to Iraq because it considers that loans to Iraq lack a reasonable expectation of repayment. EXIM points to Iraq's recent rescheduling of commercial contract payments, large transfers from Gulf governments, decreased oil production and the drop in Iraqi reserves to support its view. In addition, EXIM is concerned about the threat of war damage.

EXIM has virtually no exposure in Iraq because, until recently, EXIM was precluded from doing business with Iraq in light of that country's involvement with terrorists.

Recent analysis of Iraq's economic situation indicates that the crisis situation which prevailed during the early part of 1983 has been alleviated somewhat through imposition of an austerity program which included cutbacks in development projects and major cuts in imports. As a consequence, Iraq's estimated net foreign assets for 1983 are $11 billion although the current account balance is - $9 billion for the year. In addition, Iraq has been successful in obtaining supplier credits and deferred payments for ongoing projects. Current payments on these debts are being met. If present policies and external financing are sustained, the current account should be roughly in balance, but further rescheduling is a possibility.

Iraq's financial condition will remain dependent on petroleum export earnings and aid from the Gulf states. Iraq is determined to achieve alternative outlets for its petroleum exports in addition to the pipeline through Turkey (capacity 150,000 b/d). Iraq expects to increase its oil export capacity through Turkey to just over 1 million b/d in the spring of 1984 with a possible additional 50% increase in exports by the end of 1984. Cash transfers from the Gulf states to Iraq, at least $30 billion since the start of the war, have been and will continue to be important

EXDIS

CONFIDENTIAL
-2-

to Iraq. For the Gulf States, there appears to be no alternative to a continuation of this aid flow because of their dependence upon Iraq to resist export of the Iranian revolution.

There is the possibility, on the political side, that internal frustrations resulting from economic deprivation and a seemingly endless war may produce problems for the government. On the military front, Iraq has suffered limited setbacks on the northern front. It is uncertain how long the status quo can be maintained by Iraq in its confrontation with a much more populous Iran as long as Iran exports three times as much oil as Iraq.

Discussion:

The U.S./Iraq political relationship could be advanced by EXIM financing which had previously not been possible for political reasons. EXIM financing would benefit U.S. manufacturers and workers and could serve marginally to bolster the Iraqi economy by freeing resources for use elsewhere in the country. Most importantly, EXIM financing would signal our belief in the future viability of the Iraqi economy and secure a U.S. foothold in a potentially large export market. Viewed in combination with CCC credits already granted Iraq, an EXIM gesture would go far to show our support for Iraq in a practical, neutral context. This would be especially important in the absence of other substantial U.S. gestures, to ease the military pressures of the war, and would provide some incentive for Iraq to comply with our urgings that it show restraint in widening the war.

Although Iraq's economy is confronted with significant problems, we are guardedly optimistic regarding Iraq's ability to manage these problems through 1984.

Recommendation:

That you sign the letter attached at Tab 1 recommending that EXIM consider financing for Iraq. Our Interests Section endorses this recommendation. (Baghdad 3134 attached).

DEC 24 1983

Agree _____ Disagree _____

Attachments:

Tab 1 - Proposed Letter to William Draper
Tab 2 - Baghdad 3134

CONFIDENTIAL

125

GADIS

Under Secretary of State
for Political Affairs

Washington, D.C. 20520

December 24, 1983

Dear Bill:

I would like to bring to your attention the important role
EXIM can play in furthering long range political and economic
interests of the United States by being receptive to financing
American sales to and projects in Iraq.

I understand that there were legal constraints on EXIM
financing for sales to Iraq arising from Iraq's links to
international terrorists. Recently, the President of Iraq
announced the termination of all assistance to the principal
terrorist group of concern, among others. Iraq then expelled
this group and its leader. The terrorism issue, therefore,
should no longer be an impediment to EXIM financing for U.S.
sales to Iraq.

Although we cannot know when the heavy burden of war will
be lifted from the Iraqi economy, the threat of economic crisis
has receded. A strict austerity program, supplier credits,
foreign government project financing, and continued financial
assistance from the Gulf states should continue to sustain the
oil export capacity by 30% to one million b/d in the spring of
1984, and has plans well advanced for an additional 50%
increase in its oil exports by the end of 1984.

From the political standpoint, EXIM financing would show
U.S. interest in the Iraqi economy in a practical, neutral
context. It could provide some incentive for Iraq to comply
with our urgings that it show restraint in the war. This
evidence of our interest in increasing commercial relations
also will bring political benefits, as well as balance-of-trade
and employment benefits to our economy.

Sincerely,

Lawrence S. Eagleburger

The Honorable
    William H. Draper, III,
        President and Chairman,
            Export-Import Bank of the United States.

Appendix B: Declassified U.S. Government Documents—Knowledge and Reaction to Chemical Weapons Use during Iran–Iraq War

U.S. awareness of and reaction to Saddam's early use of chemical weapons against Iran indicates that Washington knew of his past use of poison gas against Iranian forces and "Kurdish insurgents." Washington also knew of his intention to continue using the weapons, as reflected in Saddam's famous warning (quoted below) prior to the spring 1984 Iranian offensive, that "the invaders should know that for every harmful insect there is an insecticide capable of annihilating it whatever their number and Iraq possesses this annihilation insecticide."

The documents also indicate that Washington knew of chemical shipments to Iraq, and, after the fact, condemned their use (which "confused" Baghdad—indicating that the Iraqis assumed use of chemical weapons was approved).

RELEASED IN PART B1

P91003420846

8333438

United States Department of State

Washington, D. C. 20520

UNCLASSIFIED

November 1, 1983

'83 NOV -1 P5:23

INFORMATION MEMORANDUM

S/S

NODIS REVIEW

Cat. A - Caption removed,
transferred to O/FADRC

Cat. B - Transferred to O/FADRC
with additional assets
controlled by S/S

Cat. C - Caption and custory
retained by S/S

Reviewed by: Elijah Kelly

Date: September 7   9C

TO: The Secretary

FROM: PM - Jonathan T. Howe

SUBJECT: Iraq Use of Chemical Weapons

We have recently received additional information confirming
Iraqi use of chemical weapons. We also know that Iraq has
acquired a CW production capability, primarily from Western
firms, including possibly a U.S. foreign subsidiary. In
keeping with our policy of seeking to halt CW use wherever it
occurs, we are considering the most effective means to halt
Iraqi CW use including, as a first step, a direct approach to
Iraq. This would be consistent with the way we handled the
initial CW use information from Southeast Asia and Afghanistan,
i.e., private demarches to the Lao, Vietnamese and Soviets. **B1**

As you are aware, presently Iraq is at a disadvantage in
its war of attrition with Iran. After a recent SIG meeting
on the war, a discussion paper was sent to the White House for
an NSC meeting (possibly Wednesday or Thursday this week), a
section of which outlines a number of measures we might take
to assist Iraq. At our suggestion, the issue of Iraqi CW use
will be added to the agenda for this meeting. **B1**

If the NSC decides measures are to be undertaken to assist
Iraq, our best present chance of influencing cessation of CW
use may be in the context of informing Iraq of these measures. **B1**
It is important, however, that we approach Iraq very soon in
order to maintain the credibility of U.S. policy on CW, as well
as to reduce or halt what now appears to be Iraq's almost daily
use of CW.

B1   B1

DECL: DADR

9/20/94

128

P910074-023 Department of State

8335709

ACTION MEMORANDUM

UNCLASSIFIED

ORIGINAL TO: NODIS P DUE NOV 21 N1 S0

31 NOV 1983

COPIES TO:
P
S/S
NEA
PM
S/S-S:DIR
IMA
IMB
IMC
NODIS FILE
(jab)

TO: P - Lawrence S. Eagleburger

FROM: PM - Jonathan T. Howe
        NEA - Richard W. Murphy

SUBJECT: Iraqi Use of Chemical Weapons

ISSUE FOR DECISION

Whether to instruct USINT Baghdad to raise issue of Iraqi CW use and urge cessation.

ESSENTIAL FACTORS

We have recently received additional information confirming Iraqi use of chemical weapons (CW). We also know that Iraq has acquired a CW production capability, primarily from Western firms, including possibly a U.S. foreign subsidiary. (A cable detailing U.S. CW policy and available information on Iraqi use of CW is at Tab 2.) In keeping with our policy of seeking a halt to CW use wherever it occurs, we have been considering the most effective means to halt further Iraqi CW use including, as a first step, a direct approach to Iraq.

In October Iran accused Iraq of using CW and on November 8 it requested the UNSYG to investigate. Iran also stated it would soon submit a report providing information and evidence on Iraqi CW use, but has not yet done so. We do not know whether or when this issue will develop further at the UN. It is important to make our approach to the Iraqis on this issue as early as possible, in order to deter further Iraqi use of CW, as well as to avoid unpleasantly surprising Iraq through public positions we may have to take on this issue.

If you approve the demarche to Iraq, we will submit further recommendations for your consideration on how to handle the issue in the UN if it arises there, as well as on whether we should raise with selected European governments the fact that national firms are selling to Iraq CW production related technology.

DECL: OADR

129

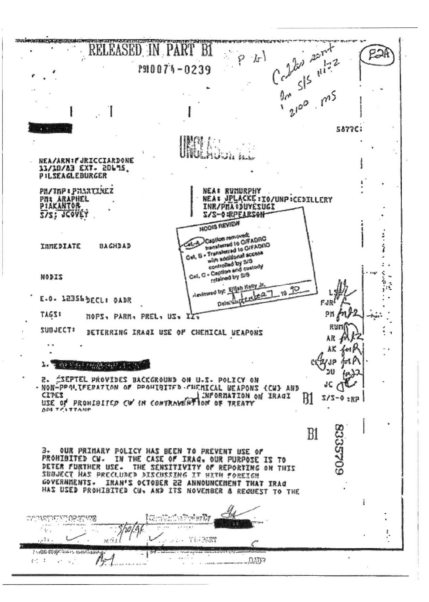

P910074-0239

P b1

Colles sent
On S/S 11:2
2100 mS

P2A

5877C:

UNCLASSIFIED

NEA/ARN:FJRICCIARDONE
11/10/83 EXT. 20675.
P:LSEAGLEBURGER

PM/TMP:PMARTINEZ
PM: ARAPHEL
P:AKANTOR
S/S; JCOVEY

NEA: RUMURPHY
NEA: JPLACKE:IO/UNP:CEDILLERY
INR/PMA:DUYESUGI
S/S-O:RPEARSON

NODIS REVIEW
Cet. A - Caption removed;
transferred to O/FADRC
Cet. B - Transferred to O/FADRO
with additional access
controlled by S/S
Cet. C - Caption and custody
retained by S/S
Reviewed by: Elijah Kelly, Jr.
Date: September 7, 19 90

IMMEDIATE   BAGHDAD

NODIS

E.O. 12356 DECL: OADR

TAGS: MOPS, PARM, PREL, US, IZ,

SUBJECT: DETERRING IRAQI USE OF CHEMICAL WEAPONS

L/
FJR
PM
RUM
AR
AK
CE/JP
DU
JC

B1 S/S-O :RP

1. ████████████████

2. SEPTEL PROVIDES BACKGROUND ON U.S. POLICY ON
NON-PROLIFERATION OF PROHIBITED CHEMICAL WEAPONS (CW) AND
CITES ██████████████ INFORMATION ON IRAQI
USE OF PROHIBITED CW IN CONTRAVENTION OF TREATY
OBLIGATIONS.

B1

B1 8335709

3. OUR PRIMARY POLICY HAS BEEN TO PREVENT USE OF
PROHIBITED CW. IN THE CASE OF IRAQ, OUR PURPOSE IS TO
DETER FURTHER USE. THE SENSITIVITY OF REPORTING ON THIS
SUBJECT HAS PRECLUDED DISCUSSING IT WITH FOREIGN
GOVERNMENTS. IRAN'S OCTOBER 22 ANNOUNCEMENT THAT IRAQ
HAS USED PROHIBITED CW, AND ITS NOVEMBER 8 REQUEST TO THE

| 2

UNSYG TO INVESTIGATE, PROVIDE BOTH AN OPENING AND THE
NECESSITY TO RAISE THIS ISSUE IN BAGHDAD, AND PERHAPS
LATER WITH FRIENDS WHO ARE IN A POSITION TO INFLUENCE THE
IRAQI DECISION TO USE PROHIBITED CW.

4. IN KEEPING WITH THE GRAVITY OF OUR LONG-STANDING CON-
CERN OVER CW PROLIFERATION AND PAST PRACTICE IN EXPRESSING
THIS CONCERN, WE ARE CONSIDERING HOW TO RESPOND TO DEVELOP-
MENT OF THE ISSUE IN THE UN. WE DO NOT WISH TO PLAY INTO
IRAN'S HANDS BY FUELING ITS PROPAGANDA AGAINST IRAQ.

5. PLEASE PRESENT THE FOLLOWING POINTS IN APPROPRIATE
MANNER TO FOREIGN MINISTER TARIQ AZIZ:

-- AS YOU ARE AWARE, THE USG IS VERY CONCERNED WITH THE
PRESENT OVERALL SITUATION IN SOUTHWEST ASIA. WE STRONGLY
SUPPORT A NEGOTIATED SETTLEMENT.

-- IT IS THUS IN A CONSTRUCTIVE SPIRIT THAT WE NOW RAISE
WITH YOU AN ISSUE OF GREAT SENSITIVITY AND IMPORTANCE TO
THE USG, NAMELY, PROHIBITED USE OF LETHAL CHEMICAL WEAPONS.

-- WE RAISE THE ISSUE NOW NEITHER TO ENTER INTO A CONFRON-
TATIONAL EXCHANGE WITH YOU, NOR TO LEND SUPPORT TO THE
VIEWS OF OTHERS; BUT, RATHER, BECAUSE IT IS A LONG-STANDING
POLICY OF THE U.S. TO OPPOSE USE OF LETHAL CW.

-- WE ALSO RAISE THE MATTER NOW BECAUSE WE BELIEVE CONTI-
NUED IRAQI USE OF CW WILL PLAY INTO THE HANDS OF THOSE
WHO WOULD WISH TO ESCALATE TENSIONS IN THE REGION, AS WELL
AS CONSTRAIN THE ABILITY OF THE USG TO PLAY A HELPFUL
ROLE IN THE REGION.

-- WE NOTE THAT IRAQ LONG AGO ACCEDED TO THE 1925 GENEVA
PROTOCOL BANNING THE USE OF CW. WE BELIEVE IRAQ'S
SCRUPULOUS ADHERENCE TO THAT PROTOCOL IS IMPORTANT TO
AVOID DANGEROUS ESCALATION OF THE WAR, TO MAINTAIN THE
HOPE OF BRINGING IRAN TO THE NEGOTIATING TABLE, AND TO
AVOID PROVIDING IRAN WITH A POTENT PROPAGANDA WEAPON
AGAINST IRAQ.

-- WE HOPE YOU WILL RECEIVE OUR REPRESENTATION IN THE
SPIRIT IT IS INTENDED. YY

B1

PN0074-0241

S673C

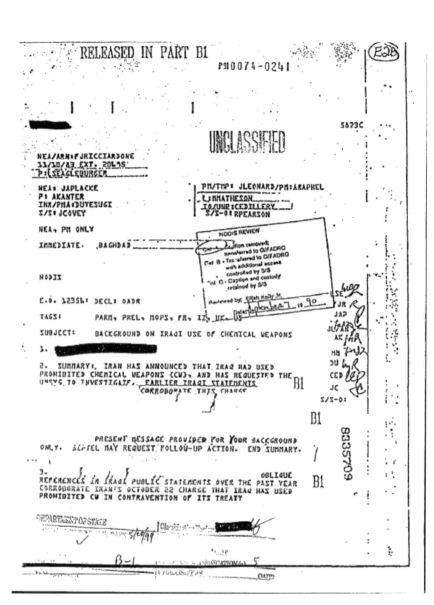

UNCLASSIFIED

NEA/ARN:FJRICCIARDONE
11/10/89 EXT. 20695
P:LSEAGLEBURGER

NEA: JAPLACKE
P: AKANTER
INR/PMA:DUYESUGI
S/S: JCOVEY

PM/TMP: JLEONARD/PM:ARAPHEL
L:HMATHESON
IO/UNP:CEDILLERY
S/S-0: RPEARSON

NEA, PM ONLY

IMMEDIATE. BAGHDAD

NODIS REVIEW

NODIS

E.O. 12356: DECL: OADR

TAGS: PARM, PREL, MOPS, FR, IZ, UK, US

SUBJECT: BACKGROUND ON IRAQI USE OF CHEMICAL WEAPONS

1.

2. SUMMARY:. IRAN HAS ANNOUNCED THAT IRAQ HAD USED
PROHIBITED CHEMICAL WEAPONS (CW), AND HAS REQUESTED THE
UNSYS TO INVESTIGATE. EARLIER IRAQI STATEMENTS
CORROBORATE THIS CHARGE

          PRESENT MESSAGE PROVIDED FOR YOUR BACKGROUND
ONLY. SEPTEL MAY REQUEST FOLLOW-UP ACTION. END SUMMARY.

3.
REFERENCES IN IRAQI PUBLIC STATEMENTS OVER THE PAST YEAR
CORROBORATE IRAN'S OCTOBER 22 CHARGE THAT IRAQ HAS USED
PROHIBITED CW IN CONTRAVENTION OF ITS TREATY

DEPARTMENT OF STATE

2

OBLIGATIONS. ON NOVEMBER 8, IRAN REQUESTED THE UNSYG TO INVESTIGATE. (IRAN HAD MADE SIMILAR CHARGES DURING THE IRAQ WAR, WHICH IRAQ HAD DENIED.)

AS LONG AGO AS JULY 1982, THE IRAQIS USED GAS AND SKIN IRRITANTS AGAINST INVADING IRANIAN FORCES QUITE EFFECTIVELY. IN OCTOBER 1982, UNSPECIFIED FOREIGN OFFICERS FIRED LETHAL CHEMICAL WEAPONS AT THE BORDERS OF SADDAM DURING BATTLES IN THE MANDALI AREA. IN JULY AND AUGUST 1988, THE IRAQIS REPORTEDLY USED A CHEMICAL AGENT WITH LETHAL EFFECTS AGAINST AND IRANIAN FORCES INVADING IRAQ AT HAJ UMRAN, AND MORE RECENTLY AGAINST KURDISH INSURGENTS.

5. IRAQI MEDIA HAVE QUOTED IRAQI PRESIDENT SADDAM HUSSEIN AS SAYING, "THERE IS A WEAPON FOR EVERY BATTLE AND WE HAVE THE WEAPON THAT WILL CONFRONT GREAT NUMBERS." MILITARY COMMUNIQUES OVER THE PAST YEAR HAVE REFERRED TO "ALL KINDS OF WEAPONS" BEING USED TO REPULSE THE IRANIANS. ON DECEMBER 18, 1982, IRAQ CLAIMED IT WOULD RETALIATE FOR AN IRANIAN-CLAIMED TERRORIST BOMBING IN BAGHDAD "WITH MORE THAN ONE MEANS...HE WHO FOREWARNS IS EXCUSED." A MILITARY COMMUNIQUE WARNED THE IRANIANS AGAINST VIOLATING INTERNATIONAL NORMS AND CHARTERS, PERHAPS TRYING TO ESTABLISH A PRETEXT FOR USING CW IN VIOLATION OF INTERNATIONAL PROTOCOLS. IN AN INTERVIEW PUBLISHED FEBRUARY 13, 1983, IN ARABIC IN AL-HAWADITH, DEFENSE MINISTER KHAYRALLAH EVADED A QUESTION ON IRAQ'S POSSESSION OF A POISON GAS WEAPON. THE AL-HAWADITH INTERVIEW DID NOT CONFIRM IRAQ'S DEVELOPMENT OF CW, BUT IT PUT THE QUESTION INTO THE PUBLIC DOMAIN. ON APRIL 12, 1983, IRAQ AGAIN WARNED OF "NEW WEAPONS...(TO) BE USED FOR THE FIRST TIME IN WAR...NOT USED IN PREVIOUS ATTACKS BECAUSE OF HUMANITARIAN AND ETHICAL REASONS...THAT WILL DESTROY ANY MOVING CREATURE."

6. IRAQ HAS A LIMITED INDIGENOUS CAPABILITY TO PRODUCE AND DEPLOY CW. FOR EXAMPLE, IRAQ MAY BE ABLE TO PRODUCE MUSTARD GAS FROM CHEMICAL INTERMEDIARIES PROCURED ABROAD. THE SOVIETS HAVE EQUIPPED AND TRAINED THE IRAQI FORCES TO FIGHT IN A CW ENVIRONMENT.

31

B1

8. OVER MANY DECADES THE U.S. HAS SOUGHT TO DETER THE
USE OF LETHAL AND INCAPACITATING CW WHEN THEIR USE
APPEARED TO LOOM AS A POSSIBILITY. IRAQ'S USE OF LETHAL
OR INCAPACITATING CW COULD FURTHER
UNDERCUT AN IMPORTANT AGREEMENT OBSERVED BY NEARLY
ALL NATIONS AGAINST CHEMICAL WARFARE. INTRODUCTION OF CW
TO THE GULF WAR REPRESENTS AN ESCALATION OF HOSTILITIES
THAT COULD RENDER STILL MORE REMOTE THE POSSIBILITY OF A
CEASEFIRE AND NEGOTIATIONS. FURTHERMORE, IRAQ'S USE OF
CW GIVES THE IRANIANS A POWERFUL PROPAGANDA TOOL AGAINST
THE IRAQI REGIME, SETTING WORLD OPINION AGAINST IRAQ AT
A TIME WHEN IRAN ENJOYS LITTLE INTERNATIONAL SYMPATHY.
BEYOND THE HUMANITARIAN AND SECURITY/PROLIFERATION
CONCERNS, THESE FACTS SHOULD OFFSET THE ATTRACTIVENESS TO
IRAQ OF USING PROHIBITED CW.

9. BOTH IRAN (IN 1929) AND IRAQ (IN 1931) HAVE RATIFIED
THE GENEVA PROTOCOL OF 1925 PROHIBITING THE USE OF
CHEMICAL WEAPONS. IRAQ ATTACHED CONDITIONS TO ITS
ACCESSION, HAVING THE EFFECT OF A "NO FIRST USE" CLAUSE,
BUT ITS COMMITMENT NOT TO USE UNLESS ATTACKED WITH SUCH
WEAPONS IS UNEQUIVOCAL. IRAN ATTACHED NO CONDITIONS TO
ITS RATIFICATION OF THE PROTOCOLS. THERE IS SOME
QUESTION WHETHER IRAN MAY HAVE USED CHEMICAL AGENTS AT
ONE POINT EARLY IN THE WAR.

10. THE EXISTING CONVENTION PROHIBITS ONLY THE USE RPT
USE OF LETHAL AND INCAPACITATING CW. NO INTERNATIONAL
TREATY YET FORBIDS DEVELOPMENT, PRODUCTION, OR DEPLOYMENT
OF LETHAL AND INCAPACITATING CW. THE U.S. AND OTHERS
HAVE BEEN NEGOTIATING FOR SUCH A TREATY FOR A NUMBER OF
YEARS. ALSO, WE DO NOT INTERPRET THE GENEVA PROTOCOL AS
APPLYING TO RIOT CONTROL AGENTS AS OPPOSED TO LETHAL AND
INCAPACITATING CHEMICALS. WE LIMIT THEIR USE TO DEFENSIVE
MILITARY MODES TO SAVE LIVES, E.G., CONTROLLING RIOTING
P.O.W.S. DISPERSING CIVILIAN "SCREENS" OF ATTACKS. RESCUE
OPERATIONS IN ISOLATED AREAS, AND PROTECTING CONVOYS
OUTSIDE THE COMBAT ZONE.

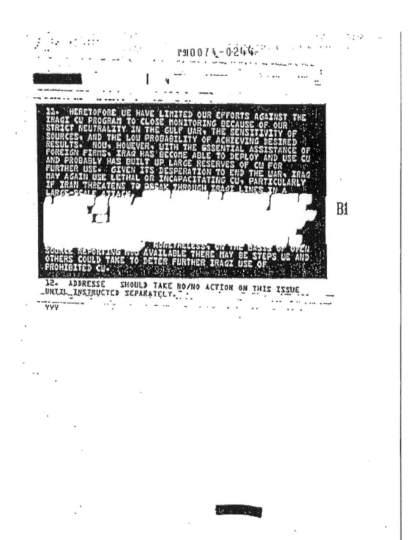

11. HERETOFORE WE HAVE LIMITED OUR EFFORTS AGAINST THE IRAQI CW PROGRAM TO CLOSE MONITORING BECAUSE OF OUR STRICT NEUTRALITY IN THE GULF WAR, THE SENSITIVITY OF SOURCES, AND THE LOW PROBABILITY OF ACHIEVING DESIRED RESULTS. NOW, HOWEVER, WITH THE ESSENTIAL ASSISTANCE OF FOREIGN FIRMS, IRAQ HAS BECOME ABLE TO DEPLOY AND USE CW AND PROBABLY HAS BUILT UP LARGE RESERVES OF CW FOR FURTHER USE. GIVEN ITS DESPERATION TO END THE WAR, IRAQ MAY AGAIN USE LETHAL OR INCAPACITATING CW, PARTICULARLY IF IRAN THREATENS TO BREAK THROUGH IRAQI LINES IN A LARGE-SCALE ATTACK.

B1

NEVERTHELESS, ON THE BASIS OF OPEN SOURCE REPORTING NOW AVAILABLE THERE MAY BE STEPS WE AND OTHERS COULD TAKE TO DETER FURTHER IRAQI USE OF PROHIBITED CW.

12. ADDRESSE SHOULD TAKE NO/NO ACTION ON THIS ISSUE UNTIL INSTRUCTED SEPARATELY.

YYY

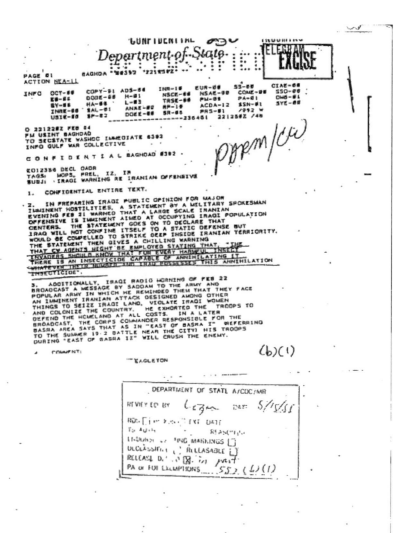

Department of State

INFO OCT-00   COPY-01 ADS-00   INR-10   EUR-00   SS-00   CIAE-00
      EB-06   DODE-00 H-01   NSCE-00   NSAE-00   COME-00 SSO-00
      SY-05   HA-08   L-03   TRSE-00   PM-00   PA-01   OMB-01
      INRE-00   SAL-01   ANAE-00   SP-10   ACDA-12   SSN-01   SYE-00
      UBIE-00   SP-03   DOEE-00   SR-00   PRS-01   /292 W
                                    236401 2212502 /48

O 2212292 FEB 84
FM USINT BAGHDAD
TO SECSTATE WASHDC IMMEDIATE 6392
INFO GULF WAR COLLECTIVE

C O N F I D E N T I A L BAGHDAD #392

EO12356 DECL OADR
TAGS: MOPS, PREL, IZ, IR
SUBJ: IRAQI WARNING RE IRANIAN OFFENSIVE

1.   CONFIDENTIAL ENTIRE TEXT.

2.   IN PREPARING IRAQI PUBLIC OPINION FOR MAJOR
IMMINENT HOSTILITIES, A STATEMENT BY A MILITARY SPOKESMAN
EVENING FEB 21 WARNED THAT A LARGE SCALE IRANIAN
OFFENSIVE IS IMMINENT AIMED AT OCCUPYING IRAQI POPULATION
CENTERS.   THE STATEMENT GOES ON TO DECLARE THAT
IRAQ WILL NOT CONFINE ITSELF TO A STATIC DEFENSE BUT
WOULD BE COMPELLED TO STRIKE DEEP INSIDE IRANIAN TERRIORITY.
THE STATEMENT THEN GIVES A CHILLING WARNING
THAT CW AGENTS MIGHT BE EMPLOYED STATING THAT, "THE
INVADERS SHOULD KNOW THAT FOR EVERY HARMFUL INSECT
THERE IS AN INSECTICIDE CAPABLE OF ANNIHILATING IT
WHATEVER THEIR NUMBER AND IRAQ POSSESSES THIS ANNIHILATION
INSECTICIDE".

3.   ADDITIONALLY, IRAQI RADIO MORNING OF FEB 22
BROADCAST A MESSAGE BY SADDAM TO THE ARMY AND
POPULAR ARMY IN WHICH HE REMINDED THEM THAT THEY FACE
AN IMMINENT IRANIAN ATTACK DESIGNED AMONG OTHER
THINGS TO SEIZE IRAQI LAND, VIOLATE IRAQI WOMEN
AND COLONIZE THE COUNTRY.   HE EXHORTED THE TROOPS TO
DEFEND THE HOMELAND AT ALL COSTS.   IN A LATER
BROADCAST, THE CORPS COMMANDER RESPONSIBLE FOR THE
BASRA AREA SAYS THAT AS IN "EAST OF BASRA I" REFERRING
TO THE SUMMER 19-2 BATTLE NEAR THE CITY) HIS TROOPS
DURING "EAST OF BASRA II" WILL CRUSH THE ENEMY.

4.   COMMENT:

(b)(1)

EAGLETON

EXCISE

SECRET

AN: D840142-0829

SECRET

PAGE 01   STATE 064124
ORIGIN SS-25

INFO OCT-00   COPY-01 ADS-00   SSO-00   /026 R
DRAFTED BY NEA/ARN:FJRICCIARDONE:VL
APPROVED BY NEA:JAPLACKE
NEA/IRN:RJHIGGINS
NEA/ARN: AEJONES
PM/THP:PMARTINEZ
S/S-O:WAGARLAND
P:RRAPHEL
DESIRED DISTRIBUTION
NEA/PM ONLY
------------------364663 040117Z /66
O 040013Z MAR 84
FM SECSTATE WASHDC
TO USINT BAGHDAD IMMEDIATE

S E C R E T STATE 064124

EXDIS   **DECAPTIONED**

E.O. 12356   DECL: OADR
TAGS: PARM, PREL, US, IZ
SUBJECT: U.S. CHEMICAL SHIPMENT TO IRAQ

1. SECRET - ENTIRE TEXT.

2. ACTION REQUESTED PARAS 4-5.

3.   MARCH 2 THAT A U.S. FIRM WAS PREPARING
TO EXPORT 22,000 POUNDS RPT POUNDS OF PHOSPHOROUS
FLOURIDE TO IRAQ. DEPARTMENT CONFIRMED MARCH 3 THAT
SHIPMENT WAS TO HAVE TAKEN PLACE BY AIR FROM JFK AIRPORT
TO IRAQ VIA EUROPE AND THAT THE CUSTOMER IN IRAQ WAS
PURCHASING THE CHEMICAL FOR USE IN THE MANUFACTURE OF
INSECTICIDES. DEPARTMENT OFFICER ADVISED THE SHIPPING
AGENT OF OUR CONCERN OVER IRAQ'S POSSIBLE INTENTION TO
SECRET

SECRET

PAGE 02   STATE 064124

USE THE CHEMICAL IN THE MANUFACTURE OF CHEMICAL WEAPONS.

SECRET

HE ASKED THE FIRM TO HOLD UP THE SHIPMENT UNTIL FURTHER
NOTICE. THE SHIPPING AGENT AGREED TO DO SO, AND
DEPARTMENT OFFICER AGREED TO GET BACK TO THE SHIPPER ON
MONDAY, MARCH 5 FOR FURTHER DISCUSSION.

4. MEANWHILE THE ISSUE OF IRAQI USE OF CHEMICAL WEAPONS
HAS BEEN RECEIVING GREATER MEDIA ATTENTION IN THE UNITED
STATES. WE ARE PREPARING PRESS GUIDANCE
THAT WILL FORCEFULLY CONDEMN IRAQ FOR ITS
USE OF CHEMICAL WEAPONS. THE GUIDANCE WILL BE
TRANSMITTED TO YOU WHEN IT IS IN FINAL FORM.

5. ACTION REQUESTED: PLEASE ADVISE THE MFA THAT, AS WE
HAD WARNED IN NOVEMBER, DECEMBER, AND EARLY FEBRUARY IN
BAGHDAD, THE CHEMICAL WEAPONS ISSUE IS OF GRAVE CONCERN
TO US, AND WE ANTICIPATE MAKING A PUBLIC CONDEMNATION OF
IRAQI USE OF CHEMICAL WEAPONS IN THE NEAR FUTURE. AS YOU
REVIEW OUR SEVERAL DISCUSSIONS OF THIS ISSUE WITH THE
IRAQIS, PLEASE EXPLICITLY LIST THE DISCUSSION IN
WASHINGTON BETWEEN NEA DAS PLACKE AND IRAQI CHIEF HAMDOUN
OF FEBRUARY 22 (REFTEL), WHICH WE SUSPECT MAY NOT HAVE
BEEN FULLY REPORTED TO THE MFA. ALSO, YOU SHOULD ADVISE
THE MFA THAT WE HAVE HELD UP A SHIPMENT OF CHEMICALS
CONSIGNED TO IRAQ OSTENSIBLY FOR USE IN THE MANUFACTURE
OF PESTICIDES. THIS SAME CHEMICAL IS ALSO A COMPONENT OF
LETHAL GASES FOUND IN CHEMICAL WEAPONS. THE U.S. WILL
NOT ALLOW ITSELF KNOWINGLY TO BECOME A SOURCE OF CHEMICAL
WEAPONS ELEMENTS. THEREFORE, WE SEEK CLARIFICATION AND
ASSURANCE BY THE GOI REGARDING THE PURPOSE AND PRECISE
USE OF THIS CHEMICAL, E.G. DETAILS OF TIMING, POINT OF
INTENDED MANUFACUTURE INTO FINISHED PRODUCT, CHEMICAL
DESCRIPTION OF FINISHED PRODUCT, AND INTENDED USE.
SECRET
SECRET

PAGE 03   STATE 064124

6. BEYOND REITERATING OUR URGENT REQUEST THAT IRAQ NOT
MAKE PROHIBITED USE OF CHEMICAL WEAPONS, YOU SHOULD
INFORM THE IRAQIS THAT WE ARE ADAMANTLY OPPOSED TO IRAQ'S
ATTEMPTING TO ACQUIRE THE RAW MATERIALS, EQUIPMENT, OR
EXPERTISE TO MANUFACTURE CHEMICAL WEAPONS FROM THE UNITED
STATES. WHEN WE BECOME AWARE OF ATTEMPTS TO DO SO, WE
WILL ACT TO PREVENT THEIR EXPORT TO IRAQ.   SHULTZ

SECRET

AN: DB40194-0217

SECRET

PAGE 01   STATE   086663
ORIGIN SS-25

INFO   OCT-00   COPY-01 ADS-00   SSO-00   /026 R

DRAFTED BY NEA/ARN: FJRICCIARDONE
APPROVED BY NEA:JAPLACKE
NEA/ARN: DLMACK
S/S-O:NRPEARSON
----------------------317365   240726Z /21
O 240512Z MAR 84
FM SECSTATE WASHDC
TO AMEMBASSY KHARTOUM IMMEDIATE
INFO USINT BAGHDAD IMMEDIATE

S E C R E T   STATE 086663

EXDIS, FOR RUMSFELD PARTY   **DECAPTIONED**

E.O. 12356: DECL: OADR
TAGS: PREL, US, IZ
SUBJECT: BRIEFING NOTES FOR RUMSFELD VISIT TO BAGHDAD

1. S - ENTIRE TEXT.

2. SETTING: TWO EVENTS HAVE WORSENED THE ATMOSPHERE IN
BAGHDAD SINCE YOUR LAST STOP THERE IN DECEMBER: (1) IRAQ
HAS ONLY PARTLY REPULSED THE INITIL THRUST OF A MASSIVE
IRANIAN INVASION, LOSING THE STRATEGICALLY SIGNIFICANT
MAJNUN ISLAND OIL FIELDS AND ACCEPTING HEAVY CASUALTIES;
(2) BILATERAL RELATIONS WERE SHARPLY SET BACK BY OUR
MARCH 5 CONDEMNATION OF IRAQ FOR CW USE, DESPITE OUR
REPEATED WARNINGS THAT THIS ISSUE WOULD EMERGE SOONER OR
LATER. GIVEN ITS WARTIME PREOCCUPATIONS AND ITS DISTRESS
AT OUR CW STATEMENT, THE IRAQI LEADERSHIP PROBABLY WILL
HAVE LITTLE INTEREST IN DISCUSSING LEBANON, THE
ARAB-ISRAELI CONFLICT, OR OTHER MATTERS EXCEPT AS THEY
MAY IMPINGE ON IRAQ'S INCREASINGLY DESPERATE STRUGGLE FOR
SECRET
SECRET

PAGE 02   STATE   086663

SURVIVAL. IF SADDAM OR TARIQ AZIZ RECEIVES YOU AGAINST

SECRET

139

CONSIDER, AND TO REJECT, A PENDING APPLICATION FROM
WESTINGHOUSE TO PARTICIPATE IN A $160 MILLION PORTION OF
A $1 BILLION HYUNDAI THERMAL POWER PLANT PROJECT IN
IRAQ. THIS DECISION WILL ONLY CONFIRM IRAQI PERCEPTIONS
THAT EXIM FINANCING FOR THE AQABA PIPELINE IS OUT OF THE
QUESTION. EAGLEBURGER TRIED TO PUT THIS PERCEPTION TO
REST, HOWEVER, EMPHASIZING TO KITTANI THE
ADMINISTRATION'S FIRM SUPPORT FOR THE LINE. THE DOOR IS
NOTYETCLOSED TO EXIM OR OTHER USG FINANCIAL ASSISTANCE
TO THIS PROJECT: FORONE THING, THE PIPELINE IS A

QUALITATIVELY MORE ATTRACTIVE PROJECT FROM A CREDITOR'S
POINT OF VIEW; SECONDLY, EXIM DOES NOW DO BUSINESS IN
JORDAN - IN WHICH SOME 60 PERCENT OF THE PIPELINE'S COSTS
WILL BE INCURRED. THE PROBLEM NOW IS FOR IRAQ, JORDAN,
AND THE COMPANY TO SETTLE THE TECHNICAL ISSUES SO THAT
THE COMPANY CAN MAKE A FORMAL PRESENTATION, FOLLOWED BY
AN APPLICATION, FOR EXIM CONSIDERATION. MEANWHILE, WE
ARE CONFUSED BY THE GOI'S OWN PRIORITIES: IT MAY BE
PLAYING OFF THE AQABA LINE AGAINST THE SAUDI LINK IN
HOPES OF GETTING ONE OR THE OTHER OFF TO A SPEEDIER START.
(MORE ON PIPELINES BY SEPTEL)
6. JORDAN: KING HUSSEIN HAS BEEN INSTRUMENTAL IN TRYING
TO IMPROVE US-IRAQI RELATIONS.

B1

HIS SUPPORT

SECRET
SECRET

PAGE 04   STATE 086663

FOR IRAQ IN ITS WAR WITH IRAN HAS SOLIDIFIED THE
JORDANIAN-IRAQI FRIENDSHIP. IT WOULD BE NATURAL FOR
SADDAM HUSSEIN TO INQUIRE ABOUT THE STATE OF US-JORDANIAN
RELATIONS. YOU COULD USEFULLY DRAW ON THE FOLLOWING
TALKING POINTS:

-- WE UNDERSTAND KING HUSSEIN'S FRUSTRATIONS, ALTHOUGH WE
DO NOT SHARE MANY OF HIS ASSESSMENTS.

-- WE CERTAINLY REJECT HIS CONCLUSIONS THAT THE PEACE
PROCESS IS DEAD AND THAT US POLICY IS IN THE HANDS OF THE
ISRAELIS. THE US HAS THE FINAL SAY IN ITS FOREIGN AND
DEFENSE OBJECTIVES, JUST AS KING HUSSEIN HAS THE FINAL
SAY IN JORDAN'S FOREIGN POLICY.

-- OUR THIRTY-YEAR FRIENDSHIP FOR JORDAN AND OUR

SECRET

COMMITMENTS TO JORDAN'S SECURITY AND UNIQUE AND ENDURING
CHARACTER ARE NOT AFFECTED BY THIS LATEST BIT OF STRAIN.

-- WE DO HOPE THAT DIPLOMACY CAN BE CONDUCTED IN THE
NORMAL CHANNELS RATHER THAN IN THE PAPER. GOOD AND CLOSE
FRIENDS SHOULD NOT RISK SENDING MISLEADING SIGNALS OF A
BREACH IN OUR RELATIONS.

-- WE WANT THE BEST POSSIBLE RELATIONSHIP WE CAN HAVE
WITH JORDAN.

7. U.S. REGIONAL POLICIES: IRAQ IS CONFUSED BY OUR
MEANS OF PURSUING OUR STATED OBJECTIVES IN THE REGION,
WHETHER IN COMBATTING KHOMEINI, IN LEBANON, WITH SYRIA,
OR WITH FRIENDS SUCH AS JORDAN, EGYPT, AND ISRAEL. IN
EACH CASE, IRAQI OFFICIALS HAVE PROFESSED TO BE AT A LOSS
TO EXPLAIN OUR ACTIONS AS MEASURED AGAINST OUR STATED
SECRET
SECRET

PAGE 05   STATE 086663

OBJECTIVES. AS WITH OUR CW STATEMENT, THEIR TEMPTATION

IS TO GIVE UP RATIONAL ANALYSIS AND RETREAT TO THE LINE
THAT U.S. POLICIES ARE BASICALLY ANTI-ARAB AND HOSTAGE TO
THE DESIRES OF ISRAEL.   SHULTZ

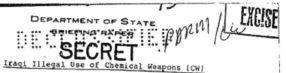

SECRET

Iraqi Illegal Use of Chemical Weapons (CW)

I.

Background:

o ~~████████~~ we concluded that Iraq had used domestically-produced lethal CW in its war with Iran ~~████~~ (b)(1) ~~████████~~ Such use violates the 1925 Geneva Protocol, to which Iraq and Iran are Parties. The Protocol prohibits first use but not possession of CW nor its retaliatory use.

o The Iraqi CW capability was developed in part through the unwitting and, in some cases, we believe witting assistance of a number of Western firms, ~~████████~~ (b)(1) ~~████████~~ We have approached the relevant States on the involvement of their national firms.

_(b)(1)

o On November 21, 1983, in Baghdad, we presented a demarche telling the Iraqis that we knew of their use of CW and strongly opposed it as a matter of principle. Other demarches to the same effect followed in succeeding months. We believe Iraqi CW use ceased after our November demarche but began again when Iran launched its February 1984 offensive.

o As a result of Iraq's renewed CW use in February, we publicly condemned Baghdad for using CW on March 5, 1984. Although adequately warned, Iraq expressed consternation with our action ~~████████~~ (b)(1) ~~████████~~ In subsequent contacts with Iraq, we have reiterated our opposition to their illegal use of CW.

Later in March, at the request of Iran, the UN Secretary General dispatched experts to Iran to investigate. The final report, submitted to the Security Council, concluded that lethal CW (both mustard and nerve agents) had been used but did not name Iraq as the user. Soon thereafter, the Security Council unanimously condemned CW use in the Gulf War, again without naming Iraq.

In March we also instituted export controls on certain chemicals suitable for the manufacture of CW to both Iraq and Iran and sought the establishment of

SECRET

SECRET

- 2 -

similar controls by other nations -- many have
followed our lead.

o   To date, Iraq has not admitted, publicly or otherwise,
    to having or using CW.

(b)(1)

II.   Current Status

o   We know of no Iraqi CW use since the end of the spring
    Iranian offensive.

(b)(1)

(b)(1)

o   Our efforts to curtail the flow of CW-related
    materials and to end the complicity of Western firms
    in the CW programs of Iraq and Iran have met with some
    success.

(b)(1)

However, because of the
dual purpose nature of many materials, we cannot stop
all shipments or technical assistance that might be
used for CW purposes short of a complete trade embargo
on both nations.

SECRET

Fact Sheet - Iraqi CW Use - Visit of FM Aziz

Drafted by PM/TMP, :dLeonard
11/16/84 ph 632-8847

Clearances:PM:AKanter
          PM/TMP:OGrobel
          PM/NESA:PTheros
          INR/PMA:GCrocker
          NEA/ARN:FRicciardone

WANG # 1034M

Appendix C: Charging of Saddam Hussein (Anfal)

The text of the Iraqi High Tribunal's charging of Saddam Hussein and the letter dropping the charges against him for the Anfal campaigns against the Iraqi Kurds.

In The Name of God All Merciful All Compassionate
Iraqi High Tribunal
Second Court of Felonies
Baghdad – Iraq
Ref. No 1/C Second/2006
Date: 2007 Jun 24
The Verdict

. . .

Convict Saddam Hussein Al-Majid: Head of the bygone Revolutionary Command Council and former Armed Forces' General Commander, he issued Decree [160] for the year 1987, granting Convict 'Ali Hasan Al-Majid full authorities of the president, Party commander, and Armed Forces General commander to execute command's objectives in the Northern Area.

The latter issued orders to carry on Al-Anfal operations, as per the aforementioned granted authority, especially the order to use "special ammunition" [meaning chemical weapons] which can not be used unless after an order from the president himself, as it had been mentioned on the voice record. Charges against him are:

Genocide: as per Article [11/First – Clauses (A) and C] by virtue of Article [15] of the court's law.
Crimes against Humanity: as per Article [12/First – Clauses (A), C, and 5] by virtue of Article [15] of the court's law.

War Crimes: as per Article [13/Fourth – Clauses (A), (D), and (L) by virtue of Article [15] of the court's law.

(page 57 of 963)

. . .

Accusing the convicts on behalf of the court:
We've already explained a detail in the previous article stating that Mr. Chief Investigative

Justice had transferred 7 convicts to this court, as follow:
1. Sultan Hashim Ahmad
2. 'Ali Hasan Al-Majid
3. Saddam Hussein Al-Majid
4. Sabir 'Abd-al-'Aziz Husayn
5. Husayn Rashid Muhammad

(page 59 of 963)

6. Tahir Tawfiq Al-Haj Yusif
7. Farhan Mutlak Al-Juburi

to prosecute them as per articles mentioned in the referral decision.

Via trials' result, after listening to the plaintiffs' testimonies, prosecution and defense witnesses, and reviewing the huge number of documents, files, compact discs (CD's) and audio tapes, and by acknowledging that the court is not bound to charges by which the **Chief of Investigative Judges transferred the convicts, the same court, on 2007 February 20, directed to each convict a charge paper, excluding Convict Saddam Husayn Al-Majid who had been executed as per First Criminal Court's verdict in Al-Dujayl case, approved to be irrevocable by cassation court.**

. . .

Chief of Judges (page 60 of 963)

Appendix D: Statute of the Iraqi High Tribunal

The 2005 Revised Statute of the Iraqi High Tribunal

Justice is the Foundation of Governance

Al-Waqa'I Al-Iraqiya

Official gazette of the Republic of Iraq

• **Iraqi High Criminal Court Law**

| No 4006 | Ramadan 14, 1426 Hijri | 47th year |
| | October 18, 2005 | |

Resolution No. (10)

In the Name of the people
The presidency Council

Pursuant to what has been approved by the National Assembly and in accordance with Article No. (33) Paragraphs A and B and Article No. (30) of the Law of Administration for the State of Iraq for the Transitional Period. The presidency Council decided in the session of October 9, 2005 to promulgate the following resolution:

Law No. (10) 2005
Law of
The Iraqi Higher Criminal Court
SECTION ONE
The Establishment and Organization
Of the Court
PART ONE
Establishment

Article 1:

First: A court is hereby established and shall be known as The Iraqi Higher Criminal Court (the "Court"). The Court shall be fully independent.

Second: The Court shall have jurisdiction over every natural person whether Iraqi or non-Iraqi resident of Iraq and accused of one of the crimes listed in Articles 11 to 14 below, committed during the period from July 17, 1968 and until May 1, 2003, in the Republic of Iraq or elsewhere, including the following crimes:
   A. The crime of genocide;
   B. Crimes against humanity;
   C. War crimes
   D. Violations of certain Iraqi laws listed in Article 14 below.

Article 2:

The Court shall have its main office in the city of Baghdad and may hold its sessions in any governorate, on the basis of a proposal by the Council of Ministers pursuant to a proposal from the President of the Court.

PART TWO
Organizational Structure of the Court

Article 3:

The court shall consist of:

First:

    A. Cassation Panel, which shall specialize in reviewing the provisions and decisions issued by one of the criminal or investigative courts.

    B. One or more criminal courts.

    C. Investigative judges.

Second: Public Prosecution.

Third: An administration, which shall provide administrative and financial services to the Court and the Public Prosecution.

Fourth:

    A. The Cassation Panel shall be composed of nine judges who shall elect a president for amongst them. The president of the Cassation Panel shall be the senior president of the court and shall supervise its administrative and financial affairs.

    B. The felony court shall be composed of five judges who shall elect a president from amongst them to supervise their work.

Fifth: The Council of Ministers may, if deemed necessary, based upon a proposal by a President of the Court, appoint non-Iraqi judges who have experience in conducting criminal trials stipulated in this law, and who are of very high moral character, honest and virtuous to work in the Court, in the event that a State is one of the parties in a complaint, and the judges shall be commissioned with the help of the International Community and the United Nations.

PART THREE
Selection of Judges, Public Prosecutors and their retirement

Article 4:

First: Judges and public prosecutors shall be of high moral character, integrity and uprightness. They shall possess experience in criminal law and shall fulfill the appointment requirements stipulated in the Judicial Organization Law No. 160 of 1979 and the Public Prosecution law No. 159 of 1979.

Second: As an exception to the provisions of paragraph (First) of this Article the candidates for the positions of judges at the Cassation Panel, the Criminal Court, the investigative judges and public prosecutors do not have to be active judges and public prosecutors. Retired judges and members of public prosecution may be nominated, without restrictions age requirement and Iraqi lawyers who possess a high level of experience, competence and efficiency and of absolute competence, in accordance with the Legal Profession Code No. 173 of 1965 and have served in judicial, legal and the legal profession fields for no less than (15) years.

Third:

    A. The Supreme Juridical Council shall nominate all judges and public prosecutors to this Court. The Council of Ministers after approving their nomination shall issue their appointment order from the Presidency Council and will be classified as class (A) judges, in an exception to the provisions of the Judicial Organization Law and the Public Prosecution Law. Their salaries and rewards shall be specified by guidelines issued by the Council of Ministers.

    B. The judges, public prosecutors and the employees appointed in accordance with the provisions of law before this legislation shall be deemed legally approved starting from the date of their appointment according to the provisions of paragraph (Third/A) of Article (4) taking into account the provisions of Article (33) of this law.

Fourth: The Presidency Council in accordance with a proposal from the Council of Ministers shall have the right to transfer Judges and Public Prosecutors from the Court to the Higher Judicial Council for any reason.

Fifth:

The term of service of a judge or a public prosecutor covered by the provisions of this law shall end for one of the following reasons:

    1. If he is convicted of a non-political felony.
    2. If he presents false information.
    3. If he fails to perform his duties without a legitimate reason.

Article 6:

First: A committee comprised of five members elected from among the Judges and public prosecutors shall be established in the Court under the supervision of the Cassation panel of the Court and they shall select a President for a term of one year. This committee shall be called "Judges and Public Prosecutors Affairs Committee". The Committee shall enjoy the authorities stipulated in the Judicial Organization Law and Public Prosecution Law. It shall consider disciplinary matters and the service of Judges and the members of the public prosecution. Its decisions shall be appealable before the extended panel of the Federal Court of Cassation if it decides to terminate the service of the judge or a member of the public prosecution.

Second: The committee shall submit a recommendations, after the appeal before the extended panel of the Federal Court of Cassation is denied, to the Council of Ministers to pass a resolution from the Presidency Council terminating the service of a judge or a public prosecutor, including the chief justice in case the provisions of Article (6) of this Law are met.

Third: At the end of the Court's work, the judges and the Public Prosecutors shall be reassigned to the Higher Judicial Council to work in the Federal Courts. Those reaching the legal age for retirement shall be retired in accordance with the Law.

PART FOUR
Presidency of the Court

Article 7:

First: The president of the court shall:
  A. Chair the proceedings of the Cassation Panel.
  B. Name the original and alternate judges of the Criminal Courts.
  C. Name any of the judges to the Criminal Court in case of absence.
  D. Accomplish the Court's administrative work.
  E. Appoint and end the service of the Administrative Director, security director, public relations director and archive and documents keeping director in the court.
  F. Name the official spokesman for the Court from among the judges or public prosecutors.

Second: The President of the Court shall have the right to appoint non-Iraqi experts to act in an advisory capacity for the Criminal Court and the Cassation Panel. The role of the non-Iraqi nationals shall be to provide assistance with respect to international law and the experience of similar Courts (whether international or otherwise). The paneling of these experts is to be done with the help from the International Community, including the United Nations.

Third: The non-Iraqi experts referred to in paragraph (Second) of this Article shall also be persons of high moral character, uprightness and integrity. It would be preferable that such non-Iraqi expert should have worked in either a judicial or prosecutorial capacity in his or her respective country or at the International War Crimes Court.

PART FIVE
Investigative Judges

Article 8:

First: Sufficient number of Investigative Judges shall be appointed.

Second: The Court's Investigative Judges shall undertake the investigation with those accused of crimes stipulated in paragraph (Second) Article (1) of this law.

Third: The Investigative Judges shall elect a Chief and his deputy from amongst them.

Fourth: The Chief shall refer cases under investigation to investigative judges individually.

Fifth: Each of the Investigative Judges' Offices shall be composed of an investigative Judge and qualified staff as may be required for the work of the investigative judge.

Sixth: An Investigative Judge shall collect evidence from any source he deems appropriate and question all relevant parties directly.

Seventh: An Investigative Judge shall act independently in the court since he is considered as a separate entity from the court. He shall not fall under nor receive requests or orders from any Government Department, or any other party.

Eight: The decisions of the Investigative Judge can be appealed in cassation before the Cassation Panel within fifteen days from the date of receipt of notification or from the date notification is considered received pursuant to law.

Ninth: The Chief Investigative Judge, after consulting with the President of the Court, have the right to appoint non-Iraqi nationals experts to assist the Investigative Judges in the investigation of cases covered by this law, whether international or otherwise. The Chief Investigative Judge can commission these experts with help from the International Community, including the United Nations.

Tenth: The non-Iraqi experts and observers referred to in paragraph (Ninth) of this Article are required to be persons of high moral character, honest and virtuous; it is preferred that the non-Iraqi expert and observer had worked in either a judicial or prosecutorial capacity in his or her respective country or in the International War Crimes Court.

PART SIX
The Public Prosecution

Article 9:

First: Sufficient number of prosecutors shall be appointed.

Second: The Public Prosecution shall be composed of a number of public prosecutors who shall be responsible for the prosecution of persons accused of crimes that fall within the jurisdiction of the Court.

Third: Public prosecutors shall elect a Chief and his Deputy from amongst them.

Fourth: Each office of public prosecution shall be composed of a prosecutor and such other qualified staff as may be required for the work of the Public Prosecutor.

Fifth: Each prosecutor shall act with complete independence since he is considered as a separate entity from the Court. He shall not fall under, nor receive instructions from, any government department or from any other party.

Sixth: The chief prosecutor shall assign individual cases to a prosecutor to investigate and to try in court based on the authority granted to the public prosecutors pursuant to the law.

Seventh: The Chief Public Prosecutor, in consultation with the President of the Court, shall have the right to appoint non-Iraqi nationals to act as experts helping the public prosecutors in the investigation and prosecution of cases covered by this law whether in an international context or otherwise. The Chief Prosecutor can commission these experts with the help of the international community, including the United Nations.

Eighth: The non-Iraqi experts, referred to in Paragraph (Seventh) of this Article are required to be persons of high moral character, honest and virtuous. It is preferred that such non-Iraqi experts had worked in a prosecutorial capacity in his respective country or in the International War Crimes Court.

PART SEVEN
The Administration Department

Article 10:

First: The Administration Department shall be managed by an officer with the title of Department Director who holds a bachelor degree in law and have judicial and administrative experience. He shall be assisted by a number of employees in managing the affairs of the department.

Second: The Administration Department is responsible for the administrative, financial and service affairs of the court and the Public Prosecution.

SECTION TWO
The Court Jurisdictions

PART ONE
The Crime of Genocide

Article 11:

First: For the purposes of this law and in accordance with the International Convention on the Prevention and Punishment of the Crime of Genocide dated December 9, 1948 as ratified by Iraq on January 20, 1959, "genocide" means any of the following acts committed with the intent to abolish, in whole or in part, a national, ethnic, racial or religious group as such:
  A. Killing members of the group.
  B. Causing serious bodily or mental harm to members of the group.
  C. Deliberately inflicting on the group living conditions calculated to bring about its physical destruction in whole or in part.
  D. Imposing measures intended to prevent births within the group.
  E. Forcibly transferring children of the group to another group.

Second: The following acts shall be punishable
  A. Genocide.
  B. Conspiracy to commit genocide.

   C. Direct and public incitement to commit genocide.

   D. Attempt to commit genocide.

   E. Complicity in genocide.

PART TWO
Crimes against Humanity

Article 12

First: For the purposes of this Law, "crimes against humanity" means any of the following acts when committed as part of a widespread or systematic attack directed against any civilian population, with knowledge of the attack:

   A. Willful Murder;

   B. Extermination;

   C. Enslavement;

   D. Deportation or forcible transfer of population;

   E. Imprisonment or other severe deprivation of physical liberty in violation of fundamental norms of international law;

   F. Torture;

   G. Rape, sexual slavery, forcible prostitution, forced pregnancy, or any other form of sexual violence of comparable gravity;

   H. Persecution against any specific party or group of the population on political, racial, national, ethnic, cultural, religious, gender or other grounds that are impermissible under international law, in connection with any act referred to as a form of sexual violence of comparable gravity.

   I. Enforced disappearance of persons.

   J. Other inhumane acts of a similar character intentionally causing great suffering, or serious injury to the body or to the mental or physical health.

Second: For the purposes of implementing the provisions of paragraph (First) of this Article, the below listed terms shall mean the stated definitions:

   A. "Attack directed against any civilian population" means a course of conduct involving the multiple panel of acts referred to in the above paragraph "First" against any civilian population, pursuant to or in furtherance of a state or organizational policy to commit such attack;

   B. "Extermination" means the intentional infliction of living conditions, such as the deprivation of access to food and medicine, with the intent to bring about the destruction of part of the population;

   C. "Enslavement" means the exercise of any or all of the powers attached to the right of ownership over a person and includes the exercise of such power in the course of human trafficking, in particular women and children;

   D. "Deportation or forcible transfer of population" means forced displacement of the concerned persons concerned by expulsion or other coercive acts from the area in which they are lawfully present, without grounds permitted under international law;

E. "Persecution" means the intentional and severe deprivation of fundamental rights contrary to international law by reason of the identity of the group or collectivity; and

F. "Enforced disappearance of persons" means the arrest, detention or abduction of persons by, or with the authorization, support or acquiescence of, the State or a political organization, followed by a refusal to acknowledge that deprivation of freedom or to give information on the fate or whereabouts of those persons, with the intention of removing them from the protection of the law for a prolonged period of time.

PART THREE
War Crimes

Article 13

For the purposes of this Law, "war crimes" means:

First: Grave breaches of the Geneva Conventions of 12 August 1949, namely, any of the following acts against persons or property protected under the provisions of the relevant Geneva Convention:

A. Willful killing;

B. Torture or inhuman treatment, including biological experiments;

C. Willfully causing great suffering, or serious injury to body or health;

D. Extensive destruction and appropriation of property not justified by military necessity and carried out unlawfully and wantonly;

E. Compelling a prisoner of war or other protected person to serve in the forces of a hostile power;

F. Willfully denying the right of a fair trial to a prisoner of war or other protected person;

G. Unlawful confinement;

H. Unlawful deportation or transfer; and

I. Taking of hostages.

Second: Other serious violations of the laws and customs applicable in international armed conflicts, within the established framework of international law, namely, any of the following acts:

A. Intentionally directing attacks against the civilian population as such or against individual civilians not taking direct part in hostilities;

B. Intentionally directing attacks against civilian objects, that is, objects which are not military objectives;

C. Intentionally directing attacks against personnel, installations, material, units or vehicles used in a peacekeeping missions in accordance with the

Charter of the United Nations or in a humanitarian assistance missions, as long as they are entitled to the protection given to civilians or civilian objects under the international law of armed conflicts;

D. Intentionally launching an attack in the knowledge that such attack will cause incidental loss of life or injury to civilians or damage to civilian objects which would be clearly excessive in relation to the concrete and direct overall military advantages anticipated;

E. Intentionally launching an attack in the knowledge that such attack will cause widespread, long-term and severe damage to the natural environment, which would be clearly excessive in relation to the concrete and direct overall military advantage anticipated;

F. Attacking or bombarding, by whatever means, towns, villages, dwellings or buildings which are undefended and which are not military objectives;

G. Killing or wounding a combatant who, having laid down his arms or having no longer means of defense, has surrendered at discretion;

H. Making improper use of a flag of truce, of the flag or of the military insignia and uniform of the enemy or of the United Nations, as well as of the distinctive emblems of the Geneva Conventions, resulting in death or serious personal injury;

I. The transfer, directly or indirectly, by the Government of Iraq or any of its instrumentalities (which includes for clarification any of the instruments of the Arab Ba'ath Socialist Party)), of parts of its own civilian population into any territory it occupies, or the deportation or transfer of all or parts of the population of the occupied territory within or outside this territory;

J. Intentionally directing attacks against buildings that are dedicated to religion, education, art, science or charitable purposes, historic monuments, hospitals and places where the sick and wounded are collected, provided they are not military objectives;

K. Subjecting persons of another nation to physical mutilation or to medical or scientific experiments of any kind that are neither justified by the medical, dental or hospital treatment of the person concerned nor carried out in his or her interest, and which cause death to or seriously endanger the health of such person or persons;

L. Killing or wounding treacherously individuals belonging to the hostile nation or army;

M. Declaring that no one remained alive;

N. Destroying or seizing the property of an adverse party unless such destruction or seizure be imperatively demanded by the necessities of war;

O. Declaring abolished, suspended or inadmissible in a court of law, or otherwise depriving, the rights and actions of the nationals of the hostile party;

P. Compelling the nationals of the hostile party to take part in the operations of war directed against their own country, even if they were in the belligerent's service before the commencement of the war;

Q. Pillaging a town or place, even when it is taken by force;
R. Using poison or poisoned weapons;
S. Using asphyxiating, poisonous or other gases, and all analogous liquids, materials or devices;
T. Using bullets, which expand or flatten easily in the human body, such as bullets with a hard envelope, which does not entirely cover the core or is pierced with incisions;
U. Committing outrages upon personal dignity, in particular humiliating and degrading treatment;
V. Committing rape, sexual slavery, enforced prostitution, forced pregnancy, or any other form of sexual violence of comparable gravity;
W. Utilizing the presence of a civilian or other protected person to render certain points, areas or military forces immune from military operations;
X. Intentionally directing attacks against buildings, material and medical units, transport, and personnel using the distinctive emblems of the Geneva Conventions in conformity with international law;
Y. Intentionally using starvation of civilians as a method of warfare by depriving them of objects indispensable to their survival, including willfully impeding relief supplies as provided for under international law; and
Z. Conscripting or enlisting children under the age of fifteen years into the national armed forces or using them to participate actively in hostilities.

Third: In the case of an armed conflict, any of the following acts committed against persons taking no active part in the hostilities, including members of armed forces who have laid down their arms and those placed *hors de combat* by sickness, wounds, detention or any other cause:

A. Use of violence against life and persons, in particular murder of all kinds, mutilation, cruel treatment and torture;
B. Committing outrages upon personal dignity, in particular humiliating and degrading treatment;
C. Taking of hostages;
D. The passing of sentences and the carrying out of executions without previous judgment pronounced by a regularly constituted court, affording all judicial guarantees which are generally recognized as indispensable.

Fourth: Other serious violations of the laws and customs of war applicable in armed conflict not of an international character, within the established framework of international law, namely, any of the following acts:

A. Intentionally directing attacks against the civilian population as such or against civilian individuals not taking direct part in hostilities;
B. Intentionally directing attacks against buildings, materials, medical transportation units and means, and personnel using the distinctive emblems of the Geneva Conventions in conformity with international law;

C. Intentionally directing attacks against personnel, installations, materials, units, or vehicles used in humanitarian assistance or peacekeeping missions in accordance with the Charter of the United Nations, as long as they are entitled to the protection given to civilians or civilian targets under the international law of armed conflict;

D. Intentionally directing attacks against buildings that are dedicated to religious, educational, artistic, scientific or charitable purposes, and historic monuments, hospitals and places where the sick and wounded are collected, provided they are not military objectives;

E. Pillaging any town or place, even when taken over by assault;

F. Committing rape, sexual slavery, forced prostitution, forced pregnancy, or any other form of sexual violence of comparable gravity;

G. Conscripting or listing children under the age of fifteen years into armed forces or groups or using them to participate actively in hostilities;

H. Ordering the displacement of the civilian population for reasons related to the conflict, unless the security of the civilians involved or imperative military reasons so demand;

I. Killing or wounding treacherously a combatant adversary;

J. Declaring that no person is still alive;

K. Subjugation persons who are under the power of another party of the conflict to physical mutilation or to medical or scientific experiments of any kind that are neither justified by the medical, dental or hospital treatment of the person concerned nor carried out in his or her interest, causing death to such person or persons, or seriously endangering their health; and

L. Destroying or seizing the property of an adversary, unless such destruction or seizure is imperatively demanded by the necessities of the conflict.

PART FOUR
Violations of Iraqi Laws

Article 14

The Court shall have the power to prosecute persons who have committed the following crimes:

First: Intervention in the judiciary or the attempt to influence the functions of the judiciary.

Second: The wastage and squander of national resources, pursuant to, item G of Article 2 of the Law punishing those who conspire against the security of the homeland and corrupt the regime No. 7 of 1958.

Third: The abuse of position and the pursuit of policies that were about to lead to the threat of war or the use of the armed forces of Iraq against an Arab country, in accordance with Article 1 of Law Number 7 of 1958.

Fourth: If the court finds a default in the elements of any of the crimes stipulated in Articles 11, 12, 13 of this law, and it is proved to the Court that the act constitutes a crime punishable by the penal law or any other criminal law at the time of its commitment, then the court shall have jurisdiction to adjudicate this case.

SECTION THREE
Individual Criminal Responsibility

Article 15

First: A person who commits a crime within the jurisdiction of this Court shall be personally responsible and liable for punishment in accordance with this Law.

Second: In accordance with this Law, and the provisions of Iraqi criminal law, a person shall be criminally responsible if that person:
  A. Commits such a crime, whether as an individual, jointly with another or through another person, regardless of whether that this person is criminally responsible or not;
  B. Orders, solicits or induces the commission of such a crime, which in fact occurs or is attempted;
  C. For the purpose of facilitating the commission of such a crime, aids, abets or by any other means assists in its commission or its attempted commission, including providing the means for its commission;
  D. Participating by any other way with a group of persons, with a common criminal intention to commit or attempt to commit such a crime, such participation shall be intentional and shall either:
    1. Be made for the aim of consolidating the criminal activity or criminal purpose of the group, where such activity or purpose involves the commission of a crime within the jurisdiction of the Court; or
    2. Be made with the knowledge of the intention of the group to commit the crime;
  E. In respect of the crime of genocide, directly and publicly incites others to commit genocide;
  F. Attempts to commit such a crime by taking action that commences its execution, but the crime does not occur because of circumstances independent of the person's intentions. However, a person who abandons the effort to commit the crime or otherwise prevents the completion of the crime shall not be liable for punishment under this Law for the attempt to commit that crime if that person completely and voluntarily gave up the criminal purpose.

Third: The official position of any accused person, whether as president, chairman or a member of the Revolution Command Council, prime minister, member of the counsel of ministers, a member of the Ba'ath Party Command, shall not relieve such person of criminal penal, nor mitigate punishment. No person is entitled to any immunity with respect to any of the crimes stipulated in Articles 11, 12, 13, and 14 of this law.

Fourth: The crimes that were committed by a subordinate do not relieve his superior of criminal responsibility if he knew or had reason to know that the subordinate was about to commit such acts or had done so, and the superior failed to take the necessary and appropriate measures to prevent such acts or to submit the matter to the competent authorities for investigation and prosecution.

Fifth: The fact that an accused person acted pursuant to an order of the Government or of his superior, shall not relieve him of criminal responsibility, but may be considered in mitigation of punishment if the Court determines that justice so requires.

Sixth: Pardons issued prior to this law coming into force, do not apply to the accused in any of the crimes stipulated in it.

SECTION FOUR
Rules of Procedure and Evidence

Article 16

The Court shall apply the Criminal Procedure Law No. 23 of 1971, and the Rules of Procedure and Evidence appended to this law, which is an indivisible and integral part of the law.

SECTION FIVE
General Principles of Criminal Law

Article 17

First: In case a stipulation is not found in this Law and the rules made there under, the general provisions of criminal law shall be applied in connection with the accusation and prosecution of any accused person shall be those contained in:

- A. The Baghdadi Penal Law of 1919, for the period starting from July 17, 1968, till Dec. 14, 1969.
- B. The Penal law no.111 of 1969, which was in force in1985 (third version), for the period starting from Dec.15, 1969, till May, 1, 2003.
- C. The Military Penal Law no.13 of 1940, and the military procedure law no.44 of 1941.

Second: To interpret Articles 11, 12, 13 of this law, the Cassation Court and Panel may resort to the relevant decisions of the international criminal courts.

Third: Grounds for exclusion of criminal responsibility under the Panel Law shall be interpreted in a manner consistent with this Law and with international legal obligations concerning the crimes within the jurisdiction of the Court.

Fourth: The crimes stipulated in Articles 11, 12, 13, and 14 shall not be subject to limitations that terminate the criminal case or punishment.

SECTION SIX
Investigations and Indictment

Article 18

First: The Investigative Judge shall initiate investigations *ex-officio* or on the basis of information obtained from any source, particularly from the police, or governmental and nongovernmental organizations. The Investigative Judge shall assess the information received and decide whether there is sufficient basis to proceed.

Second: The Court Investigative Judge shall have the power to question suspects, victims and witnesses, or their relatives to collect evidence and to conduct on-site investigations. In carrying out his task the Court Investigative Judge may, as appropriate, request the assistance of the relevant governmental authorities concerned, who shall be required to provide full co-operation with the request.

Third: Upon a determination that a *prima facie* case exists, the Investigative Judge shall prepare an indictment containing a concise statement of the facts of the crime with which the accused is charged under the Statute and shall refer the case to the criminal court.

PART ONE
Guarantees of the Accused

Article 19

First: All persons shall be equal before the Court.

Second: The accused shall be presumed innocent until proven guilty before the Court in accordance with this law.

Third: Every accused shall be entitled to a public hearing, in pursuance with the provisions of this law and the Rules issued according to it.

Fourth: In directing any charge against the accused pursuant to the present Law, the accused shall be entitled to a just fair trial in accordance with the following minimum guarantees:
   A. To be informed promptly and in detail of the content nature and cause and of the charge against him;
   B. To have adequate time and facilities for the preparation of his defense and to communicate freely with counsel of his own choosing and to meet with him privately. The accused is entitled to have non-Iraqi legal representation, so long as the principal lawyer of such accused is Iraqi;
   C. To be tried without undue delay;
   D. To be tried in his presence, and to use a lawyer of his own choosing, and to be informed of his right assistance of his own choosing; to be

informed, if he does not have legal assistance, of this right; and to have legal assistance and to have the right to request such aid to appoint a lawyer without paying the fees, case if he does not have sufficient means to pay for it; if he does not have the financial ability to do so.

E. The accused shall have the right to request the defense witnesses, the witnesses for the prosecution, and to discuss with them any evidence that support his defense in accordance with the law.

F. The defendant shall not be forced to confess and shall have the right to remain silent and not provide any testimony and that silent shall not be interpreted as evidence of convection or innocence.

SECTION SEVENTH
Trial Proceedings

Article 20

First: A person against whom an indictment has been issued shall, pursuant to an order or an arrest warrant of the Investigative Judge, be taken into custody, immediately informed of the charges against him and transferred to the Court.

Second: The Criminal Court shall ensure that a trial is fair and expeditious and that proceedings are conducted in accordance with this Statute and the Rules of Procedure and Evidence annexed to this Law, with full respect for the rights of the accused and due regard for the protection of the victims, their relatives and the witnesses.

Third: The Criminal Court shall read the indictment, satisfy itself that the rights of the accused are respected and guaranteed, insure that the accused understands the indictment, with charges directed against him and instruct the accused to enter a plea.

Fourth: The hearings shall be public unless the Criminal Court decides to close the proceedings in accordance with the Rules of Procedure and Evidence annexed to this Statue, and no decision shall be adopted under the session secrecy unless for extreme limited reasons.

Article 21
The Criminal Court shall, in its Rules of Procedure and Evidence annexed to this Statue, provide the protection for victims or their relatives and witnesses and also for the secrecy of their identity.

Article 22
Families of victims and Iraqi persons harmed may file a civil suit before this court against the accused for the harm they suffered through their actions constituting crimes according to the provisions of this Statue. The court shall have the power

to adjudicate these claims in accordance with the Iraqi Criminal procedure Code No. 23 for the year 1971, and other relevant laws.

Article 23

First: The Criminal Court shall pronounce judgments and impose sentences and penalties on persons convicted of crimes within the jurisdiction of the Court.

Second: The judgment shall be issued by a majority of the judges of the Criminal Court, and shall announce it in public. The judgment shall not be issued except pursuant to the indictment decision. The opinion of the dissenting Judges can be appended.

Article 24

First: The penalties that shall be imposed by the Court shall be those prescribed by the Iraqi Penal Code No (111) of 1969, except for sentences of life imprisonment that means the remaining natural life of the person. With considering the provisions of Article (17) of this Statute.

Second: It shall be applied against the crimes stipulated in article (14) of this Statute the sentences provided under the Iraqi Penal Code and other punishable laws

Third: The penalty for crimes under Articles 11, 12, 13 shall be determined by the Criminal Court, taking into account the provisions contained in paragraphs fourth and fifth.

Fourth: A person convicted of sentences stipulated under Iraqi Penal Code shall be punished if:

    A. He committed an offence of murder or rape as defined under Iraqi Penal Code.
    B. He participated in committing an offence of murder or rape.

Fifth: The penalty for any crimes under Articles 11, 12, 13 which do not have a counterpart under Iraqi law shall be determined by the Court taking into account such factors like the gravity of the crime, the individual circumstances of the convicted person, guided by judicial precedents and relevant sentences issued by the international criminal courts.

Sixth: The Criminal Court may order the forfeiture of proceeds, property or assets derived directly or indirectly from a crime, without prejudice to the rights of the *bona fide* third parties.

Seventh: In accordance with Article 307 of the Iraqi Criminal Procedure Code, the Criminal Court shall have the right to confiscate any material or goods prohibited by law regardless of whether the case has been discharged for any lawful reason.

SECTION EIGHT
Appeals Proceedings

PART ONE
Cassation

Article 25

First: The convicted pr the public prosecutor has the right to contest the judgments and decisions before the Cassation Panel for any of the following reasons:

1. If a judgment issued is in contradiction with the law or there is an error in interrupting it.
2. An error in procedures.
3. Material error in the facts which has led to violation of justice.

Second: The Cassation Panel may affirm, reverse or revise the decisions taken by the Criminal Court or the decisions of the Investigative Judge.

Third: When the Cassation Panel issues its verdict to revoke the judgment of acquittal or release issued by the Criminal Court or the Investigative Judge, the case shall be referred back to the Court for retrial of the accused or for the Investigative Judge to implement the decision.

Fourth: The period of appeal shall be in accordance with the provisions of the Iraqi Criminal procedure Code No. 23 for the year 1971 that is in effect, in case there is no specific provision in that regard

PART TWO
Retrial

Article 26

First: Where a new findings or facts have been discovered which were not known at the time of the proceedings before the Criminal Court or the Cassation Panel and which could have been a decisive factor in reaching the decision, the convicted person or the Prosecution may submit to the Court an application for a retrial.

Second: The Court shall reject the application if it considers it to be unfounded. If it determines that the application has merit, and for the purpose of reaching a modification of the court decision after hearing the parties in the case, may:

1. Send case back to the original Criminal Court that issued the ruling; or
2. Send case back to another Criminal Court; or
3. The Cassation Panel takes jurisdiction over the matter.

SECTION NINE
Enforcement of Sentences

Article 27

First: Sentences shall be carried out in accordance with the Iraqi legal system and its laws.

Second: No authority, including the President of the Republic, may grant a pardon or mitigate the punishment issued by the Court. The punishment must be executed within 30 days of the date when the judgment becomes final and non-appealable.

SECTION TEN
General and Final Provisions

Article 28

Investigative judges, Judge of the criminal courts, members of the public prosecution committee, the director of the administrative department and the court's staff must be Iraqi nationals with due considerations given to the provisions of Article 4 (Third) of this statute.

Article 29

First: The Court and the national courts shall have concurrent jurisdiction to prosecute persons for those offences stipulated in Article 14 of this statute.

Second: The Court shall have primacy over all other Iraqi courts with respect to the crimes stipulated in Articles 11, 12, and 13 of this statute.

Third: At any stage of the proceedings, the Court may demand of any other Iraqi court to transfer any case being tried by it involving any crimes stipulated in Articles 11, 12, 13, and 14 of this statue, and such court shall be required to transfer such case upon demand.

Fourth: At any stage of the proceedings, the Court may demand of any other Iraqi court to transfer any case being tried by it involving any crimes stipulated in Articles 13, 14, 15, 16 of this statue, and such court shall be required to transfer such case upon demand.

Article 30

First: No person shall be tried before any other Iraqi court for acts for which the Court, in accordance with Articles 300 and 301 of the Iraqi Criminal Procedure Code, has already tried him or her.

Second: A person, who has been tried by any Iraqi court for acts constituting crimes within the jurisdiction of the Court, may not be subsequently tried by the Court except if the Court determines that the previous court proceedings were not impartial or independent, or were designed to shield the accused from criminal responsibility. When decisions are made for a retrial, one of the conditions contained in Article 196 of the Iraqi Civil Procedure Code and Article (303) of the Iraqi Criminal Procedure Code must be met.

Third: In determining the penalty to be imposed on a person convicted of a crime under the present Statute, the Court shall take into account the time served of any penalty imposed by an Iraqi court on the same person for the same crime.

Article 31

First: The President of the Court, the Judges, the Court's Investigative Judges, the Public Prosecutors, the Director of the Administration Department and their staffs shall have immunity from civil suits in respect to their official functions.

Second: Other persons, including the accused, required at the seat of the Court shall be accorded such treatment as is necessary for the proper functioning of the Court.

Article 32
Arabic shall be the official language of the Court.

Article 33
No person who was previously a member of the disbanded Ba'ath Party shall be appointed as a judge, investigative judge, public prosecutor, an employee or any of the personnel of the Court.

Article 34
The expenses of the Court shall be borne by the State's general budget.

Article 35
The President of the Court shall prepare and submit an annual report on the Court activities to the Council of Ministers.

Article 36
The provisions of the civil service law No. (24) of 1960, Personnel law No. (25) of 1960, government and socialist sector employees disciplinary law No (14) of 1991 and civil pension law No.(33) of 1966 shall apply to the court's employees other than the judges and members of public prosecution.

Article 37
Law No. 1 for the year 2003 the Iraqi Special Tribunal and the Rules of Procedure and Evidence issued in accordance with the provisions of Article (16) thereof are revoked from the date this statute comes into force.

Article 38
All decisions and Orders of Procedure issued under law No. 1 for the year 2003 are correct and conform to the law.

Article 39
The Council of Ministers in coordination with the President of the Court shall issue instructions to facilitate the implementation of this statute.

Article 40
This law shall come into force on the date of its publication in the Official Gazette.

Jalal Talabani	**Adil Abdul-Mahdi**	**Ghazi Ajil Al-Yawir**
President of the Republic	Vice- President	Vice-President

Justifying Reasons

In order to expose the crimes committed in Iraq from July 17, 1968 until May 1, 2005 against the Iraqi people and the peoples of the region and the subsequent savage massacres, and for laying down the rules and punishments to condemn after a fair trial the perpetrators of such crimes for waging wars, mass extermination and crimes against humanity, and for the purpose of forming an Iraqi national high criminal court from among Iraqi judges with high experience, competence and integrity to specialize in trying these criminals.

And in order to reveal the truth and the agonies and injustice caused by the perpetrators of such crimes, and for protecting the rights of many Iraqis and alleviating injustice and for demonstrating heaven's justice as envisaged by the Almighty God. . . .

This law has been legislated.

Notes

INTRODUCTION

   1. Telegram from British Embassy Baghdad to Foreign and Commonwealth Office, "Saddam Hussein," December 20, 1969 (Public Record Office, London, FCO 17/871), National Security Archives, available at http://www.gwu.edu/~nsarchiv/NSAEBB/ NSAEBB107/iraq02.pdf.

   2. Vera Beaudin Saeedpour, Establishing State Motives for Genocide: Iraq and the Kurds, in *Genocide Watch* (Helen Fien, ed.) (1992), pp. 67–68 (citing Sir Arnold T. Wilson, *Mesapotamia, 1917–1920: A Clash of Loyalties; A Personal and Historical Record* (1931)).

CHAPTER 1

   1. Treaty of Sevres, Article 62–64 (August 10, 1920).

   2. Letter from President Woodrow Wilson to the Supreme Council of the Allied Power (November 22, 1922) in Foreign Relations of the United States 1920, vol. III, p. 790 (1936).

   3. Margaret MacMillan, *Paris 1919* (Random House, 2001), p. 369.

CHAPTER 2

   1. Memorandum from Jonathan Howe to Secretary of State Eagleburger, Iraqi Use of Chemical Weapons (November 21, 1983), available at http://www2.gwu.edu/~nsarchiv/ NSAEBB/NSAEBB82/iraq25.pdf.

   2. Middle East Watch, *Genocide in Iraq: The Anfal Campaign Against the Kurds*, Introduction (Human Rights Watch, 1993), available at http://www.hrw.org/reports/1993/ iraqanfal/.

   3. CBS News, Chemical Ali: Alive and Held (August 21, 2003), available at www.cbsnews.com/stories/2003/04/07/iraq/printable 548099.shtml.

4. David McDowall, *A Modern History of the Kurds* (St. Martin's Press, 1997), p. 353.

5. Middle East Watch, *supra* note 7, at Ch. 3 (quoting Middle East Watch interview, Piramagroun complex, July 30, 1992).

6. *Id.* at Ch. 4.

7. *Id.* at Ch. 5.

8. *Id.*

9. *Id.*

10. *Id.* at Ch. 6.

11. *Id.* at Ch. 7.

12. *Id.* at Ch. 10.

13. *Id.*

14. *Id.* at Ch. 11.

CHAPTER 3

1. McDowall, *supra* note 9, p. 358.

2. *Id.*, p. 359.

3. Guy Dinsmore, The Enduring Pain of Halabja, *Financial Times*, July 10, 2002.

4. *Id.*

5. Saddam's Chemical Weapons Campaign: Halabja, March 16, 1988, U.S. Department of State, Bureau of Public Affairs (March 14, 2003), available at http://www.state.gov/r/pa/ei/rls/18714.htm.

6. McDowall, *supra*, p. 363.

7. U.S. Senate Committee on Banking, Housing, and Urban Affairs, U.S. Chemical and Biological Exports to Iraq and Their Possible Impact on the Health Consequences of the Persian Gulf War (1994), *reprinted in* 140 CONG. REC. S15045 (1994), LEXIS 140 Cong. Rec. S15045*15047. For recently declassified primary sources acknowledging U.S. support of Iraq's chemical weapons program, see The National Security Archive, *The Saddam Hussein Sourcebook*, at www2.gwu.edu/~nsarchiv/special/iraq/index.htm (December 18, 2003).

8. Christopher Hitchens, Remember Halabja, *Salon*, March 2, 1998, available at http://archive.salon.com/col/hitc/1998/03/nc_02hitc2.html.

9. Christine M. Gosden, The 1988 Chemical Weapons Attack on Halabja, Iraq, in *Super Terrorism: Biological, Chemical, and Nuclear* (Yonah Alexander and Milton Hoenig, eds.) (Transnational Publishers, 2001), pp. 7–11.

10. INDICT, Witness Statements, First Hand Accounts from Saddam's Brutal Regime, available at http://www.indict.org.uk/ witnessdetails.php?target=Saddam (last visited April 24, 2005). INDICT, a London-based NGO, collected witness statements with support from the British Parliament and U.S. Congress.

CHAPTER 6

1. BBC News, *No-fly Zones: The Legal Position*, February 19, 2001, available at http://news.bbc.co.uk/1/hi/world/middle_east/1175950.stm.

2. Judith Richards Hope and Edward N. Griffin, The New Iraq: Revising Iraq's Commercial Law Is a Necessity for Foreign Direct Investment and the Reconstruction of Iraq's

Decimated Economy, *Cardozo Journal of International & Comparative Law*, 11 (2004), 875, 881.

3. White House, The National Security Strategy of the United States of America 13–16 (September 2002), available at www.whitehouse.gov/nsc/nss.html.

4. Hope and Griffin, *supra* note 31, 882.

5. John Hendren, Pentagon Labels Hussein a POW, Conferring Him Special Rights, *L.A. Times*, January 10, 2004, A1. For the criteria of prisoner of war status, see Jordan J. Paust, Post-9/11 Overreaction and Fallacies Regarding War and Defense, Guantanamo, the Status of Persons, Treatment, Judicial Review of Detention, and Due Process in Military Commissions, *Notre Dame Law Review*, 79 (2004), 1335, 1352.

CHAPTER 7

1. The Statute of the Iraqi Special Tribunal, December 10, 2003, available at http://www.cpa-iraq.org/human_rights/Statute.htm.

2. Salem Chalabi, interview with Mary Lou Finley, *As It Happens*, CBC Radio Broadcast, April 21, 2004.

3. Thanassis Cambanis, Despite Allawi's Vow, U.S. Official Says Trial Won't Be This Year, *Boston Globe*, September 25, 2004, A9.

4. Gregory Kehoe, interview with Bill Hemmer, *American Morning* (CNN television broadcast, May 12, 2004), transcript available at http://cnnstudentnews.cnn.com/ TRANSCRIPTS /0405/12/ltm.04.html.

5. Cambanis, *supra* note 37.

6. Charles Crain, Saddam Is Placed under Iraqi Control, *Atlanta Journal Constitution*, July 1, 2004, A6.

CHAPTER 9

1. BBC News, *Killing of Iraq Kurds* 'Genocide,' December 23, 2005, available at http://news.bbc.co.uk/2/hi/europe/4555000.stm.

2. NBC News, *Saddam Hussein Executed, Ending Era in Iraq*, MSNBC, December 30, 2006, available at http://www.msnbc.msn.com/id/16389128/.

3. Sudarsan Raghavan, Saddam Is Put to Death, *Washington Post*, December 30, 2006.

4. BBC News, *Saddam Hanged*, December 30, 2006, available at http://news.bbc.co.uk/2/hi/middle_east/6218597.stm.

5. *Id.*

6. Raghavan, *supra* note 43.

7. Fereydun Hilmi, Multiple Jeopardy, *KurdishMedia*, January 1, 2007, available at http://www.kurdmedia.com/article.aspx?id=13830.

8. Alaskan Librarian, Kurdish Reaction to Saddam Execution (drawn from Kurdish-Media.com), December 31, 2006, available at http://alaskanlibrarian.wordpress.com/2006/ 12/31/kurdish-reaction-to-saddam-execution/.

9. Convention on the Prevention and Punishment of the Crime of Genocide, *opened for signature* December 9, 1948, article 2, 102 Stat. 3045, 78 U.N.T.S. 277.

10. M. Cherif Bassiouni, Observations Concerning the 1997–98 Preparatory Committee's Work, *Denver Journal of International Law & Policy*, 25(1997), 397, 413 (indicating that the requirement for specific intent is a flaw in the definition of genocide).

11. Prosecutor v. Akayesu, ICTR-96-4-T, 1998 WL 1782077, ¶ 523 (ICTR, September 2, 1998).

12. Prosecutor v. Radislav Krstić, IT-98-33-A, ¶ 3 (2004), available at http://www.un.org/icty/krstic/Appeal/judgement/krs-aj040419e.pdf.

13. *Id.* at ¶ 134.

14. Foreign & Commonwealth Office, Saddam Hussein: Crimes and Human Rights Abuses 14–16 (2002).

15. Eric Pape and Marie Valla, Defending Saddam, Newsweek Web Exclusive, December 30, 2003, available at http://www.msnbc.msn.com/id/3840489/.

16. BBC News, *Saddam Trial Head Vows Justice*, July 2, 2004, available at http://news.bbc.co.uk/2/hi/middle_east/3859007.stm.

17. For an argument that the United States, as an occupying power, has the responsibility under international law to restore law and order in Iraq, see Jordan J. Paust, The U.S. as Occupying Power Over Portions of Iraq and Relevant Responsibilities Under the Laws of War, American Society of International Law, available at http://www.asil.org/insights/insigh102.htm.

18. Argument of Curtis F. Doebbler in debate with Professor Michael Scharf, Can Saddam Hussein Receive a Fair Trial? Debate at Case Western Reserve School of Law, January 13, 2005 (broadcast on C-SPAN, January 30, 2005), transcript available at http://www.c-spanstore.org/shop/index.php?main_page=product_video_info&products_id=184702-1.

19. MSNBC News, *Transcript of Saddam in Court*, July 1, 2004, available at http://www.msnbc.msn.com/id/5345118/.

20. Mass Killings in Iraq: Hearing before the Senate Committee on Foreign Relations, 102d Cong. 1 (1992) (statement of Claiborne Pell, Chairman).

21. Vera Beaudin Saeedpour, Establishing State Motives for Genocide: Iraq & The Kurds, in *Genocide Watch* (Helen Fien ed.) (1992), p. 66.

22. George Black, Report on al-Anfal, in *The Saddam Hussein Reader* (Turi Munthe ed.) (Basic Books, 2002), pp. 189, 199.

23. CBC News, *The Fifth Estate—The Forgotten People: The Attack at Halabja*, March 26, 2003, available at http://www.cbc.ca/fifth/kurds/attack.html.

24. Nicolas Rothwell, Town's "Justice" Awaits Saddam, *The Australian*, July 22, 2004, 7.

25. Sienho Yee, The Tu Quoque Argument as a Defense to International Crimes, Prosecution or Punishment, *Chinese Journal of International Law*, 3 (2004), 87.

26. Amir Taheri, Put Saddam on Trial—Now, *Jerusalem Post*, October 1, 2004, 16.

27. International Military Tribunal for the Trial of German Major War Criminals, Judgment, October 1, 1946, part 13: The Law of the Charter, available at http://www.yale.edu/lawweb/avalon/imt/proc/judlawch.htm.

28. BBC News, *Milosevic Hearing Transcript*, July 3, 2001, available at http://news.bbc.co.uk/2/hi/europe/1419971.stm.

29. Prosecutor v. Dusko Tadic, IT-94-1, Decision on the Defence Motion on Jurisdiction, August 10, 1995, available at http://www.un.org/icty/tadic/trialc2/decision-e/100895.htm.

30. Al-DuJail case 1/9 First/2005, Introduction to the Judgement Decision, November 5, 2006 (English translation), available at http://law.case.edu/saddamtrial/documents/dujail_opinion_pt1.pdf.

CHAPTER 10

1. Ayaan Hirsi Ali, Speech, The Role of Journalism Today, National Press Club (Washington, DC), June 19, 2007, transcript available at http://www.aei.org/publications/pubID.26367,filter.all/pub_detail.asp. Others, like Shireen Hunter, disagree on the compatibility question. See Shireen T. Hunter, *The Future of Islam and the West: Clash of Civiliazations or Peaceful Coexistence?* (Praeger, 1998).

2. Samuel P. Huntington, *The Clash of Civilizations and the Remaking of World Order* (Simon & Schuster, 1998).

3. Samuel P. Huntington, The Clash of Civilizations? *Foreign Affairs*, 72 (Summer 1993).

4. Interview, So, Are Civilisations at War? *Guardian*, October 11, 2001, available at http://observer.guardian.co.uk/islam/story/0,1442,577982,00.html.

5. Marlise Simons, Hussein's Case Won't Bolster International Human Rights Law, Experts Fear, *New York Times*, December 31, 2006.

6. U.S. Department of State, Iran Human Rights Practices, 1995, March 1996, available at http://dosfan.lib.uic.edu/ERC/democracy/1995_hrp_report/95hrp_report_nea/Iran.html.

7. For an electronic version of The Holy Qur'an, translated by M.H. Shakir and published by Tahrike Tarsile Qur'an, Inc., translated in 1983, courtesy of the University of Michigan, see: http://quod.lib.umich.edu/cgi/k/koran/koran-idx?type=DIV0&byte=783591.

8. Matthew Lippman, Sean McConville, and Mordechai Yerushalmi, *Islamic Criminal Law and Procedure* (Praeger, 1988), pp. 28–29.

9. CRS Report for Congress, *Islam: Sunnis and Shiites*, Christopher M. Blanchard, Analyst in Middle Eastern Affairs, Foreign Affairs, Defense, and Trade Division, Order Code RS21745, updated December 11, 2006, available at http://fas.org/sgp/crs/misc/RS21745.pdf.

10. Ali Khan, Professor of Law, Washburn University, The Reopening of the Islamic Code: The Second Era of Ijtihad, available at http://www.washburnlaw.edu/faculty/khan-a-fulltext/2003-1univstthomlj341.pdf.

11. Rudolph Peters, *Crime and Punishment in Islamic Law* (Cambridge University Press, 2005), 6.

12. *Id.* at 53.

13. *Id.* at 27.

14. *Id.* at 47.

15. *Id.* at 20.

16. *Id.* at 144.

17. Mohamed Al Awabdeh, History and Prospect of Islamic Criminal Law with Respect to the Human Rights 10:2, (Dissertation, Humboldt University – Berlin, 2005), available at http://edoc.hu-berlin.de/dissertationen/al-awabdeh-mohamed-2005-07-07/HTML/front.html.

18. Bringing Bigwigs to Justice, *Economist*, January 12, 2008.

CONCLUSION

1. Prosecutor v. Milosevic, IT-02-54-T, Order Terminating the Proceedings, March 14, 2006, available at http://www.un.org/icty/milosevic/trialc/order-e/060314.htm.

Bibliography

Ajami, Fouad. *The Foreigner's Gift: The Americans, The Arabs, and the Iraqis in Iraq* (Free Press, 2006).

Ali, Ayaan Hirsi. *Infidel* (Free Press, 2007).

Amanat, Abbas and Griffel, Frank, eds. *Sharia, Islamic Law in the Contemporary Context* (Stanford University Press, 2007).

Anderson, Dale. *Saddam Hussein, A Biography* (Lerner, 2003).

Arabi, Oussama. *Studies in Modern Islamic Law and Jurisprudence* (Kluwer, 2001).

Baderin, Mashood A. *International Human Rights and Islamic Law* (Oxford University Press, 2003).

Balaghi, Shiva. *Saddam Hussein, A Biography* (Greenwood, 2006).

Bantekas, Ilias and Nash, Susan. *International Criminal Law* 2nd Ed. (Cavendish, 2003).

BBC News. *Timeline: Saddam Hussein Dujail Trial*, December 4, 2006, available at: http://news.bbc.co.uk/2/hi/middle_east/4507568.stm.

BBC News. *Timeline: Anfal Trial*, January 8, 2007, available at: http://news.bbc.co.uk/2/hi/middle_east/5272224.stm.

Berman, Harold J. *Law and Revolution: The Formation of the Western Legal Tradition* (Harvard University Press, 1983).

Black, Eric. Iraq through the Ages: From the Dawn of History to Tomorrow's Headlines, the Territory of Iraq Has Been the Scene of More Than Its Share of Humankind's Momentous Events. *Minneapolis Star Tribune*, February 9, 2003, sec. A.

Boas, Gideon. *The Milosevic Trial, Lessons for the Conduct of Complex International Criminal Proceedings* (Cambridge University Press, 2007).

Burns, John F. Hussein Displays Courtesy After Death Sentence Fury. *New York Times*, November 8, 2006.

———. In New Hussein Trial, a Grisly Portrait of Mass Killings. *New York Times*, December 4, 2006.

Cairo Declaration of Human Rights in Islam (1990).

Cave, Damien. Lawyers for Hussein Accuse Kurd of Treason. *New York Times*, August 24, 2006.

Dobbs, Michael. U.S. Had Key Role in Iraq Buildup: Trade in Chemical Arms Allowed Despite Their Use on Iranians, Kurds. *Washington Post*, December 30, 2002, A1.

Fisher, Ian. Threats and Responses: Weapons Inspections; Top Iraqi Advisor Says He Believes War Is Inevitable. N*ew York Times*, January 26, 2003, 1.

Galbraith, Peter W. *The End of Iraq: How American Incompetence Created a War Without End* (Simon & Schuster, 2006).

Gunter, Michael M. *The Kurds of Iraq: Tragedy and Hope* (Palgrave MacMillan, 1993).

———. *The Kurdish Predicament in Iraq: A Political Analysis* (Palgrave MacMillan, 1999).

Hassanpour, Amir. The Kurdish Experience, *Middle East Report* (July–August 1994), available at: http://www.xs4all.nl/~tank/kurdish/htdocs/lib/kurdish_ex.html.

Hilterman, Joost R. Halabja: American Didn't Seem to Mind Poison Gas. *International Herald Tribune*, January 17, 2003.

Hooglund, Eric. The Other Face of War. Middle East Report, No. 171, The Day After (July–August 1991), available at: http://www.jstor.org/view/08992851/di011516/01p0022t/0.

Human Rights Watch. *Middle East Watch Report: Genocide in Iraq: The Anfal Campaign against the Kurds* (Human Rights Watch, 1993).

Huntington, Samuel P. *The Clash of Civilizations and the Remaking of World Order* (Simon & Schuster, 1998).

Kelly, Michael J. Can Sovereigns be Brought to Justice? The Crime of Genocide's Evolution and the Meaning of the Milosevic Trial, 76. *St. John's Law Review* 257–378 (2002).

———. *Nowhere to Hide: Defeat of the Sovereign Immunity Defense for Crimes of Genocide & the Trials of Slobodan Milosevic and Saddam Hussein* (Peter Lang, 2005).

Lippman, Matthew, McConville, Sean, and Yerushalmi, Mordechai. *Islamic Criminal Law and Procedure* (Praeger, 1988).

Lombardi, Clark B. and Brown, Nathan J. Do Constitutions Requiring Adherence to Shari'a Threaten Human Rights? How Egypt's Constitutional Court Reconciles Islamic Law with the Liberal Rule of Law, 21. *American University International Law Review* 379–435 (2006).

MacMillan, Margaret. *Paris 1919* (Random House, 2001).

McDowall, David. *A Modern History of the Kurds* (St. Martins Press, 1997).

Nasr, Vali. *The Shia Revival: How Conflicts in Islam Will Reshape the Future* (W.W. Norton, 2007).

Oppel, Richard A., Jr. After Remark, Judge in Trial of Hussein Loses His Post. *New York Times*, September 19, 2006.

Paust, Jordan J., Bassiouni, M. Cherif, Scharf, Michael, Gurulé, Jimmy, Sadat, Leila, Zagaris, Bruce, Williams, and Shannon A. *International Criminal Law* 2nd Ed. (Carolina Academic Press, 2000).

Pelletiere, Stephen C. *The Iran–Iraq War* (Praeger, 1992).

Peters, Rudolph. *Crime and Punishment in Islamic Law* (Cambridge University Press, 2005).

Power, Samantha. *A Problem from Hell: America and the Age of Genocide* (Basic Books, 2002).

Santora, Marc. Iraq Is Preparing for Saddam's Hanging. *International Herald Tribune*, December 29, 2006.

Scharf, Michael P. Can This Man Get a Fair Trial? *Washington Post*, December 19, 2004, B1.

Scharf, Michael P. and McNeal, Gregory S., eds. *Saddam on Trial, Understanding and Debating the Iraq High Tribunal* (Carolina Academic Press, 2006).

Souryal, Sam S. The Religionization of a Society: The Continuing Application of Shariah Law in Saudi Arabia. *Journal for the Scientific Study of Religion* 26, 429–449 (1987). Available at http://www.jstor.org/sici?sici=0021-8294(198712)26%3A4%3C429% 3ATROAST%3E2.0.CO%3B2-X&cookieSet=1.

Sterling, Joe. Saddam Facing Poison Gas Charges. CNN, August 20, 2006, available at: http://www.cnn.com/2006/WORLD/meast/08/20/saddam.trial/index.html.

Universal Declaration of Human Rights (1948).

Universal Islamic Declaration of Human Rights (1981).

Von Zielbauer, Paul. Kurds Tell of Gas Attacks by Hussein's Military. *New York Times*, August 23, 2006.

Wise, Edward M., Podgor, Ellen S., and Clark, Roger S. *International Criminal Law* 2nd Ed. (LexisNexis, 2004).

Wong, Edward. Prosecutors Detail Atrocities in Hussein's Trial. *New York Times*, August 22, 2006.

Zanders, John Pascal. Iranian Use of Chemical Weapons: A Critical Analysis of Past Allegations. SIPRI Chemical and Biological Warfare Project (March 7, 2001), briefing available at: http://cns.miis.edu/pubs/programs/dc/briefs/030701.htm.

Index

Rahman, Judge Raouf Abdul, 69–75, 85
Ramadan, Taha Yassin, 66, 69, 72–76
Ramadi, 32
Reagan, Ronald, 20, 29, 36–37, 44, 94, 96

Saladin, 12, 122
Saudi Arabia, 26, 43–45, 52, 119
  Shari'a, practiced in, 108–14
Sèvres, Treaty of, 2, 14–15, 16
Shari'a, 109–19
Stalin, Josef, 3, 7
Suleimaniyeh, 21–22, 24–26, 98
Syria, 14, 17, 50, 51, 91, 116–17
  Kurdish, minority in, 2, 11, 48

Talabani, Jalal, 24, 28–29, 48–49, 167
Topzawa Prison Camp, 26–27, 29, 31, 32
Turkey, 2, 14–16, 45–46, 88, 87, 108–10, 116, 119
  Kurdish minority in, 2, 11, 21, 30–31, 45–46, 48–51

United Kingdom, 2, 3–5, 14–18, 25, 35–36, 43, 46, 49, 52–53, 119
United Nations, 44, 53, 80, 101–2, 105, 114, 149, 151, 152, 153, 156, 158
  Security Council of the, 37, 44–45, 52–53, 62, 100–102, 115–17

United States, 15, 18, 21, 29, 35, 37, 43–47, 52–57, 62, 64, 94, 98, 111, 113
  As an element of the Anfal Trial, 83, 88
  As an element of the Dujail Trial, 68, 69, 71, 75, 76

Vilayet of Baghdad, 5–6
Vilayet of Basra, 5–6
Vilayet of Mosul, 15

War Crimes, xii, 2, 44, 61, 62, 63, 65, 81, 97, 100, 103, 106, 115–18, 146
Weapons of Mass Destruction, 35, 53, 68
Wilson, Woodrow, 15–16

Xenophon, 11

Yugoslavia, rule by Tito, 3
Yugoslav War Crimes Tribunal (see International Criminal Tribunal for the former Yugoslavia)

Zangana Tribe, 26
Zargos Mountains, 30
Zerda Mountain, 25
Zewa Shkan, 30

About the Author

MICHAEL J. KELLY is Professor of Law at Creighton University School of Law. His 2005 book, *Nowhere to Hide: Defeat of the Sovereign Immunity Defense for Crimes of Genocide*, received the Book of the Year Award from the U.S. Chapter of L'Association International du Droit Pénal. He is a member of the International Association of Genocide Scholars, a contributing editor to the online legal news site JURIST, and Chair of the National Security Law Section of the Association of American Law Schools.